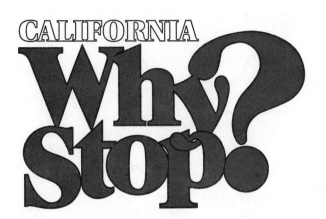

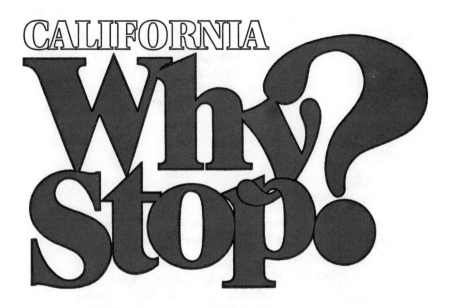

CALIFORNIA Why Stop?

A Guide to California Roadside Historical Markers

Marael Johnson

Gulf Publishing Company
Houston, Texas

Dedicated to
the many organizations
who have worked to preserve
the rich history of California

California
Why Stop?

A Guide to California Roadside Historical Markers

Gulf Publishing Company
Book Division
P.O. Box 2608 • Houston, Texas 77252-2608

10 9 8 7 6 5 4 3 2 1

Library of Congress Cataloging-in-Publication Data
Johnson, Marael.
    California, why stop? : a guide to California roadside historical
markers / Marael Johnson.
        p. cm.
    Includes bibliographical reference (p.   ) and index.
    ISBN 0-88415-923-X
        1. Historical markers—California—Guidebooks.
    2. California—Guidebooks.   3. California—History,
    Local.   I. Title.
    F862.J69   1995
    917.9404′53—dc20   95-7747
                                                                CIP

Printed in the United States of America.

Contents

Acknowledgments

Many thanks to the California Department of Parks and Recreation State Historical Resources Commission and Sandra J. Elder, Assistant Executive Secretary, for making their files available and for their courtesy and cooperation in compiling this book, and also to Dr. Eugene Chamberlain (Squibob Chapter of E Clampus Vitus).

I also wish to extend grateful acknowledgment to AMTRAK, whose trains and buses offer service to many of the historical landmark areas, for generous assistance with the research of this book.

Preface

California must certainly qualify as the most diverse state in the nation. Its nearly 160,000 square miles spin a kaleidoscope of ethereal mountain ranges, majestic forests, lush valleys, rushing rivers, placid lakes, and arid deserts, all prismed by Mt. Whitney (the lower 48's highest peak) and Death Valley (the country's lowest point). Within this landscape are renowned vineyards, historic gold rush towns, Spanish missions and adobe dwellings, low-key San Diego, ritzy-glitzy L.A., super-sophisticated San Francisco, and more than 1,000 miles of Pacific coastline ranging from golden "Riviera-esque" sandy shores in the southern half of the state to dramatic wild seas and pounding waves in the northern part.

Along the highways and byways crisscrossing this geographical and cultural phantasmagoria, you will encounter most of the state's 1,013 official historical markers. *Why Stop? A Guide to California Roadside Historical Markers* enables you to experience the whole plethora of California's historical events—from Junipero Serra's benevolent missions to Mark Twain's "jumping frog" visions, whether relaxing in your armchair or whooshing past in your car. *Why Stop?* can also be a useful planning tool for your California trip, allowing you to pick and choose routes and destinations before leaving home. Ride along the pony express route one day, relive gold rush excitement the next, and visit prehistoric tar pits on another. Most state and local tourist organizations can provide additional information on marker sites, and many towns and cities publish "walking-tour" maps of heritage areas. To the best of my knowledge, inscriptions contained herein are identical to wording on the actual plaques. Any errors are unintentional and, upon notification, will be corrected in future editions. Additionally, markers occasionally are relocated (usually due to highway construction) or removed by vandals. Again, upon notification, errors will be corrected. Enjoy *Why Stop?*. Discover the rhyme, the rhythm, the hymn, and the hum. California, here *you* come!

Marael Johnson

About California Historical Markers . . .

The official landmark program, instigated in 1931, originally was administered by the California State Chamber of Commerce with individual evaluations made by the Historic Sites Marking Committee, a group of prominent California historians. Once the sites were approved, the Division of Highways of the Department of Public Works erected the plaques.

In 1948, the California Centennial Commission, appointed by the State Legislature in the centennial year of gold discovery, took over the program. A year later, Governor Earl Warren established the California Historical Landmarks Advisory Committee to ensure "quality control" of the marker program. For some years, the California State Park Commission had final say-so.

In 1974, the California Historical Landmarks Advisory Committee became known as the State Historical Resources Commission—an advisory body of the California Department of Parks and Recreation and current overseer of official historical landmarks.

To qualify as an official landmark, the site must meet the following criteria: It is of lasting significance to the state's history; it is of significant historical importance to the state; it is a historic trail or route; or it is a significant architectural landmark.

The nine-member advisory committee which reviews each application includes a historian, architectural historian, architect, historic archaeologist, prehistoric archaeologist, ethnic historian, folklorist, and two public members.

Thus far, California has a total of 1,013 official historical landmarks. Official plaques, made of brass, sport the "California bear" symbol flanked by a star on either side. Inscriptions on the plaques are suggested by locals, edited by staff of the State Historical Resources Commission, then returned to locals for approval.

Other official landmarks are designated by plaques made of granite, wood, sandstone, marble, or other materials, and have been placed by civic organizations or patriotic and historical associations such as Daughters of the American Revolution, Sons and Daughters of the Golden West, and E Clampus Vitus.

How To Use This Guide

The marker inscriptions selected for this book have been compiled for the convenience and enjoyment of both the traveler and the history enthusiast. They occur in the order of the alphabetized cities or towns nearest them. By locating the name of the town you are approaching, you can determine the location of nearby markers by the information in italics. Indicated distances are measured from the nearest town within the county in which the marker is located. The index includes 57 California counties and lists the key persons and events responsible for the markers.

HIGHWAY AND ROAD LEGEND:
- **US**   U.S. highway
- **I**   Interstate highway
- **SH**   State highway
- **CH**   County highway
- **CR**   County road

CALIFORNIA
Why?
Stop?

AGUA CALIENTE SPRINGS (San Diego Co.)   *3.7 mi. NW, at SH 78 and CH S2 intersection*

Vallecito-Butterfield Stage Station
19 Miles

One of the chief remaining landmarks of famous old stageline coaches and spring wagons carried passengers and mail. Stations were built at 20-mile intervals. The first stage on the line left St. Louis on Sept. 15, 1858.

Placed by Department of Public Works, Division of Highways.

AGUA CALIENTE SPRINGS (San Diego Co.)   *3.7 mi. NW, at Vallecito Stage Station County Park, on CH S2*

Vallecito Stage Station

A reconstruction (1934) of Vallecito Stage Station at the edge of the Great Colorado Desert. Original was built 1852. Important stop on first official transcontinental route, serving the San Diego-San Antonio ("Jackass") mail line (1857–1859), the Butterfield Overland Stage Line, and the Southern Route emigrant caravans.

Placed by San Diego County Board of Supervisors and Historical Markers Committee, 1956.

ALAMEDA (Alameda Co.)   *NW corner Lincoln Ave. and Webster St.*

First Transcontinental Railroad

On Sept. 6, 1869, first transcontinental railroad train linking two great oceans, and consisting of 12 cars and three locomotives, passed here on way to a wharf terminal west of here, a location now covered by lagoon for take-off trans-Pacific planes, and within confines of present U.S. Naval Air Station. Original celebration held near this spot.

Placed by California Centennial Commission in cooperation with Alameda Historical Society, 1951.

ALAMEDA (Alameda Co.)   *Alameda Naval Air Station, Naval Air Station Mall, in front of Bldg. 1*

Pan Am China Clipper
(Contact Public Affairs Office
for permission to see plaque)

Pan American World Airways fabled China Clipper (Martin M/130 flying boat) left Alameda Marina on Nov. 22, 1935. Under the command of Captain Edwin C. Musick, the flight would reach Manila via Honolulu, Midway, Wake, and Guam. The inauguration of ocean airmail service and commercial air flight across the Pacific was a significant event for both California and the world.

Placed in cooperation with Pan American Airlines and Alameda Naval Air Station, 1985.

ALLEGHANY (Sierra Co.)

3.3 mi. W, at SW corner Ridge and Henness Pass rds.

Henness Pass Road

Pioneer Emigrant Trail Henness Pass Road. The main emigrant trail leading from Virginia City, Nevada, to Marysville, California. Traveled by the pioneer as early as 1849.

Placed by Sierra Parlor No. 268 of Native Daughters of the Golden West, 1941.

ALLEGHANY (Sierra Co.)

9 mi. W, on Ridge Rd., 8.6 mi. E of SH 49

Plum Valley House Site

The Plum Valley House, built in 1854 by John Bope, was constructed of hewn logs and whip sawn lumber. It was a toll house station on the Henness Pass road between Marysville and Virginia City. It is named for the wild plums which grow in the area.

Placed in cooperation with Sierra Parlor No. 268 of Native Daughters of the Golden West, 1962.

ALTADENA (Los Angeles Co.)

Santa Rosa Ave., between Woodbury Ave. and Altadena Dr.

Christmas Tree Lane

The 135 deodar cedar trees were planted in 1885 by the Woodbury family, the founders of Altadena. First organized by F.C. Nash in 1920, the "Mile of Christmas Trees" has been strung with 10,000 lights each holiday season through the efforts of volunteers and the Christmas Tree Lane Association. It is the oldest large-scale Christmas lighting spectacle in Southern California.

Placed in cooperation with Altadena Heritage, 1990.

ALTAVILLE (Calaveras Co.)

298 S. Main St., near SH 4 junction

Prince-Garibardi Building

This structure was erected in 1852 by B. R. Prince and G. Garibardi for a general merchandise business. Improved in 1857, with living quarters on the second floor, it is still used for living and warehouse purposes.

Placed in cooperation with Princess Parlor No. 84 of Native Daughters of the Golden West, 1960.

ALTAVILLE (Calaveras Co.)

State Dept. of Forestry Station, 125 N. Main St.,

Altaville Grammar School

This brick building, erected in 1858 with funds raised by a dance in the billiard saloon of the N. R. Prince Building (which still stands), is one of the oldest schools of California. Used as a school until 1950, it was then replaced by the present Mark Twain Elementary School in Altaville.

Placed by California State Park Commission in cooperation with Princess Parlor No. 84 of Native Daughters of the Golden West, 1955.

ALTURAS (Modoc Co.)   *7.7 mi. N, beside railroad track*
along US 395

Chimney Rock

Site of pioneer cabin built by Thomas A. Denson in 1871. This marker is dedicated to the pioneers of Modoc County by Alturas Parlor 159 of Native Daughters of the Golden West, Sept. 21, 1932.

Private plaque.

ANAHEIM (Orange Co.)   *775 Anaheim Blvd., at North St.*

Anaheim
Founded 1857
Location of
North Gate

Private plaque.

ANAHEIM (Orange Co.)   *414 N. West St., near Sycamore St.*

Mother Colony House

First house built in Anaheim, 1857, by George Hanson, founder of "The Mother Colony," group selecting name given settlement. This German group left San Francisco to form grape growing colony in Southern California. Vineyards became largest in California until destroyed, 1885, by grape disease. Colony started producing Valencia oranges. Here once resided Madame Helena Modjeska, and Henryk Sienkiewicz, author of *Quo Vadis.*

Placed by California Centennial Commission in cooperation with Grace Parlor No. 242 of Native Daughters of the Golden West and Mother Colony Parlor No. 281 of Native Sons of the Golden West, 1950.

ANDERSON (Shasta Co.)   *10 mi. E, Rt. 1, Box 273, Dersch Rd.*
at Bear Creek

Dersch Ranch

First owned by a Dr. Baker before 1858. Later became the George Dersch home. Mrs. Dersch killed by Indians, Aug. 16, 1866.

Placed by Trails West, Inc., 1976.

ANDERSON (Shasta Co.)   *.6 mi. E of Deschutes and Dersch rds.*
intersection

Fort Reading

Located 80 rods north. Established May 26, 1852, by Co. E, 2nd infantry, U.S.A. Evacuated June 1867.

Placed by U.S. Army and Shasta Historical Society, 1934.

ANDERSON (Shasta Co.)   *1.7 mi. N, NW corner SH 99*
and Spring Gulch Rd.

Mt. Shasta—14,161 feet

Official Emblem of Shasta Historical Society

"The pioneers in their journeys marked the roads and trails so that others recognizing them might safely follow."

This spot marks the location of the California-Oregon road main artery of travel of the pioneer blazed by them in the "fifties" and followed at this place by the Pacific Highway "linking the past with the future."

Placed by McCloud Parlor No. 149 of Native Sons of the Golden West of Redding, 1931.

ANDRADE (Imperial Co.)
On Algondes Rd., SH 186, .5 mi. S of I-8, .4 mi. N of Andrade border

Hernando de Alarcon Expedition, 1540

Alarcon's mission was to provide supplies for Francisco Coronado's expedition in search of the fabled Seven Cities of Cibola. The Spaniards led by Hernando de Alarcon ascended the Colorado River by boat from the Gulf of California past this point, thereby becoming the first non-Indians to sight Alta California on Sept. 5, 1540.

Placed in cooperation with Quechan Tribal Council, Imperial Irrigation District, Imperial Valley Pioneers, and Squibob Chapter of E Clampus Vitus, 1982.

ANGELS CAMP (Calaveras Co.)
NE corner Main St. and Bird Way

Angels Camp
Home of the Jumping Frog—Romance—Gold—History

Founded in 1849 by George Angel, who established a mining camp and trading store 200 feet below this marker. A rich gravel mining area and one of the richest quartz mining sections of the Mother Lode. Production records of over 100 million dollars for Angels Camp and vicinity. Prominent in early day California history. Townsite established in 1873. The locale of Mark Twain's famous story, *The Jumping Frog of Calaveras.* Frequented by Joaquin Murietta, Black Bart, and other early day bandits.

Placed by Calaveras County Chamber of Commerce, 1931.

ANGELS CAMP (Calaveras Co.)
NE corner Main St. and Bird Way

Angels Hotel

C. C. Lake erected here a canvas hotel in 1851. It was replaced by a one-story wooden structure, and then by one of stone in 1855, with a second story being added in 1857. Here, Samuel Clemens first heard the yarn, which was later to bring him fame as Mark Twain, author of *The Jumping Frog of Calaveras.*

Placed in cooperation with Princess Parlor No. 84 of Native Daughters of the Golden West, 1960.

ANGELS CAMP (Calaveras Co.)
3.7 mi. S, on SH 4

To Honor Archie Stevenot
"Mr. Mother Lode"

He was born Sept. 25, 1882, on the old Stevenot homestead, one-half mile west of this marker, son of Emile K. and Sarah E. Stevenot and the grandson of Gabriel K. Stevenot, Calaveras County pioneer who pitched tent there in April, 1850.

Student, salesman, miner, rancher, postmaster, schoolboard member, and general superintendent of the nearby Carson Hill mine, he has spent a productive lifetime in this region. He established the Mother Lode Highway Association in 1919, serving as president or director until 1950 when it joined into the Golden Chain Council. One of the organizers of the California State Chamber of Commerce. One of organizers of Mother Lode Baseball League. A native son and one of the state's favorites, there is hardly an activity for the benefit of California and the Mother Lode with which he has not been identified.

To our supreme noble grand humbug of the Grand Council of E Clampus Vitus, Inc., this marker is affectionately dedicated this 14th day of October, 1961.

Placed by Matuca Chapter No. 1849 of E Clampus Vitus.

ANGELS CAMP (Calaveras Co.)   *5.4 mi. S, at vista point on SH 49*
Robinson's Ferry

In 1848, John W. Robinson and Stephen Mead established ferry transport for freight, animals and persons across river. In 1856 Harvey Wood purchased interest and later acquired property which was maintained by Wood Family until 1911. Charges were 50 cents for each passenger, horse, jenny, or other animal.

Placed by California Centennial Commission and Angels Camp Lions Club, 1949.

ANTIOCH (Contra Costa Co.)   *Black Diamond Mines Regional Park, off SH 4, 3.9 mi. S on Somersville Rd.*
Mount Diablo Coal Field

From 1860 to 1906, this area was the largest coal mining district in California. Five towns (Nortonville, Somersville, Stewartville, Judsonville, and West Hartley) grew up around twelve major mines. Today the towns are gone, the buildings having been moved to nearby communities after the mines closed. Mine openings, tailings, railroad beds, and a pioneer cemetery are being preserved by the East Bay Regional Park District.

Placed in cooperation with East Bay Regional Park District and Joaquin Murietta Chapter No. 13 of E Clampus Vitus, 1980.

ANZA (Riverside Co.)   *7 mi. SE, on Cary Ranch, 60901 Coyote Canyon Rd.*
Site of de Anza Camp, March 1774

On Mar. 16, 1774, Juan Bautista de Anza, Indian fighter, explorer, and colonizer, led through this pass (named by him San Carlos) the first white explorers to cross the mountains into California; the party traveled from Tubac, Arizona, to Monterey, California. On Dec. 27, 1775, on a second expedition into California, Anza led through this pass the party of Spaniards from Sonora who became the founders of San Francisco.

Placed by Historic Landmarks Committee of Native Sons of the Golden West, 1924.

ANZA-BORREGO DESERT (San Diego Co.)   *Anza-Borrego Desert State Park, on CH S2, 8.6 mi. S of SH 78*
Box Canyon

The old way variously known as Sonora, Colorado River, or Southern Emigrant Trail and later as Butterfield Overland Mail Route traversed Box Canyon just east of here. January 19, 1847, the Mormon Battalion, under command of Lt. Col. Philip St. G. Cooke, using hand tools, hewed a passage through the rocky walls of the narrow gorge for their wagons and opened the first road into Southern California.

Placed by San Diego County Board of Supervisors and the Historical Markers Committee, 1953.

ANZA-BORREGO DESERT (San Diego Co.) *Blair Valley, Anza-Borrego Desert State Park, .5 mi. E of CH S2, 5.8 mi. S of SH 78*

Butterfield Overland Mail Route

This pass, Puerta, between the desert and the cooler valleys to the north, was used by the Mormon Battalion, Kearny's Army of the West, the Butterfield Overland Mail stages, and emigrants who eventually settled the West. The eroded scar on the left was the route of the Butterfield stages, 1858–61. The road on the right served as a county road until recent years.

Placed by California State Park Commission in cooperation with Sierra Club of California, San Diego Chapter, 1958.

ANZA-BORREGO DESERT (San Diego Co.) *Anza-Borrego Desert State Park, 6 mi. NW of Borrego Springs, on Borrego Springs Rd.*

The Anza Trail

This route was opened by Captain Juan Bautista de Anza and Father Francisco Garces in 1774. Anza's expedition of 1775, a group of 240 soldiers and settlers being led from Sonora to found San Francisco, encamped near this place El Vado (The Ford), for three days and two nights, Dec. 20–22, 1775.

Placed by California State Park Commission in cooperation with the Kiwanis Club of Borrego Springs.

ANZA-BORREGO DESERT (San Diego Co.) *Anza-Borrego Desert State Park, on Vallecito Creek Rd., 1.6 mi. E of CH S2, 6.3 mi. SE of Agua Caliente Springs*

Palm Springs

Here was a palm-studded desert resting place, 1826–1866, for Mexican pioneers, mountain men, the army of the West, Mormon Battalion, Boundary Commission, forty-niners, railway survey, Butterfield Overland Mail stages, and California Legion. It is the site of the Butterfield stage station built in 1858 by Warren F. Hall.

Placed in cooperation with Fremont-Kearny Historians of Old San Diego, 1958.

ANZA-BORREGO DESERT (San Diego Co.) *Anza-Borrego Desert State Park, Henderson Canyon Rd., 1,000 ft. N of Peg Leg Rd.*

Peg Leg Smith

Thomas L. Smith, better known as "Peg Leg Smith," 1801–66, was a mountain man, prospector, and spinner of tall tales. Legends regarding his lost mine have grown through the years. Countless people have searched the desert looking for its fabulous wealth. The gold mine possibly could be within a few miles of this monument.

Placed in cooperation with Borrego Springs Chamber of Commerce, 1960.

ANZA-BORREGO DESERT (San Diego Co.)

*On CH S2,
.9 mi. NW of SH 78
intersection, near
Anza-Borrego Desert
State Park*

San Felipe

Here the southern trail of explorers, trappers, soldiers, and emigrants crossed ancient trade routes of Kamia, Cahuilla, Diegueño, and Luiseno Indians. On the flat, southwest across the creek, Warren F. Hall built and operated the San Felipe home station of the Butterfield Mail, 1858–61, used later by Banning stages and by the military during the Civil War.

Placed in cooperation with Squibob Chapter No. 1853 of E Clampus Vitus, 1964.

ANZA-BORREGO DESERT (San Diego Co.)

*Anza-Borrego Desert
State Park, Borrego Sink,
3 mi. SE of Palm Canyon
and Peg Leg rds.*

San Gregorio

Somewhere in this narrow valley, perhaps on this very spot, the Anza expeditions of 1774 and 1775 made their camps. Water for the 240 people and over 800 head of stock on the 1775 march was obtained from a series of wells, deeper than the height of a man, dug into the sandy bottom of the wash.

Placed by California State Park Commission in cooperation with Borrego Springs Chamber of Commerce, 1959.

ANZA-BORREGO DESERT (San Diego Co.)

*Anza-Borrego Desert
State Park, Santa Catarina Spring,
10 mi. NW of Borrego Springs*

Santa Catarina

This spring area was named by Capt. Juan Bautista de Anza when his overland exploration party camped here on Mar. 14, 1774, during the opening of the Anza Trail from Sonora into Alta California. Anza's colonizing expedition of 1775, consisting of 240 persons and over 800 head of livestock, camped here the night of December 23.

Placed in cooperation with the Squibob Chapter of E Clampus Vitus, 1963.

ARCADIA (Los Angeles Co.)

*Los Angeles State and
County Arboretum,
301 N. Baldwin Ave.*

Hugo Reid Adobe
1839
Furnished by National Society
of Colonial Dames in California
1961

Private plaque.

ARCADIA (Los Angeles Co.)

Los Angeles State and County Arboretum, 301 N. Baldwin Ave.

Queen Anne Cottage

Constructed by Elias Jackson ("Lucky") Baldwin in 1881. Designed by A. A. Bennett, and intended for entertaining. There being no kitchen, meals were served from the nearby adobe (built by Hugo Reid in 1839) where Baldwin actually lived. Restored and dedicated May 18, 1954, as part of Los Angeles State and County Arboretum.

Placed by California State Park Commission, 1954.

ARCATA (Humboldt Co.)

US 101 to Sunset Ave., N .9 mi. on L.K. Wood Blvd. frontage rd.

Camp Curtis 1862–1865

In memory of
Co. E & I 2nd California Volunteer Infantry
1862–1863
Co. B 1st Battalion Mountaineers
California Volunteers 1863–1864
Co. A 1st Battalion Native California
Volunteer Calvary 1864
and
Marie Brizard Todd
A Pioneer of 1847

Placed by Pioneer Society of Humboldt County.

ARCATA (Humboldt Co.)

Plaza Park, Eighth and H sts.

Jacoby Building

(Plaque at NE corner, structure at SE corner)

The basement and first story of the building, at 8th and H streets (opposite), was constructed in 1857 for Augustus Jacoby. For many years it was a principal supply point for the Klamath-Trinity mining camp trade. From 1858 through 1864 it served periodically as a refuge in time of Indian troubles. Housing various mercantile firms during its early years, it was acquired by A. Brizard in 1880.

Placed in cooperation with Humboldt County Historical Society, City of Arcata, and Brizard Company, 1963.

ARVIN (Kern Co.)

350 E. Bear Mountain Blvd., courtyard of Saint Thomas the Apostle Church

Francisco Garces O.F.M.

Padre Garces, first recorded white man in this locality, came in April of 1776, seeking a new route from Mexico to California. This epic journey covered more than 2,000 miles of uncharted desert and wilderness, opening trails later to become highways and railroads.

Placed by Kern County Chamber of Commerce, Kern County Historical Society, Bakersfield El Tejon Parlor No. 239 of Native Daughters of the Golden West, Bakersfield Parlor No. 42 of Native Sons of the Golden West.

ASTI (Sonoma Co.)   *SE corner Asti and Asti Post Office rds.*
Italian Swiss Colony
Here in 1881 Italian Swiss immigrants established an agricultural colony. Choice wines, produced from grape plantings from the old world, soon brought wide acclaim. By 1905, ten gold medals were awarded these wines at international competitions.
Placed by California State Park Commission, 1957.

ATASCADERO (San Luis Obispo Co.)   *6500 Palma Ave.*
Atascadero Administration Building
This building, dedicated in 1914 and completed in 1918, was the headquarters for the Atascadero Colony, a model community envisioned by Edward G. Lewis. Designed by Walter D. Bliss of San Francisco and built of reinforced concrete and locally produced brick, it has also served as a private school for boys, a veterans' memorial building, and county offices. It is currently the seat of municipal government.
Placed in cooperation with Atascadero Historical Society, 1984.

AUBURN (Placer Co.)   *SW corner Maple St. and Lincoln Way*
City of Auburn
Gold discovered near here by Claude Chana, May 16, 1848. Area first known as "North Fork" or "Wood's Dry Diggings." Settlement given name of Auburn in Fall of 1849. Soon became important mining town, trading post, and stage terminal. County Seat of Sutter County 1850 and Placer County 1851. Destroyed by fire 1855, 1859, and 1863.
Placed by California Centennial Commission and Placer County Historical Society, 1950.

AUBURN (Placer Co.)   *639 Lincoln Way*
First Transcontinental Railroad—Auburn
After an eleven-month delay due to political opposition and lack of money, Central Pacific tracks reached Auburn May 13, 1865, and regular service began. Government loans became available when the railroad completed its first 40 miles, four miles east of here. With the new funds, Central Pacific augmented its forces with the first Chinese laborers, and work began again in earnest.
Placed in cooperation with Conference of California Historical Societies and Placer County Historical Society, 1969.

AUBURN (Placer Co.)   *3 mi. W, SW corner Lozanos and Bald Hill rds.*
Town of Ophir
Founded in 1849 and first known as "The Spanish Corral." Area proved so rich that biblical name of Ophir adopted in 1850. Most populous town in Placer County in 1852, polling 500 votes. Almost totally destroyed by fire, July 1853. Later became center of quartz mining in this country.
Placed by California Centennial Commission and Placer County Historical Society, 1950.

AVALON (Los Angeles Co.)

On Catalina Island,
at 100 St. Catherine Way

The Tuna Club of Avalon

The Tuna Club of Avalon marks the birthplace of modern big game sportfishing in 1898. Led by Dr. Charles Frederick Holder, the club's founding members adopted the rules of conduct stressing conservationist ethics and sporting behavior. Today their work remains the basis for the sport's internationally accepted principles.

Placed in cooperation with Tuna Club of Avalon, 1991.

BAGDAD (Trinity Co.)

SH 299, 1,000 ft. S of Helena turnoff

Bagdad

On this site once stood the town of Bagdad. Founded in the year of 1850 by pioneers Crayen Lee and David Weed. Peak of population 500.

Placed by Mt. Bally Parlor No. 87 of Native Sons of the Golden West and Eltapome Parlor No. 55 of Native Daughters of the Golden West, 1953. (Unofficial marker)

BAKER (San Bernardino Co.)

30 mi. N, 4 mi. S, Death Valley
National Monument, on SH 127

Harry Wade Exit Route

After being in Death Valley with the ill-fated 1849 caravan, Harry Wade found this exit route for his ox-drawn wagon, thereby saving his life and those of his wife and children. At this point the Wade party came upon the known Spanish Trail to Cajon Pass.

Placed by descendants of Harry Wade and Death Valley '49ers in cooperation with San Bernardino County Board of Supervisors and California State Park Commission, 1957.

BAKERSFIELD (Kern Co.)

City Hall, SW corner Chester
and Truxtun aves.

Colonel Thomas Baker
Civil Engineer—Lawyer—Farmer—Soldier
1810–1872

In 1863 Col. Baker came to this location. A friend to all travelers, his settlement became known as "Baker's Field." This civic center is his dream come true. His motto—"Time will justify a man who means to do right."

Placed by Kern County Historical Society, Bakersfield City Council, El Tejon Parlor No. 239 of Native Daughters of the Golden West, Bakersfield Parlor No. 42 of Native Sons of the Golden West, Kern County Board of Supervisors, Kern County Chamber of Commerce, and public donations, 1942.

BAKERSFIELD (Kern Co.)

7 mi. NE, on Round Mountain Rd.,
7 mi. E of China Grade Loop

Discovery Well
Kern River Field

Oil was discovered at 70 feet in 1899 when Tom Means persuaded Roe Elwood and Frank Wiseman to dig for oil, aided by Jonathan, Bert, Jud, Ken Elwood, George Wiseman, and John Marlowe.

June 1, 1899, 400 feet north, Horace and Milton McWhorter drilled the first commercial well.

Placed by Bakersfield Parlor No. 42 of Native Sons of the Golden West, El Tejon Parlor No. 239 of Native Daughters of the Golden West, Kern County Historical Society, and Kern County Chamber of Commerce, 1940.

BAKERSFIELD (Kern Co.)   *Chester Ave. and 30th St. intersection*
Francisco Garces
1738–1781 Spanish Franciscan

Padre Garces seeking a new route between Sonora, Mexico, and Monterey crossed Rio de San Felipe (Kern River May 7, 1776) at Rancheria San Miguel, now Bakersfield. First recorded white man in this locality, he brought Christianity to the Indian and on Rio Colorado his brave life was crowned with martyrdom. "Greater love hath no man than this—that a man lay down his life for his friends."

Placed by Kern County Historical Society, Bakersfield Council No. 977 K of C, Garces Memorial Committee, Bakersfield Parlor No. 42 of Native Sons of the Golden West, City of Bakersfield, Kern County Chamber of Commerce, El Tejon Parlor No. 239 of Native Sons of the Golden West, Bakersfield Chamber of Commerce, public donations, and Union Oil Company, 1939.

BAKERSFIELD (Kern Co.)   *SE side of Kern River Bridge, on China Grade Loop, 1,000 ft. S of Round Mountain Rd.*
Gordon's Ferry

Gordon's Ferry was an overhead cable type of ferry operated during the 1850s by Maj. Gordon. An adobe station house was located on the south bank of Kern River, just a few yards to the west of this marker. It was also a station of the Butterfield Overland Mail stage route from 1858 to 1860.

Placed by Bakersfield Parlor No. 42 of Native Sons of the Golden West, El Tejon Parlor No. 239 of Native Daughters of the Golden West, and Kern County Chamber of Commerce, 1937.

BAKERSFIELD (Kern Co.)   *NW corner W. Columbus and Isla Verde sts.*
Home of Elisha Stevens

Near this spot stood the last home of Elisha Stevens, noted American pathfinder and scout. Born in Georgia, Apr. 5, 1804, he learned blacksmithing during his youth. Drifting west he became a trapper on the Upper Missouri for more than two decades. In 1844 he led the 50-member Murphy-Townsend wagon train safely from Council Bluffs to Sutter's Fort. During the Mexican War he served as an ordnance mechanic under Commodore Stockton. For a time he lived in Santa Clara County, then settled here on a 38-acre tract, the first permanent settler in the Bakersfield district. He died Sept. 9, 1887, and is buried in Union Cemetery.

Placed by California State Park Commission in cooperation with Kern County Historical Society, El Tejon Parlor No. 239 of Native Daughters of the Golden West, Bakersfield Parlor No. 42 of Native Sons of the Golden West, and Kern County Museum, 1964.

BAKERSFIELD (Kern Co.) — 414 19th St.
Last Home of Alexis Godey

Near this site stood the last home of Alexis Godey, frontiersman and scout. Born in St. Louis, Mo., in 1818, he acted as guide for John C. Fremont's expedition through the Kern area in 1843–44, and was honored for his services at the battle of San Pasqual in 1846. Moving here in 1883, Godey died Jan. 19, 1889.

Placed in cooperation with Kern County Historical Society, El Tejon Parlor No. 239 of Native Daughters of the Golden West, and Kern County Museum, 1960.

BAKERSFIELD (Kern Co.) — 11 mi. E, SH 178 at Rancheria Rd.
Rio de San Felipe

One mile north of here on May 1, 1776, Francisco Garces of the Franciscan Order crossed Kern River in his search for a shorter route from Sonora, Mexico, to Monterey, California. He was the first known explorer to describe this river, which he named Rio de San Felipe.

Placed by Bakersfield Parlor No. 42 of Native Sons of the Golden West, El Tejon Parlor No. 239 of Native Daughters of the Golden West, Kern County Historical Society, and Kern County Chamber of Commerce, 1938.

BAKERSFIELD (Kern Co.) — 11 mi. NE, NE corner of Round Mountain and Bakersfield-Glennville rds.
Posey Station

Two and one-half miles east of this point stood the Butterfield Overland stage site called Posey Station. Operating through present Kern County during 1858–61, this famous line ran from St. Louis, Missouri, to San Francisco until the outbreak of the Civil War.

Placed by Kern County Historical Society, El Tejon Parlor No. 239 of Native Daughters of the Golden West, and Kern County Museum, 1956.

BALBOA (Orange Co.) — 400 Main St.
Balboa Pavilion

This is one of California's last surviving examples of the great waterfront recreational pavilions from the turn of the century. Built in 1905 by the Newport Bay Investment Company, it played a prominent role in the development of Newport Beach as a seaside recreation area. In 1906, it became the southern terminus for the Pacific Electric Railway connecting the beach with downtown Los Angeles. The railway's red cars connected the beach with Los Angeles in only one hour.

Placed in cooperation with the Balboa Pavilion Company, Inc., 1984.

BARD (Imperial Co.) — 4.4 mi. NE, on CH S24, .2 mi. W of Levee and Mehring rds. intersection
Site of Mission San Pedro
y San Pedro de Bicuner

To protect the Anza Trail where it forded the Colorado River, the Spanish founded a pueblo and mission nearby on Jan. 7, 1781. Threatened with the loss of their land, the Quechans (Yumas) attacked this strategic settlement on July 17, 1781. The

Quechan victory closed this crossing and seriously crippled future communications between upper California and Mexico.

Placed in cooperation with E Clampus Vitus, Imperial Valley Pioneers, Phil Porretta and family, Bureau of Land Management, Yuma County Historical Society, and Quechan Tribal Council, 1980.

BARSTOW (San Bernardino Co.)

Santa Fe Depot, SW corner First Ave. and Riverside Dr.

Barstow Harvey House
(Plaque at Mojave River Museum, 270 E. Virginia Way)

Harvey Houses were legendary in the history of western rail travel. Operated by Fred Harvey in conjunction with the Santa Fe Railway, the network of restaurant-hotels set a new standard in quality meal service. Barstow's Spanish-Moorish "Casa del Desierto" opened in 1911 and closed in 1971. It was registered as one of the last and finest remaining examples of the west's famous Harvey Houses.

Placed in cooperation with Billy Holcomb Chapter of E Clampus Vitus, Mojave River Valley Museum, San Bernardino County Museum, and Fred Harvey, Inc., 1983.

BARSTOW (San Bernardino Co.)

25 mi. NE via I-15 to Harvard Rd. exit, then 2.5 mi S to unmarked sandy road, S .5 mi. to site

Camp Cady
(1860–1871)

Camp Cady was located on the Mojave Road which connected Los Angeles to Albuquerque. Non-Indian travel on this and the nearby Salt Lake road was beset by Paiutes, Mohaves, and Chemehuevis defending their homeland. To protect both roads, Camp Cady was established by U.S. Dragoons in 1860. The main building was a stout mud redoubt. Improved camp structures were built one-half mile west in 1868. After peace was achieved, the military withdrew in 1871. This protection provided by Camp Cady enabled travelers, merchandise, and mail using both roads to boost California's economy and growth.

Placed in cooperation with Billy Holcomb Chapter of E Clampus Vitus, State Department of Fish and Game, Mojave River Valley Museum, and Daggett Historical Society, Inc., 1994.

BARSTOW (San Bernardino Co.)

30 mi. NE, on I-15, at Midway rest area

Mojave Road

Long ago, Mohave Indians used a network of pathways to cross the Mojave Desert. In 1826, American trapper Jedediah Smith used their paths and became the first non-Indian to reach the California coast overland from mid-America. The paths were worked into a military wagon road in 1859. This "Mojave Road" remained a major link between Los Angeles and points east until a railway crossed the desert in 1885.

Placed in cooperation with Billy Holcomb Chapter of E Clampus Vitus, Bureau of Land Management, and Mojave River Valley Museum Association, 1988.

BEAR VALLEY (Mariposa Co.)   *On SH 49*

Bear Valley

First called Johnsonville, Bear Valley had a population of 3,000, including Chinese, Cornish, and Mexicans. During 1850–60 when Col. John C. Fremont's Ride Tree and Josephine mines were producing, Fremont's elegant hotel, Oso House, built with lumber brought around the Horn, no longer stands. After fire in 1888, structures were rebuilt. Some still standing are Bon Ton Saloon, Trabucco Store, Odd Fellows Hall, schoolhouse, and remains of jail. All reminders of Bear Valley's colorful past.
Placed by Matuca Chapter 1849 of E Clampus Vitus, 1985.

BELL GARDENS (Los Angeles Co.)   *7000 E. Gage*

Casa de Rancho San Antonio

Casa de Rancho San Antonio
Built 1810 for
Antonio Maria Lugo
Restored 1888 by
Henry Tift Gage
Governor State of California 1899–1903
Dedicated March 31, 1941

Placed by Native Sons and Daughters of the Golden West, Rio Hondo Parlor No. 284, and Los Angeles Parlor No. 43, 1941.

BELMONT (San Mateo Co.)   *College of Notre Dame,*
1500 Ralston Ave.

Ralston Hall

This redwood structure was completed in 1868 by William Chapman Ralston, San Francisco financier. Incorporating Count Cipriani's earlier villa, this enlarged mansion with its mirrored ballroom became the symbol of the extravagance of California's Silver Age. It anticipated features later incorporated into Ralston's Palace Hotel of San Francisco.
Placed in cooperation with the California Historical Society, 1972.

BENICIA (Solano Co.)   *Main gate of port area, Jefferson*
and Adams sts. intersection

Benicia Arsenal

On this historic site, for more than a century, military history was written. The loyalty, courage, and devotion of the military and the civilians who served their country here furnished material for a brilliant page in the saga of the Far West. What we say here—will like autumn leaves, soon fall and fade away. What they did here will live forever. As the final curtain falls on the 115th anniversary of the founding of Benicia Arsenal, a grateful nation salutes you.
Placed by the Historic Landmarks Committee of the Native Sons of the Golden West and Benicia Parlor No. 89 of Native Sons of the Golden West, 1964.

BENICIA (Solano Co.)   NE corner Military E. and E. 7th St.
Site of Benicia Arsenal

Captain Charles P. Stone with 12 enlisted men established Benicia Arsenal in August, 1851. As an ordnance depot, first building being erected in September 1851. Between 1853 to 1863, Congress authorized an expenditure of $555,000.00 on the establishment and at the same period some 15 stone and frame buildings were constructed. The depot was first called "California Ordnance Depot," then Benicia Arsenal Depot, finally in the spring of 1852 "Benicia Depot." The arsenal played an important role in all crises, from Indian wars to the Korean War of 1950. Descendants of the men who established Benicia Arsenal are still living in Benicia and parts of California. After 112½ years of supplying the Pacific Coast and Far East bases, Benicia Arsenal is part of the City of Benicia, adding 2,300 acres to the city.

Placed by Native Sons of the Golden West.

BENICIA (Solano Co.)   NW corner 1st and G sts.
Old State Capitol

Erected in 1852, this historic building was ostensibly intended for Benicia City Hall, offered as the state capitol, and promptly accepted. It has that honor from Feb. 4, 1853, to Feb. 25, 1854. Deeded to the state in 1951, it was one of the four locations of the "Capitol on Wheels."

Placed in cooperation with the Solano County Historical Society, 1975.

BENICIA (Solano Co.)   Benicia City Park, Military W. St.,
                                       between 1st and 2nd sts.
Site of Benicia Seminary

The birthplace of Mills College, founded in 1852 as the Young Ladies' Seminary of Benicia. Acquired from Mary Atkins by Cyrus and Susan Mills in 1865, it was moved to its present site in Oakland in 1871 and chartered as a college by the State of California in 1885.

Placed in cooperation with the Alumnae Associates of Mills College, 1965.

BENICIA (Solano Co.)   110 W. J St.
First Masonic Hall Built in California

The first Masonic Hall built in California was begun in the summer of 1850, occupied by the Lodge Oct. 14, 1850, and formally dedicated Dec. 27, 1850. This building served as the Masonic Temple for Benicia Lodge No. 5 until 1888, when the new temple was occupied. Used by a boys' club prior to World War I and by the American Legion shortly after the war. It was reacquired by Benicia Lodge No. 5 in 1950.

Placed by the Historic Landmark Committee Native Sons of the Golden West, Benicia Parlor No. 89 of Native Sons of the Golden West, and Benicia Parlor No. 287 of Native Daughters of the Golden West, 1950.

BENICIA (Solano Co.)   135 W. G St.
Fischer-Hanlon House

In 1849, Joseph Fischer, a Swiss immigrant, came to Benicia. After joining a butcher partnership, Fischer purchased this lot on July 1, 1858. The house, reputed to be an old hotel, was relocated here. The converted building is an outstanding example of East Coast Federalist styling, which illustrates architectural diffusion during the gold rush.

Placed in cooperation with the Solano County Historical Society, 1976.

BENICIA (Solano Co.)   *120 E. J St.*
Saint Paul's Episcopal Church

Designed in 1859 by Lt. Julian McAllister and built by shipwrights of the Pacific Mail and Steamship Company, St. Paul's is an outstanding example of early California Gothic ecclesiastical architecture. Notable for its fine craftsmanship, this building has continuously served the Episcopal Church since its consecration by the Rt. Rev. William Ingraham Kip in 1860.

Placed in cooperation with Exxon U.S.A., 1973.

BENICIA (Solano Co.)   *Benicia City Park, K St.*
between 1st and 2nd sts.
Site of the First Protestant Church

On this site was organized by the Rev. Sylvester Woodbridge, Jr., on Apr. 15, 1849, the First Presbyterian Church of Benicia. This was the first Protestant church established in California with an ordained resident pastor. The church was disbanded in 1875.

Placed by the Historic Landmark Committee Grand Parlor Native Sons, and Benicia Parlor No. 89 and Benicia Parlor No. 287 Native Sons and Daughters of the Golden West.

BENICIA (Solano Co.)   *Francesca Terrace Park, 711 Hillcrest Ave.*
Benicia Barracks Site

Benicia Barracks, established on Apr. 30, 1849, and organized by brevet Lt. Col. Silas Casey, 2nd U.S. Infantry, was the U.S. Army headquarters for the Department of the Pacific from 1852–57. Also known as the "Post near Benicia," it remained a garrison installation until 1898. The post hospital, built in 1856, is the only remaining structure associated with the original barracks. The barracks became part of the Benicia Arsenal, which closed in 1964.

Placed in cooperation with the City of Benicia and the Benicia Historical Society, 1982.

BENICIA (Solano Co.)   *Matthew Turner Shipyard*
Park, foot of W. 12th St.
Turner/Robertson Shipyard, 1883–1918

In 1882, Matthew Turner of San Francisco relocated his shipyard to Benicia. Turner, the most prodigious shipbuilder in North America, constructed 228 vessels, 169 of which were launched here. In 1913, the shipyard was purchased by James Robertson, who operated it until 1918. The yard's ways, and the whaler *Stamboul,* used as a shipyard work platform, are visible at low tide.

Placed in cooperation with the City of Benicia, 1987.

BERKELEY (Alameda Co.)   *2315 Durant Ave.*
Berkeley City Club
The Berkeley City Club, organized in 1927, was one of the area's earliest attempts by women to contribute to social, civic, and cultural progress. The building, constructed in 1929, is one of the outstanding works of noted California architect Julia Morgan, whose successful interpretation of Moorish and Gothic elements in this monumental structure created a major landmark of California design.
Placed in cooperation with the Berkeley City Club, 1977.

BERKELEY (Alameda Co.)   *Piedmont Ave., between Dwight Way*
                                                     and Gayley Rd.
Piedmont Way
Piedmont Way was conceived in 1865 by Frederick Law Olmsted, America's foremost landscape architect. As the centerpiece of a gracious residential community close beside the College of California, Olmsted envisioned a roadway that would follow the natural contours of the land and be sheltered from sun and wind by "an overarching bowery of foliage." This curvilinear, tree-lined parkway was Olmsted's first residential street design. It has served as the model for similar parkways across the nation.
Placed in cooperation with the Friends of the Frederick Law Olmsted Papers, 1990.

BERKELEY (Alameda Co.)   *Main entrance on Oxford St.*
University of California, Berkeley Campus
These landmarks form the historic core of the first University of California campus, opened in 1873: Founders' Rock, University House, Faculty Club and Glade, Hearst Greek Theatre, Hearst Memorial Mining Building, Doe Library, Sather Tower and Esplanade, Sather Gate and Bridge, Hearst Gymnasium, and California, Durant, Wellman, Hilgard, Giannini, Wheeler, North Gate, and South halls.
Placed in cooperation with the Regents of the University of California, 1985.

BEVERLY HILLS (Los Angeles Co.)   *1740 Green Acres Pl.*
Greenacres
Greenacres, one of the greatest estates of Hollywood's Golden Era, was built in 1929 for the internationally known silent screen comedian, Harold Lloyd. With its formal gardens, it is one of the finest Mediterranean/Italian Renaissance style residential complexes remaining in the state. The 44-room house was designed by Sumner Spaulding and the gardens planned by A. E. Hansen. The estate is patterned after the Villa Gamberaia near Florence, Italy.
Placed in cooperation with the Dona Powell Corporation, 1985.

BEVERLY HILLS (Los Angeles Co.)   *300 block of S. La Cienega Blvd.,*
                                         between Gregory and Olympic
Portola Trail 1769
The expedition of Don Gaspar de Portola from Mexico passed this way en route to Monterey to begin the Spanish colonization of California. With Captain Don Fernando Rivera y Moncada, Lt. Don Pedro Fages, Sgt. Jose Francisco Ortega, and

Fathers Juan Crespi and Francisco Gomez, Portola and his party camped near this spot on August 3, 1769.

Placed by California State Park Commission in cooperation with the City of Beverly Hills and Los Fiesteros de Los Angeles, 1959.

BIEBER (Lassen Co.)
County of Lassen Library-Historical Museum, NE corner Bridge St. and Veterans Ln.

Lassen Emigrant Trail

Peter Lassen opened the Lassen Emigrant Trail in 1848 when he led a 12-wagon emigrant train from Missouri to California. The route, which passed near this place, was extensively traveled during the years 1848–53 by emigrants seeking gold, adventure, and a new life in the west. Because of the route and the hospitality of the Indians, the trail was little used after 1853.

Placed by California State Park Commission in cooperation with Bieber and Lassen County Chambers of Commerce and Lassen County Historical Society, 1961.

BIG BASIN (Santa Cruz Co.)
Slippery Rock Memorial, Big Basin Redwoods State Park, SH 236

The First State Park

A group of conservationists led by Andrew P. Hill camped at the base of Slippery Rock on May 15, 1900, and formed the Sempervirens Club to preserve the redwoods of Big Basin. Their efforts resulted in deeding 3,500 acres of primeval forest to the State of California on Sept. 20, 1902. This marked the beginning of the California State Park system.

Placed in cooperation with the Conservation Associates, 1968.

BIG BEAR CITY (San Bernardino Co.)
4.3 mi. NW Belleville Holcomb Valley, on CR 3N16

Holcomb Valley
Named for
William Francis "Bill" Holcomb
Pioneer prospector
who, in this valley, discovered
Southern California's richest
gold field—May 5, 1860
Placed by Platrix Chapter E Clampus Vitus, 1955.

BIG BEAR LAKE (San Bernardino Co.)
4.8 mi. W of Big Bear Lake Village, on W edge of lake, at SH 28 and SH 38 intersection

Old Bear Valley Dam

In 1884 Frank Brown built an unusual dam here to supply irrigation water for the Redlands area. The single-arch granite dam formed Big Bear Lake, then the world's largest man-made lake. Engineers claimed the dam would not hold, and declared it "The Eighth Wonder of the World" when it did. The old dam is usually underwater because of the 20-foot higher dam built 200 feet west in 1912.

Placed in cooperation with Billy Holcomb Chapter of E Clampus Vitus, U.S. Forest Service, San Bernardino County Museum, and Big Bear Valley Historical Society, 1982.

BIG OAK FLAT (Tuolumne Co.) — *On SH 120*
Mark Twain Bret Harte Trail
Big Oak Flat

First called Savage Diggings after man who discovered gold here, 1848. Renamed Big Oak Flat about 1850 after giant oak tree that stood in center of town near this spot. Oak was about 13 feet in diameter and was undermined in 1869 and burned in 1890. Pieces remain. Rich placer and lode mines reported to have yielded $28,000,000 during heyday. Stone buildings, erected 1852, still standing 1949.

Placed by California Centennial Commission and Boys Service Club, Sonora Union High School, 1949.

BISHOP (Inyo Co.) — *5.2 mi. SW, SE corner SH 168 and Bishop Creek Rd. intersection*
Bishop Creek Battleground

On Apr. 6, 1862, a battle took place around this site between newly arrived citizens of the Owens River Valley and the Paiute and Shoshone Indians, original inhabitants of the land. The reason for this battle is lost in obscurity, but brave men on both sides died here for a cause which they held to be inviolate.

Placed in cooperation with California Historical Landmarks Advisory Committee and Eastern California Museum Association, Inc., 1966.

BISHOP (Inyo Co.) — *4 mi. NE of Bishop, US 6 and Silver Canyon Rd. intersection*
Owensville

The first white man's settlement in northern Owens Valley was built here in 1861 and two years later prospectors named it Owensville. It thrived for some time; but in 1864, as mining in the White Mountains petered out, the miners moved on to better diggings, leaving the town deserted.

Placed by Slim Princess Chapter of E Clampus Vitus, 1977.

BISHOP (Inyo Co.) — *4.5 mi. NE, on Silver Canyon Rd., in old townsite of Laws*
Laws Station

In 1883, the Carson & Colorado Railroad was built between Mound House (near Carson City, Nevada) through Laws to Keeler, California, a distance of 300 miles. Laws Station was named in honor of Mr. R. J. Laws, Assistant Superintendent of the railroad. Between 1883 and about 1915, this railroad provided the only dependable means of transportation in and out of Owens Valley. Train service was stopped on Apr. 30, 1960.

Placed in cooperation with Bishop Museum and Historical Society, 1983.

BISHOP (Inyo Co.)
3 mi. SW, on S side of SH 168, between Mumy Ln. and Redhill Rd.

San Francis Ranch

In 1861 Samuel A. Bishop, his wife, and party left Fort Tejon for the Owens Valley driving 650 head of stock. On Aug. 22, Bishop reached a creek later named for him and southwest of this spot. Established San Francis Ranch. There a peace treaty was signed by the settlers and the chiefs of the Paiute Indians.

Placed by Slim Princess Chapter 395 of E Clampus Vitus, 1985.

BLAIRSDEN (Plumas Co.)
5 mi. SW, Plumas-Eureka State Park, S on SH 89 from SH 70, then W on CH A14

Jamison City
Eureka Mine and Mill
Johnstown

Along the pioneer trail lies Jamison City and Mine, large producer, famous for its 52-pound nugget; Eureka Mill and Mine yielding $17 million to Cornish miners and others. Johnstown, now Johnsville, well preserved '49 town.

BLAIRSDEN (Plumas Co.)
5 mi. SW, Plumas-Eureka State Park, S on SH 89 from SH 70, then W on CH A14

Pioneer Ski Area of America

The first sport ski area in the western hemisphere was in the Sierra Nevada. By 1860 races were held in the Plumas-Sierra region. The mining towns of Whisky Diggins, Poker Flat, Port Wine, Onion Valley, La Porte, Jamison City, and Johnsville organized the earliest ski clubs and annual competitions.

Placed by California State Park Commission in cooperation with California Historical Society, Plumas County Historical Society, and Plumas Ski Club, 1961.

BLUE LAKE (Humboldt Co.)
Railroad Depot, 330 Railroad Ave.

Arcata and Mad River Railroad Company

Incorporated Dec. 15, 1854, as the Union Plank Walk, Rail Track, and Wharf Company, the Arcata and Mad River Railroad is the oldest line on the north coast. Originally using a horse-drawn car, the railroad served as a link between Humboldt Bay and the Trinity River mines. Later, locomotives were added as the line grew to serve the redwood industry.

Placed in cooperation with Humboldt County Historical Society and the Arcata and Mad River Railroad Company, 1970.

BLYTHE (Riverside Co.)
9.5 mi. N, on US 95, Intake Service, at Palo Verde Diversion Dam

Blythe Intake

On July 17, 1877, Thomas Blythe, a San Francisco financier, filed the first legal claim for Colorado River water rights. Oliver Callaway planned a diversion dam and canal which opened in 1877 to irrigate the Palo Verde Valley. This made possible the settlement and development of the valley.

Placed in cooperation with Billy Holcomb Chapter of E Clampus Vitus, Palo Verde Valley Historical Society, and Riverside County Parks and Recreation, 1986.

BLYTHE (Riverside Co.)   *16 mi. N, on SH 95*
Giant Desert Figures

Times of origin and meaning of these giant figures, the largest 167 feet long, the smallest 95 feet, remain a mystery. There are three figures, two of animals and a coiled serpent, and some interesting lines.

Placed by Department of Public Works, Division of Highways.

BODEGA BAY (Sonoma Co.)   *.5 mi. S, Doran Park, on*
Doran Beach Rd., 1.6 mi. W of SH 1
Bodega Bay and Harbor

Discovered in 1602–03 by the expedition of Vizcaino. It was named by Bodega in his survey of 1775. The harbor was used in 1790 by Colnett and by the Kusov Expeditions in 1809 and 1811. The Russian-American Company and their Aleut hunters used the bay as an outpost until 1841. Stephen Smith took control in 1843. Pioneer ships of many nations used Bodega Bay as an anchorage.

Placed in cooperation with the Westerners and Sonora County Parks and Recreation, 1970.

BODEGA BAY (Sonoma Co.)   *Bodega Hwy. near Bodega Ln.*
Church of St. Teresa of Avila

Constructed of redwood in 1859 by New England ships' carpenters on Spanish land grant donated by Jasper O'Farrell. On Mar. 8, 1860, Father Louis Rossi was appointed pastor. Archbishop Alemany dedicated the church in the town of Bodega in June 2, 1861, and it has served this coastal community continuously for over a century.

Placed in cooperation with the Roman Catholic Church and Sonoma County Parks and Recreation Department, 1968.

BODFISH (Kern Co.)   *In front of post office, NE corner*
Miller St. and Kern River Canyon Rd.
Havilah
7 Miles

Founded 1863 by Aleck Harpending, who named it from verse in *Genesis* as "A Place Rich in Gold." Made Kern County seat, 1866. A station of stagelines running between Los Angeles and San Francisco. Declined after county seat moved to Bakersfield, 1872.

Placed by Department of Public Works, Division of Highways.

BREA (Orange Co.)   *Carbon Canyon Regional*
Park, 4442 Carbon Canyon Rd.
Olinda

The course of oil production was changed in 1899 when the Olinda area became the first site in California to use the technique of drilling with the hole full of water. Having been developed as a source of fuel oil for the Santa Fe Railroad, Olinda became a bustling boomtown at the turn of the century. Its demise came with the construction of Carbon Canyon Dam in 1959.

Placed in cooperation with Orange County Board of Supervisors, 1978.

BRIDGEPORT (Mono Co.)   *19.8 mi. SE, Bodie State Historic Park, on SH 270, 12.8 mi. E of US 395*
Bodie
Gold was discovered here in 1859 by W.S. Bodey after whom the town was named. Once the most thriving metropolis of the Mono country, Bodie's mines produced gold valued at more than 100 million dollars. Tough as nails, "the bad man from Bodie" still carries his guns and Bowie knife down through the pages of western history.

Placed by California State Park Commission in cooperation with Mono County Department of Parks and Recreation and Mono County Historical Society, 1964.

BRIDGEPORT (Mono Co.)   *7 mi. S, on US 395*
Dog Town
1857
Site of the first major gold rush to California's eastern slope of the Sierra Nevada, Dog Town derived its name from a popular miners' term for camps with huts or hovels. Ruins, lying close to the cliff bordering Dog Town Creek, are all that remain of the makeshift dwellings which here formed part of the "diggins."

Placed by California State Park Commission in cooperation with Mono County Department of Parks and Recreation and Mono County Historical Society, 1964.

BUENA PARK (Orange Co.)   *Knott's Berry Farm, 8039 Beach Blvd., Ghost Town area, N side of Mott's Miniatures*
Rivera (Old Maizeland) School
This was the first school in the Rivera district, constructed in 1868, and previously located on Shugg Lane, now Slauson Avenue.

Placed by California State Park Commission in cooperation with East Los Angeles Parlor No. 266 of Native Daughters of the Golden West, 1960.

BURLINGAME (San Mateo Co.)   *290 California Dr.*
Burlingame Railroad Station
This first permanent building in the Mission Revival style of architecture was designed by George H. Howard and J. B. Mathison and financed by local residents and the Southern Pacific Railroad. It opened for service on October 10, 1894. The roof used 18th century tiles from the Mission San Antonio de Padua at Jolon and the Mission Dolores Asistencia at San Mateo.

Placed in cooperation with San Mateo County Historical Association and the Society of California Pioneers, 1971.

BUTTONWILLOW (Kern Co.)   *On Butterfield Dr., .5 mi. N of SH 58*
Buttonwillow Tree
A lone tree landmark on an old trans-valley trail. It was an ancient Yokuts Indian meeting place, later a location for white stock rodeos. Miller and Lux established their headquarters and store here about 1885. The town of Buttonwillow takes its name from this old tree and rodeo grounds.

Placed by Kern County Historical Society and Kern County Museum, 1952.

CALABASAS (Los Angeles Co.) *23537 Calabasas Rd.*
Plummer Park and Oldest House in Hollywood
(Old location: 7377 Santa Monica Blvd., Hollywood)
Known as the "oldest house in Hollywood." This house was built in the 1870s by Eugene Raphael Plummer.
Placed by Milly Barrett Chapter, Daughters of the American Revolution, 1956.

CALAVERITAS (Calaveras Co.) *4.5 mi. SE of San Andreas,*
on Calaveras Rd. at Costa Rd.
Calaveritas
Calaveritas, settled in 1849 by Mexicans, was a flourishing mining town with stores, saloons, and fandango halls. Joaquin Murietta is reported to have frequently visited its fandango halls and gambling houses. Destroyed by fire in 1858.
Placed by California Centennial Commission and Calaveras County 20–30 Club, 1950.

CALEXICO (Imperial Co.) *Rockwood Plaza,*
Sixth St. E. at Heber Ave.
Camp Salvation
Here on Sept. 23, 1849, Lt. Cave J. Couts, Escort Commander, International Boundary Commission, established Camp Salvation. From September till the first of December 1849, it served as a refugee center for distressed emigrants attempting to reach the gold fields over the Southern Emigrant Trail.
Placed by California State Park Commission in cooperation with the City of Calexico and Squibob Chapter of E Clampus Vitus, 1965.

CALIENTE (Kern Co.) *1.3 mi. S, .9 mi. N of SH 58, on Bealville Rd.*
Bealville
Named for Edward F. Beale, this station on the Southern Pacific rail line was established in 1876 as a depot and telegraph office. Service was discontinued in 1943. Beale was superintendent of California Indian Affairs during the 1850s. In 1865 he became owner of the adjacent Rancho El Tejon.
Placed by Kern County Historical Society, Kern County Museum, and El Tejon Parlor No. 239 of Native Daughters of the Golden West, 1962.

CALIENTE (Kern Co.) *2.3 mi. N of SH 58, on Bealville Rd.*
Caliente
Caliente, formerly Allen's Camp. Was renamed when the Southern Pacific Railroad established construction headquarters here in 1875 while track was laid over Tehachapi Pass. It was a freighting center for Havilah and other mining towns as well as shipping point for cattle from Walker's Basin and Bear Mountain.
Placed by Kern County Historical Society, Bakersfield Parlor No. 42 of Native Sons of the Golden West, El Tejon Parlor No. 239 of Native Daughters of the Golden West, and Kern County Museum, 1961.

CALISTOGA (Napa Co.)   *1458 Lincoln Ave.*
Calistoga Depot
Built by Sam Brannan for the Napa Valley Railroad in 1868 one year before the completion of the transcontinental railroad. Second oldest remaining station in California. Northern terminus of the Napa Valley Railroad and its successors, the Napa Valley branches of the Central Pacific Railroad and the Southern Pacific Railroad. Restored in 1978 by Calistoga Depot Associates.
Placed by Sam Brannan Chapter No. 1004 of E Clampus Vitus, 1979.

CALISTOGA (Napa Co.)   *3.1 mi. S, end of Schramsberg Rd. off SH 29*
Schramsberg
Founded in 1862 by Jacob Schram, this was the first hillside winery of the Napa Valley. Robert Louis Stevenson, visiting here in 1880, devoted a chapter of his *Silverado Squatters* to Schramsberg and its wines. Ambrose Bierce and Lilly Hitchcock Coit were other cherished friends. The original house and winery have been excellently preserved.
Placed by California State Park Commission in cooperation with Napa County Historical Society, 1957.

CALISTOGA (Napa Co.)   *SW corner SH 29 and Lincoln Ave.*
Site of John York's Cabin
Among the first houses of Calistoga was John York's cabin. Constructed in October 1845. Rebuilt as part of the home of the Kortum family, it was used as a residence until razed in 1930. Nearby was the cabin of David Hudson, also built in October 1845. Calistoga was named by Samuel Brannan in 1859.
Placed by California State Park Commission in cooperation with the City of Calistoga and Napa County Historical Society, 1959.

CALISTOGA (Napa Co.)   *7.5 mi. NE, on SH 29*
Robert Louis Stevenson State Park
In the spring of 1880, Robert Louis Stevenson brought his bride to Silverado. He and Fannie Osbourne Stevenson lived here from May 19 until July, while he gathered the notes for *Silverado Squatters.*

CALISTOGA (Napa Co.)   *7.5 mi. NE, on SH 29*
Robert Louis Stevenson State Park
This tablet placed by the Club Women of Napa County marks the site of the cabin occupied in 1880 by Robert Louis Stevenson and bride while he wrote *The Silverado Squatters.* "Doomed to know not winter, only spring, a being trod the flowery April blithely for awhile, took his fill of music, joy of thought and seeing, came and stayed and went, nor ever ceased to smile." *R.L.S.*
Private plaque.

CALISTOGA (Sonoma Co.)   *5 mi. NW, 4100 Petrified Forest Rd.*
Petrified Forest
The petrified forest, dating from the Eocene Period, is the only known example of petrified forest in California. Its size, scope, and variety of petrification is unique in

the world. Opalized wood, obsidian, quartz, crystal, petrified coral, and fossilized insects number among its wonders.

Placed in cooperation with Ollie Orre Bockee, Jeanette Orre Hawthorne, and Davida Conway, 1978.

CAMANCHE (Calaveras Co.)

S. Camanche Shore Park, picnic area near S entrance, Camanche Parkway S., 3 mi. NW of Burson

Camanche

Named Camanche in 1849 after Camanche, Iowa. Once called Limerick. Peak population 1,500. Rich mining at nearby Cat Camp, Poverty Bar, and Sand Hill. Mokelumne River water brought in by Lancha Plana and Poverty Bar ditch. Fire June 21, 1873, destroyed large Chinatown. Buhach manufactured on nearby Hill Ranch.

Placed by Calaveras County Historical Society and residents of Camanche in cooperation with California State Park Commission, 1956.

CAMBRIA PINES (San Luis Obispo Co.)

Nitt Witt Ridge, 881 Hillcrest Dr.

Nitt Witt Ridge

Nitt Witt Ridge, one of California's remarkable twentieth century folk art environments, is the creation of Arthur Harold Beal (Der Tinkerpaw or Captain Nitt Witt), a Cambria Pines pioneer, who sculpted the land using hand tools and indigenous materials, remarkable inventiveness, and self-taught skills. A blend of native materials and contemporary elements, impressive in its sheer mass and meticulous placement, it is a revealing memorial to Art's unique cosmic humor and zest for life.

Placed in cooperation with Saving and Preserving Arts and Cultural Environments and the Art Beal Foundation, 1986.

CAMPO (San Diego Co.)

SH 94, at Campo corner

Old Campo Store

Dedicated to the pioneers of San Diego County
Built in 1868 by L. H. and S. E. Gaskill
Historic stone store—post office—bank and stage station
Scene of famous bandit raid December 5, 1875

Placed by Ellsworth M. Statler, San Diego County Board of Supervisors 1943–48, California State Historical Association, San Diego Historical Society, and Native Sons and Daughters of the Golden West, 1948.

CAMPO SECO (Calaveras Co.)

Intersection Campo Seco and Penn Mine rds.

Campo Seco

Settled in 1849 by Mexicans who worked placers on Oregon Gulch. Rich copper deposits discovered in 1859. Largest living cork oak tree in California planted here 1858. Ruins of Adams Express Building with iron doors still standing.

Placed by California Centennial Commission and Campo Seco Community Club, 1950.

CANBY (Modoc Co.)

4.9 mi. SE, on top of hill,
500 ft. S of Centerville Rd.

Evans and Bailey Fight

In memory of S. D. Evans, Sr., of Roseburg, Ore. and Joe Bailey of Eugene, Ore. Killed by Indians on this spot Aug. 1, 1861, and 800 head of cattle stolen. 1929.
Private plaque, placed 1929.

CANBY (Modoc Co.)

9.3 mi. NW, and 5 mi. NW of CR 84

Old Emigrant Trail

Bend of the Pit River
Lassen Trail 1848
Placed by Trails West Inc., 1974.

CANTIL (Kern Co.)

3.7 mi. E of Cantil Post Office,
SE corner of Pappas Ranch,
.5 mi. S of Valley Rd., on Pappas Rd.

Desert Spring

This spring was on the old Indian Horsethief Trail and later (1834) Joe Walker Trail. The famished Manly-Jayhawk Death Valley parties (1849–50) were revived here after coming from Indian Wells through Last Chance Canyon. This was also a station on the Nadeau Borax Freight Road.
Placed by California Centennial Commission in cooperation with Kern County Historical Society and Kern County Museum, 1950.

CANTIL (Kern Co.)

13.4 mi. NE of Cantil Post Office,
7.4 mi. W of US 395, on Garlock Rd.

Garlock

In 1896 Eugene Garlock constructed a stamp mill near this spot for the crushing of gold ore from the Yellow Aster Mine on Rand Mountain. Known originally as Cow Wells by prospectors and freighters during the 1880s and early 1890s, the Town of Garlock continued to thrive until water was piped from here to Randsburg in 1898, and the Kramer-Randsburg rail line was completed in the same year.
Placed by California State Park Commission in cooperation with Kern County Historical Society, El Tejon Parlor No. 239 of Native Daughters of the Golden West, and Kern County Museum, 1960.

CANYON COUNTRY (Los Angeles Co.)

4.7 mi. E, .4 mi. S of
SH 14, Lang Station Rd.,
Soledad Canyon

Lang Southern Pacific Station

On Sept. 5, 1876, Charles Crocker, President, Southern Pacific Railroad, drove a gold spike here to complete his company's San Joaquin Valley line, first rail connection of Los Angeles with San Francisco and transcontinental lines.
Placed by California State Park Commission in cooperation with Historical Society of Southern California, 1957.

CAPITOLA (Santa Cruz Co.) *201 Monterey Ave.*
Camp Capitola—Superintendent's Office
California's first seaside resort community was established here in 1869 by Mr. F. A. Hihn. The grand opening was held on July 4, 1874, for the 15-acre resort, located in the present village and depot hill areas. The superintendent's office, built from local redwood in the 1880s, served as the headquarters for Camp Capitola until 1930.

Placed in cooperation with Capitola Historical Society, 1973.

CARPINTERIA (Santa Barbara Co.) *Carpinteria Valley Museum of History, 950 Maple Ave.*
La Carpinteria (1769)
(Second plaque at 1000 S. Carpinteria Ave.)

The Chumash Indian village of "Mishopshnow," discovered by Juan Rodriguez Cabrillo, Aug. 14, 1542, was located one-fourth mile southwest of here. Fray Juan Crespi of the Gaspar de Portola Expedition named it "San Roque," Aug. 17, 1769. Portola's soldiers, observing the Indians building wooden canoes, called the village "La Carpinteria"—the Carpenter Shop.

Placed by California State Park Commission in cooperation with the County of Santa Barbara.

CARSON (Los Angeles Co.) *18501 S. Wilmington Ave.*
First United States Air Meet
About one-half mile southeast of this spot, on Dominquez Hill in historic Rancho San Pedro, the first air meet in the United States was held during Jan. 10–20, 1910. Subsequently, this area has evolved into one of the world's leading aviation-industrial centers.

Placed by California State Park Commission in cooperation with the City of Compton and the Co. of Los Angeles, 1960.

CARSON HILL (Calaveras Co.) *3.7 mi. S of Angels Camp, on SH 4*
Carson Hill
Gold discovered in creek just below town by James H. Carson in 1848, whose name was given to creek, hill, and town. In November 1854, at Morgan Mine, was found the largest gold nugget in California, weighing 195 pounds troy, worth at that time $43,000.

Placed by California Centennial Commission and Angels Camp Lions Club, 1949.

CARTAGO (Inyo Co.) *7 mi. N, 1 mi. E of US 395*
Cottonwood Charcoal Kilns
In June 1873 Col. Sherman Stevens built a sawmill and flume on Cottonwood Creek high in the Sierras directly west of this spot. The flume connected with the Los Angeles bullion road. The lumber from the flume was used for timbering in the mine and buildings, and the wood was turned into charcoal in these kilns, then hauled to Steven's Wharf east of here on Owens Lake. There it was put on the steamer the "Bessie Brady," or the "Mollie Stevens," hauled directly across the lake, and from there wagons took it up the "Yellow Grade" to Cerro Gordo Mine, high in the Inyo Mountains above Keeler. M.W. Belshaw's furnaces had used all available wood around the Cerro Gordo, and this charcoal was necessary to continued production.

The bullion, which was then taken out by the reverse of this route, was hauled to Los Angeles on Remi Nadeau's 14, 16, 18 animal freight wagons and played a major part in the building of that little pueblo into the city of today.

Placed by California Eastern Sierra Museum Association, 1955, and Slim Princess Chapter No. 395 of E Clampus Vitus, 1976.

CASTELLA (Shasta Co.)

Castella Crags State Park, 1 mi. W of I-5, on lawn at entrance station

Battle Rock

Battle of the Crags was fought below Battle Rock in June 1855. This conflict between the Modoc Indians and the settlers resulted from miners destroying the native fishing waters in the Lower Soda Springs area. Settlers led by Squire Reuben Gibson and Mountain Joe Doblondy, with local Indians led by their Chief Weilputus, engaged Modocs, killed their Chief Dorcas Dalla, and dispersed them. Poet Joaquin Miller and other settlers were wounded.

Placed in cooperation with the Trinitarianus Chapter No. 62 of E Clampus Vitus, 1984.

CASTELLA (Shasta Co.)

6.9 mi. S, on old Hwy. 99, .7 mi. SW of Sims exit

Southern's Stage Station

This tablet marks the location of the famous Southern Hotel and Stage Station. The original building was a log cabin built in 1859. During a half century, many noted people who made early California history were entertained in this hotel.

Placed by May H. and Fannie E. Southern, daughters of Simeon Fisher Southern and Sarah Lafferty Southern, 1931.

CASTRO VALLEY (Alameda Co.)

19200 Redwood Rd., between James and Alma

**Site of First Public School
in Castro Valley**

This site was part of the original Don Castro Land Grant. In 1866 pioneer settler Josiah Grover Brickell made a land grant of this site for "educational purposes only" and paid the teacher's salary, who taught children by day, in the one room school house, and farm hands at night by candlelight.

Placed by California State Park Commission in cooperation with Vallecito Parlor No. 308 of Native Daughters of the Golden West, 1962.

CEDAR GROVE (El Dorado Co.)

5622 Old Pony Express Trail

Sportsman's Hall

This was the site of Sportsman's Hall, also known as Twelve-Mile House, the hotel operated in the late 1850s and 1860s by John and James Blair. A stopping place for stages and teams of the Comstock, it became a relay station of the California Overland Pony Express. Here, at 7:40 a.m., Apr. 4, 1860, pony rider William (Sam) Hamilton, riding in from Placerville, handed the express mail to Warren Upson, who two minutes later sped on his way eastward.

Placed by California State Park Commission in cooperation with James W. Marshall Chapter No. 49 of E Clampus Vitus and the California Overland Pony Express Trail Association, 1960.

CEDARVILLE (Modoc Co.)
Cedarville Park, Center St., between Townsend and Bonner sts.

Cressler and Bonner Trading Post, 1865

The first building erected in Deep Creek Settlement, now Cedarville, was built in 1865 as a trading post by James Townsend, who was killed in an Indian fight in 1866. Purchased by William T. Cressler and John H. Bonner in 1867, the building was used as a trading post and general store until larger quarters were built in 1874. The mercantile, banking, and ranching firm of Cressler and Bonner played a major role in the settlement and development of Surprise Valley and Modoc County. The land for the Cedarville Park was donated to Modoc County by descendants of Mr. Cressler in 1957, and the building was reconstructed in 1977 with funds provided by the State Recreational Bond Act of 1974.

Private plaque.

CENTRAL VALLEY (Shasta Co.)
6 mi. N, at Bridge Bay Resort parking lot, I-5 and Bridge Bay turnoff

Bass Hill

In loving memory to these pioneers who "held the ribbons" but have turned the bend in this road. This stage driver's monument marks the Sacramento River where it connects with U.S. Highway 99.

Placed by Mae Helene Bacon Boggs, niece of Williamson Lyncoya Smith, 1930.

CHICO (Butte Co.)
Bidwell Nature Center, Cedar Grove Picnic Area, Bidwell Park, Cedar Grove and E. 8th St.

Chico Forestry Station and Nursery

In 1888, the State Board of Forestry established an experimental forestry station and nursery, a companion to the Santa Monica station established in 1887. The two were the first such stations in the nation. Exotic and native trees were tested and produced for scientific and conservation purposes. The station was operated by the Board of Forestry until 1893.

Placed in cooperation with the California Division of Forestry and the City of Chico, 1972.

CHICO (Butte Co.)
Hooker Oak Recreation Area, Bidwell Park, Manzanita Ave., between Vallombrosa and Hooker Oak Ave.

Hooker Oak

Height of tree 96 ft. Circum. of tree 8 ft. From ground 29 ft. Spread of north & south branches 153 ft. Circum. of outside branches 481. Lineal measurement—largest so. branch 111 ft. Diameter of trunk 8 ft. From ground 9 ft. Estimated age of tree 1,000 years. Allowing 2 ft. per person 8,000 people can stand under this tree.

Placed by Annie K. Bidwell Parlor 168 of Native Daughters of the Golden West, 1953.

CHICO (Butte Co.)

Bidwell Mansion State Historic Park, 525 The Esplanade

Rancho del Arroyo Chico

A vast expanse covering 26,000 acres, Rancho Chico was purchased in 1849–50 by John Bidwell. In 1865 he began construction of the mansion nearby, which in time became the social and cultural center of the upper Sacramento Valley. It was through his advancement of agriculture, however, that Bidwell made his greatest contribution. The introduction here of plants from all over the world opened the door to California's present agricultural treasure house.

Placed in cooperation with historical groups of Butte County, 1966.

CHILCOOT (Plumas Co.)

1.5 mi. E, rest area, Beckwourth Pass, SH 70

Emigrant Trail
Beckwourth Pass

Elevation 5,221. Lowest pass in the Sierra Nevada Mountains. Discovered in 1851 by James R. Beckwourth. "No desert's waste nor redskins bold could swerve them from this western strand. Naught could their courage e'er dismay in onward trudging day by day." *A.W. Wern*

Placed by Las Plumas Parlor No. 254 of Native Daughters of the Golden West, 1937.

CHILES VALLEY (Napa Co.)

3.6 mi. N on SH 128, SW corner of hillside, Chiles and Pope and Lower Chiles Valley rds.

Chiles Grist Mill

Built by Joseph Ballinger Chiles who first came to California in 1841. He erected the mill on Rancho Catacula 1845–46, the first American flour mill in Northern California. The mill was still used in the 1880s. Chiles was a vice-president of the Society of California Pioneers, 1850–53.

Placed by Society of California Pioneers in cooperation with California State Park Commission, 1956.

CHILI GULCH (Calaveras Co.)

On SH 49, 1.4 mi. S of Mokelumne Hill

Chili Gulch

Richest placer mining section, extending five miles, in Calaveras County. Received name from Chileans who worked gulch in 1848 and 1849, and scene of the so-called Chilean War. Largest known quartz crystals recovered from mine on south side of gulch.

Placed by California Centennial Commission and Mokelumne Lions Club, 1949.

CHINESE CAMP (Tuolumne Co.)

NW corner SH 120 and Main St.

Mark Twain Bret Harte Trail
Chinese Camp

Reportedly founded about 1849 by a group of Englishmen who employed Chinese as miners. Much surface gold found on hills and flats. Headquarters for stage lines in early 1850s, and for several California Chinese mining companies. First Chinese

Tong war in state fought near here between Sam Yap and Yan Woo Tongs. Present stone and brick post office built 1854, still standing. St. Francis Xavier Catholic Church built 1855, restored 1949. First pastor, Father Henry Aleric.

Placed by California Centennial Commission and Tuolumne County Council No. 2165 of Knights of Columbus, 1949.

CHINESE CAMP (Tuolumne Co.)

3.5 mi. SE, on SH 120 vista point at north approach to Don Pedro Bridge

Jacksonville

Near this site, now inundated by the waters of Don Pedro Reservoir, stood the historic town of Jacksonville. It was settled by Julian Smart who planted the first garden and orchard in the spring of 1849. Named for Col. A. M. Jackson. In 1850 it was the principal river town in the area. It was the gathering center for thousands of miners working the rich bed of the Tuolumne River.

Placed in cooperation with Golden Chain Council of the Mother Lode and 120 Highway Association, 1971.

CHINO (San Bernardino Co.)

3 mi. SW, Chino Fire Station No. 2, 4440 Eucalyptus Ave.

Rancho Chino Adobe Site

Near this site, Isaac Williams in 1841 built a large adobe home, located on the 22,000-acre Rancho Chino which he acquired from his father-in-law, Antonio Lugo. The "Battle of Chino" occurred at the adobe on Sept. 26–27, 1846, during which 24 Americans were captured by a group of about 50 Californios. Located on the Southern Immigrant Trail to California, the adobe later became an inn and stage stop famous for its hospitality.

Placed in cooperation with Chino Valley Historical Society, Billy Holcomb Chapter of E Clampus Vitus, and San Bernardino County Museum, 1982.

CHINO (San Bernardino Co.)   *5.5 mi. S, 17127 Pomona-Rincon Rd.*

Yorba-Slaughter Adobe

This example of early California architecture was built in 1850–53 by Raimundo Yorba. Purchased in 1868 by Fenton Mercer Slaughter, it was preserved as a memorial to him by his daughter, Julia Slaughter Fuqua.

Placed by California State Park Commission in cooperation with Ontario Parlor No. 251 of Native Daughters of the Golden West, 1960.

CITY OF INDUSTRY (Los Angeles Co.)   *15415 E. Don Julian Rd.*

Workman Family Cemetery

"El Campo Santo," this region's earliest known private family cemetery, was established in 1850 by William Workman. The miniature classic Grecian mausoleum was built in 1919 by grandson Walter P. Temple. Included in this cemetery are the remains of Workman, his family and descendents, partner John Rowland, friend Pio Pico (the last California governor under Mexican rule), and his wife Maria Ygnacia Pico.

Placed in cooperation with City of Industry, 1976.

CITY OF INDUSTRY (Los Angeles Co.)   *15415 E. Don Julian Rd.*
William Workman Home
Home of pioneer William Workman. Workman and co-owner John Rowland developed the 48,790-acre La Puente Rancho. Workman and co-leader Rowland organized the first wagon train of permanent eastern settlers which arrived in Southern California on Nov. 5, 1841. Workman first began this home in 1842, then remodeled it in 1872 to resemble an English manor house.

Placed in cooperation with City of Industry, 1976.

CLAREMONT (Los Angeles Co.)   *8.1 mi. N of SH 66, on Camp Baldy Rd., San Antonio Canyon*
Pomona Water Power Plant
The first hydro-electric installation in California for long-distance tranmission of alternating current at high voltage was built in 1892 on San Antonio Creek below this spot by the San Antonio Light and Power Company organized by Dr. Cyrus Grandison Baldwin, president of Pomona College. The first high-voltage transformers built by George Westinghouse for this installation provided for 10,000-volt transmission of electric service from this plant to Pomona.

Placed in cooperation with Historical Society of Pomona Valley, Inc., 1955.

CLARKSVILLE (El Dorado Co.)   *.5 mi. W, on frontage road adjacent to US 50, .5 mi. S on El Dorado Hills Blvd., 9 mi. NE on Old White Rock Rd., then .3 mi. W on PG&E Clarksville Substation Rd.*
Mormon Tavern
At this site on the old Clarksville-White Rock emigrant road was Mormon Tavern, constructed in 1849, and enlarged and operated by Franklin Winchell in 1851. A popular stop for teams and stages, it became a remount station of the California Overland Pony Express. Here on Apr. 4, 1860, Pony Express rider William (Sam) Hamilton changed horses on the first trip eastward of the Pony Express.

Placed by California State Park Commission in cooperation with James W. Marshall Chapter No. 49 of E Clampus Vitus, Marguerite Parlor No. 12 of Native Daughters of the Golden West, and California Overland Pony Express Trail Association, 1960.

CLEARLAKE OAKS (Lake Co.)   *1.5 mi. S, SH 20 and Sulphur Bank Rd. intersection*
Sulphur Bank Mine
This sulphur mine also produced quicksilver and became one of the most noted producers in the world. First worked for sulphur in 1865 and in four years produced a total of 2,000,000 pounds. Reopened and developed for quicksilver in 1873 and credited with a total output of 92,400 flasks. Was important producer in World Wars I and II.

Placed by California Centennial Commission and County of Lake, 1950.

CLEMENTS (San Joaquin Co.)

*1 mi. N, entrance to Stillman
L. Magee Park, Mackwille Rd.*

Lone Star Mill

First built in 1855 by Hodge and Terry. Burned in 1856 and was rebuilt on its present site. Purchased by S. L. Magee in 1860 and was operated by him for the next 25 years when it was abandoned for lack of business.

Placed by Clements 4-H Club, 1950.

CLOVERDALE (Sonoma Co.)

*On W side of Asti Rd., 1.68 mi. N
of Asti post office, S of town*

Icaria-Speranza Utopian Colony

Icaria-Speranza was a Utopian community based on the writings of French philosopher Etienne Cabet. In 1881, at Cloverdale, French immigrant families led by the Dehay and Leroux families began their social experiment in cooperative living based on solidarity and depending on an agrarian economy. It lasted until 1886. Icaria-Speranza was the only Icarian colony in California and the last of seven established throughout the United States. On this site stood the Icarian schoolhouse, deeded to the county in 1886.

Placed in cooperation with National Icarian Heritage Society and Cloverdale Historical Society, 1989.

COALINGA (Fresno Co.)

*Three large rocks in foothills
SW of Cantua Creek Bridge*

Arroyo de Cantua

(Plaque located on SH 198, 9 mi. N of Coalinga)

Headquarters of notorious bandit, Joaquin Murietta. Killed here July 25, 1853, by posse of state rangers, led by Capt. Harry Love. Terrorized mining camps and stage operations during his career.

Placed by Department of Public Works, Division of Highways.

COLFAX (Placer Co.)

*Red Caboose Museum, NE
corner Main and Grass Valley sts.*

First Transcontinental Railroad—Colfax

Central Pacific rails reached Colfax, formerly Illinoistown, Sept. 1, 1865, and train service began four days later. Colfax was a vital construction supply depot and junction point for stage lines for ten months. It was renamed by Governor Stanford in honor of Schuyler Colfax, Speaker of the House of Representatives, and later Ulysses S. Grant's vice president. The assault on the Sierra began here.

Placed in cooperation with Conference of California Historical Societies and Placer County Historical Society, 1969.

COLOMA (El Dorado Co.)

*Marshall Gold Discovery
State Historic Park, SH 49,
in Gold Discovery parking lot*

The Coloma Road

Here in the valley of the Cul-luh-mah Indians, James W. Marshall discovered gold on Jan. 24, 1848, in the tailrace of Sutter's sawmill. The Old Coloma Road, opened in 1847 from Sutter's Fort to Coloma, was used by Marshall to carry the news of the discovery to Capt. John A. Sutter. During the goldrush, it was used by thousands of miners going to and from the diggings. In 1849 it became the route of California's first stageline, established by James E. Birch.

Placed by California State Park Commission in cooperation with Golden Key of Greenwood, El Dorado County Chamber of Commerce, and Grand Parlors of the Native Sons and Native Daughters of the Golden West, 1960.

COLOMA (El Dorado Co.)

Marshall Gold Discovery State Historic Park, SH 49, follow trail from Gold Discovery parking lot to American River

Sutter's Mill Site

This rock monument marks the site of John A. Sutter's sawmill in the tailrace of which James W. Marshall discovered gold, Jan. 24, 1848, starting great rush of argonauts to California. The Society of California Pioneers definitely located and marked site in 1924. Additional timbers and relics, including original tailrace unearthed in 1947, were discovered after property became state park. Marshall Monument, overlooking this spot, was erected following movement inaugurated in 1886 by Native Sons of the Golden West.

Placed by Historic Landmarks Committee of Native Sons and Native Daughters of the Golden West, 1948.

COLOMA (El Dorado Co.)

Marshall Gold Discovery State Historic Park, SH 49

Marshall Monument

Erected by the State of California
in memory of James W. Marshall
1810–1885
whose discovery of gold
January 24, 1848
in the tailrace of Sutter's Mill at Coloma
started the great rush of argonauts
Monument unveiled May 3, 1890.

Placed by Placerville Parlor of Native Sons of the Golden West.

COLTON (San Bernardino Co.)

Agua Mansa Cemetery, 270 E. Agua Mansa Rd.

Agua Mansa Cemetery

This historic site marks the resting place of the pioneers of the Agua Mansa area which was started about 1840. The preservation of this cemetery began in 1951.

Placed by Jurupa Parlor No. 296 of Native Daughters of the Golden West, 1961.

COLTON (San Bernardino Co.)

10600 Hunts Lane

Fort Benson

On this spot fort was erected, 1856, during contest over valley lands. Here stood ancient Indian village, Jumuba, headquarters first mission stock farm in valley. Here,

1821, occurred first Christian baptism credited to San Bernardino. Here, 1827, camped Jedediah Strong Smith, first American to enter California overland.

Placed by Lugonia Parlor No. 241 of Native Daughters of the Golden West and Arrowhead Parlor No. 110 of Native Sons of the Golden West, 1935.

COLUMBIA (Tuolumne Co.) *2 mi. N and S, on SH 49*

2 Miles
Columbia

One of the best preserved of early mining towns and known as "gem of southern mines." Gold discovered through cloudburst, 1850; population grew to 6,000 in six weeks. Governor Earl Warren signed bill at Columbia July 15, 1945, creating Columbia State Park.

Placed by Department of Transportation, Division of Highways.

COLUMBIA (Tuolumne Co.) *Columbia State Historic Park, NW corner Broadway and Washington sts.*

Columbia

Columbia, the "Gem of the Southern Mines," became a town of 4,000 to 5,000 in the 1850s, following the discovery of gold here by the Hildreth party Mar. 27, 1850. Gold shipments, estimated at $87,000,000, declined rapidly after 1858, but Columbia never became a "ghost town." Columbia Historic State Park was created in 1945 to preserve its historic buildings and sites.

Placed by California State Park Commission in cooperation with Tuolumne County Chamber of Commerce, 1958.

COLUMBIA (Tuolumne Co.) *5 mi. NW, vista point on Calaveras side of Columbia-Vallecito Highway bridge, over Stanislaus River*

Mark Twain Bret Harte Trail
Parrott's Ferry

Site of ferry crossing established 1860 by Thomas H. Parrott connecting mining towns of Tuttletown and Vallecito. Ferry in operation until 1903 when first bridge built. Ferry boat of flat bottom wooden construction propelled on heavy cables. Cable anchorage in large boulder Calaveras side of river still visible (1949) at low water, sandbag dam built to form small lake.

Placed by California Centennial Commision and Aronos Research Club of Sonora, 1949.

COLUMBIA (Tuolumne Co.) *2 mi. SE, 22041 Sawmill Flat Rd.*

Mark Twain Bret Harte Trail
Sawmill Flat

Name derived from two sawmills erected here to supply mining timbers early 1850s. Population at one time 1,000. Rich in pocket gold in heyday. Mining camp of Mexican woman, Dona Elisa Martinez, at north end of flat, reported to have been hideout of famous bandit, Joaquin Murietta. Site of story, *The Battle of Sawmill Flat*.

Placed by California Centennial Commission and Odd Fellows and Rebekahs of Tuolumne County, 1949.

COLUMBIA (Tuolumne Co.)

2.6 mi. SW, SE corner
Mt. Brow and Shaw's Flat rds.

Mark Twain Bret Harte Trail
Shaw's Flat

In 1850 this community was alive with gold miners. James D. Fair, after whom the Fairmont Hotel in San Francisco is named, was one of the most notable. The Mississippi House, built in 1850, contains many relics including the original bar and post office with its grill and mailboxes. On a nearby hill stands the old bell, given by miners, which summoned men to work and announced the convening of various courts. According to tradition, a local bartender added to his income by panning the gold dust dropped on his muddy boots while serving customers.

Placed by Historic Landmark Committee and Tuolumne Parlor No. 144 of Native Sons of the Golden West, 1947.

COLUMBIA (Tuolumne Co.)

1.1 mi. SW, at Springfield and
Horseshoe Bend rds. intersection

Mark Twain Bret Harte Trail
Springfield

Springfield received name from abundant springs gushing from limestone boulders. Town, with its stores, shops, and hotel, built around plaza. Once boasted 2,000 inhabitants. Believed founded by Doña Josefa Valmesada, Mexican woman of means with reputation for aiding Americans in war with Mexico. During heyday, 150 miners' carts could be seen on road, hauling gold-bearing dirt to Springfield springs for washing.

Placed by Historic Landmarks Committee and Columbia Parlor No. 258 of Native Sons of the Golden West, 1948.

COLUSA (Colusa Co.)

547 Market St.

Colusa County Courthouse

Erected in 1861, this Federal/Classic Revival style building is the oldest remaining courthouse in the Sacramento Valley. The "southern" style reflects the county's heritage from the antebellum South and states-rights sympathies during the Civil War. In its early years, the courthouse also served as the county's center of cultural, social, and religious activites.

Placed in cooperation with Colusa County Historical Society and Colusa County Board of Supervisors, 1976.

COLUSA (Colusa Co.)

6.5 mi. W of I-5, on S side
of Maxwell-Stites Rd.

Swift's Stone Corral
Restored by Colusa Parlor No. 60 N.S.G.W.

Placed by Native Sons of the Golden West.

COMPTON (Los Angeles Co.)

18127 S. Alameda St.

Dominguez Ranch House

Central portion built in 1826 by Manuel Dominguez.

Rancho San Pedro

Ten square leagues granted, provisionally by Gov. Fages to Juan Jose Dominguez in 1784. Regranted by Gov. Sola to Cristobal Dominguez in 1822.

Battle of Dominguez Ranch

Fought on this rancho Oct. 8 & 9, 1846, when Californians led by Jose Antonio Carrillo repelled United States forces under Capt. William Mervine, U.S. Navy, in an attempt to recapture the pueblo of Los Angeles.

Placed by California Parlor No. 247 of Native Daughters of the Golden West in cooperation with County of Los Angeles Board of Supervisors, 1945.

COMPTON (Los Angeles Co.)   *NW corner Myrrh St. and Willowbrook Ave.*

Heritage House

The original house of two rooms was built in 1869 by A.R. Loomis. Other rooms were added by successive occupants. It was marked as the "oldest house in Compton" in 1955; purchased by the city June 11, 1957; and removed from 209 South Acacia Street to its present site in that year. Restored, refurnished, and renamed by the citizens of Compton as a tribute to early settlers of the community, it was presented to the public Apr. 14, 1958.

Placed by California State Park Commission in cooperation with Compton City Council, Compton Parlor Native Daughters of the Golden West, and Heritage House Auxilliary, 1959.

CONCORD (Contra Costa Co.)   *3119 Grant St.*

Don Fernando Pacheco Adobe

(Plaque located at NE corner
Grant St. and Solano Way)

One-quarter mile north of this spot is located the adobe house constructed in 1843 by Don Fernando Pacheco. Reconstructed in 1941, it is preserved as a memento of the historic past of Contra Costa County.

Placed by California State Park Commission in cooperation with Contra Costa County Horsemen's Association, 1958.

CONCORD (Contra Costa Co.)   *1870 Adobe St.*

The Don Salvio Pacheco Adobe—1853

Don Salvio Pacheco—soldier—surveyor of pueblo public lands—settled here in 1828—was awarded this grant called Monte del Diablo in 1835 by Gov. Jose Figueroa—living in this vicinity from 1844 to 1875—he completed this building June 24, 1853. Settlers in 1853 located near here and named the place Pacheco— later it was visited by great floods. Don Salvio Pacheco gave land surrounding this adobe in 1868 to the Pacheco flood refugees and the settlement became known as Todos Santos, now known as Concord. Upon Don Salvio's death Aug. 8, 1876, this building was inherited by his son Don Salvador Pacheco.

Placed by Contra Costa County Historical Society, 1954.

COPPEROPOLIS (Calaveras Co.) *375 Main St., State*
Dept. of Forestry Station

Copperopolis

Copper discovered here by W. K. Reed and Thomas McCarty in 1860. Mines utilized during the Civil War and the first and second world wars. During Civil War period was principal copper producing section of United States.

Placed by California Centennial Commission and Copperopolis Community Center, 1949.

CORONA (Riverside Co.) *20730 Temescal Canyon Rd.*

Site of Butterfield Stage Station

Where mail was delivered and horses changed. First stage carrying overland mail left Tipton, Missouri, Sept. 15, 1858, and passing through Temescal, arrived Los Angeles Oct. 7, 1858.

Placed by History and Landmarks Committee, Corona Woman's Improvement Club, 1934.

CORONA (Riverside Co.) *Corona City Park, 100 block 6th St.*

1886–1936
Corona Founders

R. B. Taylor, George L. Joy, Samuel Merrill, A. E. Garretson, and Adolph Rimpau, having purchased lands of the La Sierra Rancho of Bernardo Yorba and the El Temescal Grant of Leandro Serrano on May 4, 1886, founded the citrus colony and town of Corona.

Placed by 20-30 Club of Corona, 1936.

CORONA (Riverside Co.) *11 mi. S, on old Hwy. 71, .9 mi. S of*
I-15 and Temescal Canyon Rd. junction

Old Temescal Road

This route was used by Luiseno and Gabrieleno Indians, whose villages were nearby. Leandro Serrano established here the first home of a white settler in Riverside County in 1820. Over it traveled Jackson and Warner in 1831 and Fremont in 1849. It was the southern emigrant road for gold seekers, 1849–1851; the overland mail route, 1858–1861; and a military road between Los Angeles and San Diego, 1861–1865.

Placed by California State Park Commission in cooperation with Woman's Improvement Club of Corona, 1959.

CORONA (Riverside Co.) *Off Temescal Canyon Rd., 1 mi. E on*
Dawson Canyon Rd., .1 mi. NE on
Gravel Pit Rd., .2 mi. S along railroad tracks,
site is 50 ft. W of tracks

Painted Rock

In tribute to the earliest record of any people in this region. The Santa Fe Railway has preserved this rock with ancient Indian pictograph. And the History and Landmarks Committee of the Corona Woman's Improvement Club has placed this tablet May 4, 1927.

Private plaque.

CORONA (Riverside Co.)

8 mi. SE, NE corner I-15 and Old Temescal Rd.

Site of Third Serrano Adobe

Nearby, an adobe house was built about 1867. It was occupied until 1898 by Leandro Serrano's widow, Josefa. Under Spanish law, she owned the surrounding 20,000-acre Rancho Temescal, but her ownership was denied by the U.S. Supreme Court.

Placed by Billy Holcomb Chapter of E Clampus Vitus, Hydro Conduit Corporation, and Phil Porretta family, 1981.

CORONA (Riverside Co.)

8 mi. SE, NW corner of I-15 and Old Temescal Rd.

Serrano Tanning Vats

Nearby, two vats were built in 1819 by the Luiseno Indians under the direction of Leandro Serrano, first non-Indian settler in what is now Riverside County. The vats were used in making leather from cow hides. In 1981 the vats were restored and placed here by the Billy Holcomb Chapter of E Clampus Vitus.

Placed in cooperation with Temescal Water Company, Hydro Conduit Corporation, Glen Ivy Hot Springs, Phil Porretta family, and Billy Holcomb Chapter of E Clampus Vitus, 1981.

CORONADO (San Diego Co.)

Sunset Park, 200 block of Ocean Blvd., at entrance to Gate 5, North Island Naval Air Station

Site of First Military Flying School
(U.S. Naval Air Station, North Island)

The flat lands beyond have been a part of aviation history since Glenn Curtiss founded the first military flying school in America here on Jan. 17, 1911. The Army operated Rockwell Field until Jan. 31, 1939. The Navy commissioned the present air station on Nov. 8, 1917.

Placed in cooperation with the City of Coronado, 1967.

CORONADO (San Diego Co.)

1500 Orange Ave., in hotel garden patio

Hotel del Coronado

This Victorian hotel, built in 1887, is one of America's largest wooden buildings. Few seaside resort hotels of this significant architectural style remain in America. The hotel has hosted several presidents and other national figures.

Placed in cooperation with San Diego Historical Society, Coronado Historical Association Inc., and San Diego Chapter of American Institute of Architects, 1980.

COSTA MESA (Orange Co.)

Estancia Park, NW corner Adams Ave. and Mesa Verde Dr. W.

Diego Sepulveda Adobe

This home of early Spanish Californians, erected in the 1820s, once served as an "estancia" or station for mission herdsmen. It was dedicated in 1963 for public use by the Segerstrom family and restored by the City of Costa Mesa. It is jointly maintained and operated by the Costa Mesa Parks Department and the Costa Mesa Historical Society.

Placed by the City of Costa Mesa, 1969.

COTATI (Sonoma Co.)   *Downtown Plaza, SE corner*
E. Cotati Ave. and Old Redwood Hwy.

Cotati Downtown Plaza

Cotati's hexagonal town plan, one of only two in the United States, was designed during the 1890s by Newton Smyth as an alternative to traditional grid land planning. The six-sided town plaza was designed for founder Thomas Page, and each of the surrounding streets was named after one of Page's sons. "Cotati" derives from "Kotati," a local Pomo Indian chieftain.

Placed in cooperation with the City of Cotati and all organizations, 1975.

COTTONWOOD (Shasta Co.)   *5.8 mi. E, near entrance to*
Reading Island Park, 213 Adobe Rd.

Site of Reading Adobe
Rancho Buena Ventura

Home of Pierson Barton Reading (1816–1868)—California pioneer of 1843—Major in Fremont's California Battalion, Mexican War of 1846, signer of Capitulation of Cahuenga—discoverer of second major gold strike 1848. Adobe built here 1847, designated seat of Shasta County government 1850–51, kitchen wing of Reading Mansion 1854–1881, destroyed by vandals 1942, best stock farm in California 1862. Maj. Reading buried nearby.

Placed in cooperation with Shasta Historical Society, 1968.

COULTERVILLE (Mariposa Co.)   *County Park, NE corner*
CH J20 and SH 132 intersection

Coulterville

While miners worked nearby streams and veins for gold, George W. Coulter served their needs as merchant and hotel proprietor. His first store, established in 1850, was a tent stocked with merchandise hauled in by pack train. Coulter and the town which bears his name prospered, as Coulterville became the business and social capital of this area.

Placed by California State Park Commission in cooperation with the Mariposa County Recreation and Parks Commission and the Mariposa County Historical Society, 1959.

COVELO (Mendocino Co.)   *5 mi. S, at Inspiration Point, on SH 162*

Round Valley

This valley was discovered by Frank M. Azbill, arriving from Eden Valley, on May 15, 1854. During the same year, Charles Kelsey from Clear Lake also visited it, and George E. White sighted it from Blue Nose.

Placed by California State Park Commission in cooperation with the Mendocino County Board of Supervisors and Covelo Women's Improvement Club, 1959.

CRESCENT CITY (Del Norte Co.)   *Battery Point Island,*
end of A St.

Battery Point Lighthouse

The Battery Point Lighthouse is one of the first lighthouses on the California coast. Rugged mountains and unbridged rivers meant coastal travel was essential for the economic survival of this region. In 1855 Congress appropriated $15,000 for the construction of the light station, which was completed in 1856 by the U.S. Lighthouse Service. Theophilis Magruder was the station's first keeper; Wayne Philand was its last before automation in 1953.

Placed in cooperation with Del Norte County Historical Society, 1987.

CRESCENT CITY (Del Norte Co.) *Brother Jonathan Vista Point, in park at SE corner 9th St. and Pebble Beach Dr.*

Brother Jonathan Cemetery

This memorial is dedicated to those who lost their lives in the wreck of the Pacific Mail Steamer, *Brother Jonathan,* at Point St. George's Reef, July 30, 1865.

Placed by California State Park Commission in cooperation with Del Norte Historical Society, 1960.

CRESCENT CITY (Del Norte County) *US 199 E to Kings Valley Rd., then 1.2 mi. NE*

Camp Lincoln

A United States military post was established here Sept. 12, 1862, by the men of Company G, 2nd Regiment, Infantry, California Volunteers, to keep peace between the Indians and the miners and settlers of northwestern California. It was abandoned in May 1870. Commanding officer's quarters and one barracks remain at the date of dedication of this site.

Placed by California State Park Commission in cooperation with Del Norte Historical Society, 1962.

CRESCENT CITY (Del Norte Co.) *US 199 to Parkway Dr., S 1,000 ft. to SE corner Parkway Dr. and Elk Valley Rd.*

Pioneer Stage Road to Oregon

Constructed in 1858, this was the route of the Crescent City Turnpike. Following the present Elk Valley Road to Old Camp Lincoln, it then crossed the ridge, forded Smith River to Low Divide, and continued to Jacksonville, Oregon, by way of various gold camps.

Placed by California State Park Commission in cooperation with Del Norte County Historical Society, 1958.

CRESCENT CITY (Del Norte Co.) *Beach Front Park and Picnic Area, SW corner Front and H sts.*

S.S. Emidio

Nearby are portions of the hull of the General Petroleum Corporation tanker *S.S. Emidio,* which on Dec. 20, 1941, became the first casualty of the Imperial Japanese Navy's submarine force action on California's Pacific Coast. The ship was attacked some 200 miles north of San Francisco and five crewmen were killed. Abandoned, the vessel drifted north and broke up on the rocks off Crescent City. The bow drifted into the harbor, where it lay near this marker until salvaged in 1950.

Placed in cooperation with Eureka Chapter 101 of E Clampus Vitus, 1982.

CRESCENT CITY (Del Norte Co.) *1886 Pebble Beach Dr.,*
500 ft. S of Pacific Ave.

Tolowa Indian Settlements

At the time of white contact, the principal villages of the native Tolowa Indians of northern Del Norte County were located at Battery Point in Crescent City (Ta'Atun), Pebble Beach (Meslteltun), south of Point St. George (Tatintun), and north of Point St. George (Tawiatun). The major villages were almost completely independent economic units.

Placed by California State Park Commission in cooperation with Del Norte County Historical Society, 1965.

CRESTLINE (San Bernardino Co.) *SH 18, .5 mi. W of Crestline*
interchange

Mormon Road

Built by the pioneers
Dedicated to
the pioneer women
of 1852
by the women of 1932

Private plaque.

CROCKETT (Contra Costa Co.) *993 Loring Ave.*

The Old Homestead

This was the first American home in Crockett. Constructed in 1867 by Thomas Edwards, Sr., on land purchased in 1866 from Judge J. B. Crockett. Located on an earlier Indian village near the Carquinez Straits, its timbers, some of which were brought around the Horn, have been well preserved.

Placed by California State Park Commission in cooperation with Carquinez Women's Club, 1960.

CUCAMONGA (San Bernardino Co.) *8916 Foothill Blvd.*

Cucamonga Winery

Established by Tiburcio Tapia to whom the Cucamonga Rancho was granted Mar. 3, 1839, by Governor Juan Bautista Alvarado of Mexico.

Placed by Ontario Parlor No. 251 of Native Daughters of the Golden West and Los Ranchos Parlor No. 283 of Native Sons of the Golden West, 1950.

CUCAMONGA (San Bernardino Co.) *Near 8501 Red Hill*
Country Club Dr.

Tapia Adobe Site

In 1839 Governor Juan Alvarado granted the 13,000-acre tract called Cucamonga to Tiburcio Tapia, an ex-soldier who was a prominent merchant and alcalde in Los Angeles. A half-mile west of this marker, Tapia, employing Indian laborers, immediately built an adobe house on a vantage point on Red Hill. The large adobe was abandoned in 1858 when Tapia's heirs sold the rancho. The adobe soon disintegrated into its native earth. This marker is located on land which once was a part of Tapia's rancho.

Placed in cooperation with Billy Holcomb Chapter of E Clampus Vitus, Rancho Cucamonga Historical Society, San Bernardino County Museum Association, and Thomas vineyards, 1985.

CUPERTINO (Santa Clara Co.)
Monta Vista High School, 21840 McClellan Rd., west parking lot

Arroyo de San Joseph Cupertino

This arroyo honoring San Joseph, patron saint of flight and students, was first discovered and traversed by Spanish explorers in 1769. On Mar. 25–26, 1776, Col. Juan Bautista de Anza made it his encampment No. 93, as mapped by his cartographer, Padre Pedro Font, before continuing on to the San Francisco bay area where he inititated steps to found a colony, a mission, and a presidio.

Placed in cooperation with Cupertino Historical Society, Inc., 1968.

DALY CITY (San Mateo Co.)
1100 Lake Merced Blvd.

Broderick-Terry Duel

The famous duel that ended dueling in California was fought in a ravine east of here, near the shore of Lake Merced, in the early morning of Sept. 13, 1859. The participants were U.S. Senator David C. Broderick and Chief Justice David S. Terry of the California Supreme Court. Senator Broderick was mortally wounded. The site is marked with a monument and granite shafts where the two men stood.

Placed by California Centennial Commission and the County Board of Supervisors in cooperation with San Mateo County Historical Association, 1949.

DANA POINT (Orange Co.)
Ken Sampson Overview, St. of the Blue Lantern at Santa Clara Ave.

Dana Point

Named for Richard Henry Dana, author of *Two Years Before the Mast,* who was here in 1835. El Embarcadero, the cove below, was used by hide vessels trading with Mission San Juan Capistrano. This trade reached its peak in 1830–40. Here in 1818, Hipolito Bouchard, flying an Argentine flag, anchored his fleet while raiding the mission.

Placed by California State Park Commission.

DANVILLE (Contra Costa Co.)
856 Danville Blvd., at El Portal

Historical Landmark
1772
Captain Pedro Fages Trail

Fages, commandante at Monterey, vainly looked for a way across San Francisco Bay. With Juan Crespi, Franciscan missionary, 14 soldiers, a muleteer and an Indian servant, he trekked along Carquinez Strait, thence eastward nearly to Antioch. Turning back, these first white men to explore what became Contra Costa County passed this point and camped near Danville Mar. 31, 1772.

Placed by San Ramon Valley Historical Society, 1972.

DANVILLE (Contra Costa Co.)   *14 mi. E, Mount Diablo State Park,*
on summit, 4.5 mi. E of ranger station

Mount Diablo

Mount Diablo, sacred to Native Americans who lived and worshipped there for over 5,000 years, became a critical reference point for Spanish explorers in the 18th century, and American trappers and early California settlers in the 19th. In 1851 Col. Leander Ransome established the crossing of the Mount Diablo base and meridian lines from which most of California and Nevada are surveyed.

Placed in cooperation with San Ramon Valley Historical Society, 1978.

DAVENPORT (San Mateo Co.)   *17 mi. N, Pigeon Point Light Station,*
.2 mi. W of SH 1 and Pigeon Point Rd.

Pigeon Point Lighthouse

This brick lighthouse was built to incorporate a French first order Fresnel lens. Although no longer used, the lens is still operable in the lantern room. Previously the lens had been installed at Cape Hatteras, North Carolina. It first flashed over the Pacific in November, 1872, and the lighthouse has served continuously without structural modifications since that time.

Placed in cooperation with the United States Coast Guard, 1980.

DEATH VALLEY GATEWAY (Inyo Co.)   *Death Valley National*
Monument, on SH 190,
1.3 mi. SE of Furnace Creek

Death Valley '49ers Gateway

Through this natural gateway the Death Valley Forty-Niners, more than one hundred emigrants from the Middle West, seeking a short cut to gold fields of Central California, entered Death Valley, December 1849. All suffered from thirst and starvation. Two contingents passed southward here; the others proceeded northward seeking to escape from region.

Placed by California Centennial Commission and Death Valley 49ers, Inc., 1949.

DEATH VALLEY NATIONAL MONUMENT (Inyo Co.)   *Off SH 190,*
6 mi. SW on road to Badwater,
then 9.6 mi. S to
Tule Springs, 17 mi. S
of Furnace Creek

Bennett's Long Camp

Near this spot, Bennett-Arcane contingent of Death Valley Forty-Niners, emigrants from Middle West, seeking short cut to California gold fields, were stranded for a month and almost perished from starvation. Two young companions, William Lewis Manly and John Rogers, made heroic journey on foot to San Francisquito Rancho near Newhall.

Placed by California Centennial Commission and Death Valley '49ers, Inc., 1949.

DEATH VALLEY NATIONAL MONUMENT (Inyo Co.)   *100 ft. S of SH 190, Stovepipe Wells*

Burned Wagons Point

Near this monument, Jayhawker group of Death Valley Forty-Niners, gold seekers from Middle West, who entered Death Valley in 1849 seeking short route to mines of Central California, burned their wagons, dried the meat of some oxen, and, with surviving animals, struggled westward on foot.

Placed by California Centennial Commission and Death Valley '49ers, inc., 1949.

DEATH VALLEY NATIONAL MONUMENT (Inyo Co.)   *100 ft. S of SH 190, at Stovepipe Wells*

Eichbaum Toll Road

In 1926 H.W. Eichbaum obtained a franchise for a toll road from Darwin Falls to Stovepipe Wells, the first maintained road into the valley from the west. It changed the area from mining to tourism and brought about creation of Death Valley National Monument seven years later.

Placed in cooperation with Death Valley '49ers, Inc., 1971.

DEATH VALLEY NATIONAL MONUMENT (Inyo Co.)   *On SH 190, 1.4 mi. N of Furnace Creek*

Old Harmony Borax Works

On the marsh near this point, borax was discovered in 1881 by Aaron Winters who later sold his holdings to W. T. Coleman of San Francisco. In 1882 Coleman built the Harmony Borax Works and commissioned his superintendent, H. W. S. Perry, to design wagons and locate a suitable route to Mojave. The work of gathering the ore (called "cottonball") was done by Chinese workmen. From this point, processed borax was transported 165 miles by twenty mule team to the railroad until 1889.

Placed by California State Park Commission in cooperation with Death Valley '49ers, Inc., and the National Park Service, 1962.

DEATH VALLEY NATIONAL MONUMENT (Inyo Co.)   *Off SH 190, 2.8 mi. N on Sand Dunes Access Rd., 6.1 mi. E of Stovepipe Wells*

Old Stovepipe Wells

This waterhole, only one in the sand dune area of Death Valley, was at the junction of two Indian trails. During the bonanza days of rhyolite and skidoo, it was the only known water source on the cross-valley road. When sand obscured the spot, a length of stovepipe was inserted as a marker, hence its unique name.

Placed in cooperation with the National Park Service and Death Valley '49ers, Inc., 1968.

DESERT CENTER (Riverside Co.)   *Approximately 6 mi. W of Desert Center*

Site of Contractors General Hospital

In 1933, Dr. Sidney R. Garfield opened Contractors General Hospital six miles west of here. His modest facility successfully delivered health care to Colorado

River aqueduct workers through a prepaid insurance plan. Later, in association with industrialist Henry J. Kaiser, Dr. Garfield applied the lessons he first learned at the hospital to create his enduring legacy: Kaiser Permanente, the nation's largest non-profit prepaid health care program.

Placed in cooperation with Kaiser Permanente Medical Care Program, 1992.

DEVORE (San Bernardino Co.)

7 mi. W, Glen Helen Regional Park, 2555 Devore Rd.

Sycamore Grove

This campsite on both the Mojave Trail over the mountains and the Cajon Pass route was probably first seen by Spanish and American travelers in the 1770s and was noted by them in 1806, 1849, and 1850. Michael White, grantee in 1843 of the Muscupiabe Rancho, lived nearby. The Mormon colony camped in 1851 on either side of this little pass for about four months while Amasa Lyman, Charles Rich, Jefferson Hunt, David Seely, and Andrew Lytle negotiated the purchase of the San Bernardino Rancho from the Lugo family.

Placed by San Bernardino Society of California Pioneers and Lugonia Parlor No. 241 of Native Daughters of the Golden West, 1972.

DIAMOND SPRINGS (El Dorado Co.)

NW corner SH 49 and China Garden Rd.

Diamond Springs

This town, settled in 1848, derived its name from its crystal clear springs. Among the richest spots in this vicinity, its diggings produced a 25-pound nugget, one of the largest ever found in El Dorado County. Its most thriving period was in 1851. Later it became a contender for the county seat. Through its lumber, lime production, and agriculture, Diamond Springs retained some of its early importance.

Placed in cooperation with the Citizens of Diamond Springs and Mother Lode Lions Club of Diamond Springs and El Dorado.

DOUBLE SPRINGS (Calaveras Co.)

On SH 12, 2.4 mi. E of Valley Springs

1 mile
Double Springs

Founded Feb. 18, 1850. Became county seat of Calaveras County. Old court house, said to be constructed of lumber brought from China, is still standing, but not on the original site.

Placed by the Department of Public Works, Division of Highways.

DOWNIEVILLE (Sierra Co.)

Community United Methodist Church, SH 49

First Protestant Church

This Methodist Episcopal Church, the first Protestant place of worship to be erected in Downieville, was organized in 1855 by Rev. H. Ewart who became the first regular pastor in 1856. Necessary funds were raised by Rev. John B. Hill.

Placed by California Centennial Commission, Naomi Parlor No. 36 of Native Daughters of the Golden West, and Downieville Parlor No. 92 of Native Sons of the Golden West, 1950. (Unofficial marker)

DOWNIEVILLE (Sierra Co.)   *Sierra County Jail Yard*
Sierra County Sheriff's Gallows

On Nov. 27, 1885, 20-year-old James O'Neill was hanged from this gallows for the Aug. 7, 1884, murder of Webber Lake dairyman John Woodward. That execution, conducted by Sheriff Samuel C. Stewart approximately 100 feet west of this site, was the last legal execution in Sierra County and the only time this gallows was used. Changes in state law in 1891 ended local executions in California, and further changes in 1941 ended hanging as a means of legal execution within the state.

Placed in cooperation with County of Sierra and Sgt. Lee Adams, Project Director, 1988.

DRYTOWN (Amador Co.)   *.2 mi. N of Drytown, on SH 49*
Drytown

Founded 1848. Oldest town and first in which gold was discovered in Amador County. Its venerable town hall and other picturesque structures remain. Was not "dry" as name implies, containing 26 saloons at one time.

Placed by Department of Public Works, Division of Highways.

DUTCH FLAT (Placer Co.)   *NE corner Main and Stockton sts.*
Dutch Flat

Founded in the spring of 1851 by Joseph and Charles Dornbach. From 1854 to 1882, it was noted for its rich hydraulic mines. In 1860 had the largest voting population in Placer County. Chinese inhabitants numbered about 2,000. Here Theodore Judah and Dr. D. W. Strong made the original subscriptions to build the first transcontinental railroad.

Placed by California Centennial Commission and Placer County Historical Society, 1950.

EDISON (Kern Co.)   *3.6 mi. E, SE corner Old Bena and Towerline rds.*
Jedediah Strong Smith Trail

Near this spot about the first of February 1827, Jedediah Strong Smith, first United States citizen to reach Mexican California overland, passed through the present area of Kern County with his party of fur trappers. From San Gabriel Mission the group was en route north to a land reported teeming with "plenty of beaver . . ." Smith and his men were trailblazers whose exploits soon led to the American conquest of California.

Placed by the California State Park Commission in cooperation with Kern County Historical Society, El Tejon Parlor No. 239 of Native Daughters of the Golden West, and Kern County Museum, 1959.

EL DORADO (Calaveras Co.)   *Mountain Ranch, NW corner of Whiskey Slide and Mountain Ranch rds.*
El Dorado

Patented as a townsite in 1872. This early town derived its name from a sawmill located here. A post office established at Mountain Ranch in 1856 was moved to El Dorado in 1868 and El Dorado has thus become known as Mountain Ranch. This bell was used from 1885 to 1953 in the local school established as Cave City School

District in 1855. In 1946 this school joined with the Banner District to become the El Dorado Union Elementary School District.

Placed by El Dorado Union Community Club and Calaveras County Historical Society, 1956.

EL DORADO (El Dorado Co.)

N side of Church St. and Pleasant Valley Rd. intersection

El Dorado

El Dorado, meaning "the gilded one," was first known as Mud Springs from the boggy quagmire the cattle and horses made of nearby watering place. Originally an important camp on the old Carson Emigrant Trail. By 1849–50 it had become the center of a mining district and the crossroads for freight and stage lines. At the height of the rush, its large gold production supported a population of several thousand.

Placed by California State Park Commission and Mother Lode Lions Club of Diamond Springs and El Dorado.

EL DORADO (El Dorado Co.)

SW corner Church St. and Pleasant Valley Rd.

El Dorado (Mud Springs)

Trading post, emigrant stop, and mining camp of the 1850s, this became one of the remount stations of the Central Overland Pony Express. Here at the Nevada house on Apr. 13, 1860, pony rider William (Sam) Hamilton changed horses while carrying the first west-bound mail of the Pony Express from St. Joseph, Missouri, to Sacramento, California.

Placed by California State Park Commission in cooperation with James W. Marshall Chapter No. 49 of E Clampus Vitus, Golden Chain Council of the Mother Lode, and Central Overland Pony Express Trail Association, 1960.

EL MONTE (Los Angeles Co.)

Santa Fe Trail Historical Park, Valley Blvd. and Santa Anita Ave.

El Monte

El Monte, on the bank of the San Gabriel River, played a significant part in California's early pioneer history. It was first an encampment on the Old Spanish Trail, an extension of the trail from Missouri to Santa Fe. By the 1850s, some began to call El Monte the "end of the Santa Fe Trail." Early in that decade a permanent settlement was established here by immigrants from Texas, the first settlement in Southern California founded by citizens of the United States.

Placed in cooperation with the City of El Monte, 1987.

EL TORO (Orange Co.)

8 mi. NE, 500 ft. E of Modjeska and Harding Canyon rds., Modjeska Canyon

Modjeska's Home

Famous as the home of Madame Modjeska, one of the world's great actresses, it was designed by Stanford White in 1888 on property called "Forest of Arden." Sold soon after her retirement, it remains a monument to the woman who contributed immeasureably to the cultural life of Orange County.

Placed by California State Park Commission.

EL TORO (Orange Co.)   *Heritage Hill, Serrano Regional Historic Village, NE corner Serrano Rd. and Lake Forest Dr.*

The Serrano Adobe
State of California
Historic Landmark
No. 199
La casa de adobe de Jose Serrano
Home of Jose Serrano, original grantee
of
Rancho Canada de Los Alisos
Restored A.D. 1932

Private plaque.

ELK GROVE (Sacramento Co.)   *Elk Grove Cemetery, Row C, Lot 2, Elk Grove Blvd.*

Grave of Cumi Donner Wilder

This survivor of the ill-fated Donner party was the daughter of George and Mary Blue Donner. Born near Springfield, Illinois, in 1832. She arrived in California in December 1846 with her sister, Leanna Charity Donner, and was rescued by the first relief party to reach the tragic scene. Married to Benjamin W. Wilder in 1853, she died on July 4, 1923, survived by her sister and two children.

Placed by the California State Park Commission in cooperation with Liberty Parlor No. 213 of Native Daughters of the Golden West, 1960.

ELK GROVE (Sacramento Co.)   *Near SW corner of SH 99 and Grant Line Rd.*

Murphy's Corral

This is the site of the beginning of the conquest of California by the United States. On June 10, 1846, American settlers led by Ezekial Merritt overpowered soldiers under Lt. Francisco Arce and took their Mexican army horses from the corral of the Murphy Ranch on the north bank of the Cosumnes River. The "Bear Flag" action in Sonoma followed on June 14, 1846.

Placed by the California State Park Commission in cooperation with College of the Pacific and Stockton Corral of Westerners, 1959.

ELK GROVE (Sacramento Co.)   *9125 Elk Grove Blvd.*

Site of First County Free Library Branch in California

In 1908 El Grove acquired, through the effort of Miss Harriet G. Eddy, then principal of Elk Grove Union High School, the first county free library branch in California. Subsequently, California's county free library branch system has become one of the most outstanding in California.

Placed in cooperation with Elk Grove Parlor No. 41 of Native Sons of the Golden West and Library Parlor No. 213 of Native Daughters of the Golden West, 1967.

EMIGRANT GAP (Placer Co.)   *I-80, Emigrant Gap Vista Pt.*

Emigrant Gap

The spring of 1845 saw the first covered wagons to surmount the Sierra Nevada Mountains. They left this valley, ascended to the ridge, and turned westward to old

Emigrant Gap. The wagons were lowered by ropes to the floor of Bear Valley. Hundreds followed, before, during, and after the gold rush. This was a hazardous portion of the overland emigrant trail.

Placed by California Centennial Commission and Placer County Historical Society, 1950.

EMPIRE (Stanislaus Co.)   *.1 mi. S on CH J7*
Empire City
One mile south of this spot is the site of Empire City, founded in 1850 by John G. Marvin. Head of navigation on the Tuolumne River, military supply depot, and 2nd county seat of Stanislaus County. Destroyed by flood in 1861–62.

Placed by Estanislao Chapter No. 58 of E Clampus Vitus, 1961.

ENCINO (Los Angeles Co.)   *Los Encinos State Historic Park, 16756 Moorpark St.*
De la Osa Adobe
of
Los Encinos State Historical Monument
This dwelling, built in 1849 by Don Vicente de la Osa, was a favored stopping place for the numerous travelers on El Camino Real. It stands on land that is a part of the one-square-league Rancho El Encino granted in 1845 by Governor Pio Pico to three Indians, Ramon, Francisco, and Roque, whose interests were purchased by Don Vicente. Originally the land was under the jurisdiction of Mission San Fernando Rey, founded in 1797.

Placed by Los Angeles Parlor No. 124 of Native Daughters of the Golden West, 1937 and 1950.

ESCONDIDO (San Diego Co.)   *5 mi. SE, 1 mi. E of I-15, on Pomerado Rd.*
Mule Hill
On Dec. 7, 1846, day following Battle of San Pasqual fought five miles east of here, Gen. Stephen Kearny's command while marching on San Diego was attacked by Californians. The Americans counterattacked, occupied hill until Dec. 11 when march was resumed. Short of food, they ate mule meat and named the place "Mule Hill."

Placed by California Centennial Commission and San Diego Historical Markers Committee, 1950.

ESCONDIDO (San Diego Co.)   *7 mi. SE, San Pasqual Battlefield State Historic Park, SH 78 at Old Pasqual Rd.*
San Pasqual Battlefield
While marching to the conquest and occupation of California during the Mexican War, a detachment of 1st U.S. Dragoons, under the command of Brig. Gen. Stephen W. Kearny, was met on this site by native California lancers, under the command of Gen. Andres Pico. In this battle, fought on Dec. 6, 1846, severe losses were incurred by the American forces. The native Californians withdrew after Kearny had rallied his men on the field. Gallant action on the part of both forces characterized the Battle of San Pasqual, one of the significant actions during the Mexican War of 1846–1848.

Placed by California State Park Commission, 1962.

EUREKA (Humboldt Co.)   *NW corner 3rd and E sts.*

Eureka
"I have found it"

Eureka was founded as a town in 1850 and incorporated as a city in 1874. Located on the remote northwestern coast of California, Eureka was the region's major port of entry by water in the 19th century before the construction of good access by land, and rose to historical prominence as the major social, political, and economic center of the region. "Eureka" is a Greek expression and a popular mining term meaning "I have found it."
Placed in cooperation with Eureka Chapter No. 101 of E Clampus Vitus, 1979.

EUREKA (Humboldt Co.)   *Fort Humboldt State*
Historic Park, 3431 Fort Ave.

Fort Humboldt

By the early 1850s, newly arrived white settlers had moved into the Humboldt Bay area, causing conflict with the native inhabitants. To protect both Indians and settlers, Fort Humboldt was established in 1853 and operated until 1866. It became a focal point in the violent struggle between two cultures. Many Native Americans were assembled here before removal to reservations.
Placed in cooperation with Eureka Chapter No. 101 of E Clampus Vitus, 1980.

EUREKA (Humboldt Co.)   *Fort Humboldt State*
Historic Park, 3431 Fort Ave.

Fort Humboldt

Occupied by U.S. troops from 1853 to 1865. General U.S. Grant was stationed here in 1853.
Placed by Daughters of the American Revolution of California, 1925.

EUREKA (Humboldt Co.)   *Humboldt Hill Rd., off US 101,*
at Harold Larsen Vista Pt.

Humboldt Harbor Historical District

Captain Jonathan Winship made the first recorded entry into Humboldt Bay by sea in June 1806. Encountered in 1849 by Josiah Gregg's party, new word of its existence reached San Francisco. By 1850 the Laura Virginia Association had founded Humboldt City, Union (Arcata), Bucksport, and Eureka. In subsequent years the bay became a major north coast lumber port and shipbuilding center.
Placed in cooperation with Humboldt County Historical Society, 1976.

FAIRFAX (Marin Co.)   *Marin Town and Country Club, one block S*
of Belmont and Pastori aves. intersection

Site of Birds' Nest Glen

The home of "Lord" Charles Snowden Fairfax, pioneer and political leader of the 1850s. Served California as an assemblyman (1853), speaker of assembly (1854), and clerk of the State Supreme Court (1856). Fairfax, a descendent of Scottish barons of the Cameron Fairfax family of Virginia, was involved in the last of California's historic political duels, being host to the principals and friends of the two antagonists.

Placed by California State Park Commission in cooperation with Marin County Native Sons and Daughters of the Golden West, 1960.

FALL RIVER MILLS (Shasta Co.) *.3 mi. W, on SH 299, NW of Long St.*

Lockhart Ferry

Established by Samuel Lockhart in 1856 as a link in the first wagon road from Yreka to Red Bluff, the Lockhart Ferry crossed below the confluence of the Fall and Pit rivers near this spot. After a massacre in December 1856, the ferry was reestablished in 1857 below Fall River Falls.

Placed by California State Park Commission in cooperation with Fort Crook Historical Society, 1956.

FELLOWS (Kern Co.) *On Broadway, 100 ft. W of fire station*

First Gusher—Midway Field—Well No. 2-6
The Well Which Made the Midway Oil Field Famous

Near an area of small 40- and 50-barrel wells, it blew in over the derrick top Nov. 27, 1909, with a production of 2,000 bbl a day, and started one of the greatest oil booms California ever experienced.

"For a long time it held the rank of the best producer in the whole west side, and before its glory began to wane other celebrities in the gusher line began to crown the north midway stage." *Morning Echo,* Bakersfield, Feb. 28, 1911.

Well 2-6 was located as a wildcat June 1, 1909, by Fred C. Ripley, then assistant manager of oil properties, Santa Fe Railway Coast Lines, later manager of its successor, the Chanslor-Canfield Midway Oil Company, with which he was associated 1904 to 1947.

Private plaque.

FELTON (Santa Cruz Co.) *Graham Hill and Covered Bridge rds.*

Felton Covered Bridge

Built in 1892–93 and believed to be the tallest covered bridge in the country, it stood as the only entry to Felton for 45 years. In 1937, it was retired from active service to become a pedestrian bridge and figured prominently in many films of that period. After suffering damage in the winter storms of 1982, it was restored to its original elegance in 1987 using native materials and local talent.

Placed in cooperation with Monterey Viejo Chapter 1846 and Mountain Charlie Chapter 1850 of E Clampus Vitus and the County of Santa Cruz, 1987.

FERNDALE (Humboldt Co.) *5 mi. W, on Centerville Rd.*

Centerville Beach Cross

To the memory of the 38 pioneers who lost
their lives in wreck of Northerner
Jan. 6, 1860
by
Ferndale Parlor NSGW
1921

Private plaque.

FERNDALE (Humboldt Co.)

Ferndale City Hall Park,
Herbert and Main sts. intersection

Ferndale

This pioneer agricultural community, settled in 1852, helped feed the booming population of mid-century San Francisco. Long known as "Cream City," Ferndale made innovative and lasting contributions to the dairy industry. Local creameries, and the town's role as a transportation and shipping center in the late 19th and early 20th centuries, fostered prosperity that produced Ferndale's outstanding Victorian-Gothic residential and false-front commercial architecture.

Placed in cooperation with Ferndale Chamber of Commerce Historical Committee and community effort, 1976.

FIDDLETOWN (Amador Co.)

S side of street from
Dr. Yee's Chinese Herb Shop

Fiddletown

Settled by Missourians in 1849. Suggested that settlement be called Fiddletown because residents "were always fiddling." Changed in 1878 to Oleta but original name later restored. Once trading center for American, Loafer, and French flats, Lone Hill, and other rich mining camps. Bret Harte added to community's fame in *An Episode of Fiddletown.*

Placed by California Centennial Commission and residents of Fiddletown, 1950.

FLOURNOY (Tehama Co.)

3.9 mi. N, on Osborn Rd.

1854—Indian Military Post—1866
Nomi Lackee Indian Reservation

Controlled over 300 to 2,500 militant Indians. U.S. survey of 1858 showed 25,139.71 acres in the reservation. Indians moved to Round Valley in 1866.

Placed by Mrs. Leila Masterson, Flournoy Farm Bureau Center, and Berendos Parlor No. 23 of Native Daughters of the Golden West, 1938.

FOLSOM (El Dorado Co.)

3 mi. NE, Folsom Lake State Recreation
Area, north side, Dyke 8 picnic area

Mormon Island

First gold camp after discovery at Sutter's Mill, established 1848. Originally known as Lower Mines or Mormon Diggings. The rich sand bar findings actually started the gold rush of 1849. At the same location was a settlement founded by Sam Brannan, known as Natoma, later moved south of Folsom when the gold strike was exhausted.

Placed by Lord Sholto Douglas Chapter No. 3 of E Clampus Vitus, 1981.

FOLSOM (El Dorado Co.)

4 mi. NE, Folsom Lake State
Recreation Area, Green Valley Rd.

Mormon Island, Negro Hill, Salmon Falls,
and Condemned Bar

These historic mining towns, and other mining camps of the gold rush era, now inundated by Folsom Lake, are commemorated by the Mormon Island Memorial Cemetery nearby. Here were reburied the pioneers whose graves were flooded when the lake was formed by the Folsom Dam. Their memory is a reminder that what we are today we owe to those who came before us.

Placed by California State Park Commission in cooperation with Marguerite Parlor No. 12 of Native Daughters of the Golden West, 1957.

FOLSOM (Placer Co.)
Folsom Lake State Recreation Area, Beals Point unit, 3 mi. N on levee

Pioneer Express Trail
(Plaque on riding trail)

Between 1849 and 1854, Pioneer Express riders rode this gold rush trail to the many populous mining camps on American River bars now covered by Folsom Lake, including Beals, Condemned, Dotons, Long, Horseshoe, Rattlesnake, and Oregon, on the route to Auburn and the camps beyond.

Placed by California State Park Commission, 1957.

FOLSOM (Sacramento Co.)
819 Sutter St.

Folsom Pony Express Terminus

Gold rush and railroad town, Folsom became the western terminus of the Central Overland Pony Express on July 1, 1860. During its first few months, after Apr. 4, 1860, the express mail had been run by pony to and from Sacramento. Beginning on July 1, 1860, the Sacramento Valley Railroad carried it between Sacramento and Folsom until Placerville was made the terminus during July 1–Oct. 26, 1861.

Placed by California State Park Commission in cooperation with Sacramento County Historical Society, Folsom Historical Association, Fern Parlor No. 123 of Native Daughters of the Golden West, Folsom Chamber of Commerce, and Central Overland Pony Express Trail Association, 1960.

FOLSOM (Sacramento Co.)
Folsom Powerhouse State Park, Greenback Lane

Old Folsom Powerhouse

In the 1850s, Horatio Gates Livermore and later his sons, Horatio P. and Charles E., pioneered the development of ditches and dams on the American River for industry and agriculture. One historic result was Folsom Powerhouse, which began operations in July 1895. Power was delivered to Sacramento at 11,000 volts, which was a new achievement in long distance high-voltage transmission. The Capital celebrated by a grand electric carnival Sept. 9, 1895.

The original generating plant, still in place, remained in continuous operation until 1952.

The plant was donated by Pacific Gas and Electric Co. to the State of California to preserve its historical values.

Placed by California State Park Commission in cooperation with Sacramento Section of American Institute of Electrical Engineers, 1958.

FOLSOM (Sacramento Co.)
Leidesdorff Plaza, NE corner Reading and Sutter

Folsom Terminal
California's First Passenger Railroad

Completion of the Sacramento Valley Railroad from Sacramento to Folsom was celebrated here Feb. 22, 1856, by enthusiastic residents of both cities. The new line,

22 miles in length, was commenced Feb. 12, 1885, and was built by Theodore Dehone Judah, noted pioneer engineer.

Placed by California State Park Commission in cooperation with Sacramento County Historical Society, 1956.

FONTANA (San Bernardino Co.)   *Josephine Knopf Senior Citizen*
Center of Fontana, 8384 Cypress Ave.

Site of U.S. Rabbit Experimental Station

In March 1928, the Federal Government established the first and only experimental station in the United States devoted solely to research on the breeding and raising of rabbits, on a five-acre property donated by A. B. Miller of Fontana. The station successfully pioneered new techniques of rabbit care and breeding until 1965 when the City of Fontana acquired the property for use as a senior citizens' facility.

Placed in cooperation with Fontana Historical Society, City of Fontana, and Billy Holcomb Chapter of E Clampus Vitus, 1984.

FOREST HILL (Placer Co.)   *24540 Main St.*

Forest Hill

Gold discovered here in 1850 in which year the first "forest house" was built. In 1852, the Jenny Lind Mine was found, which produced over a million dollars in gold, while the mines in this immediate vicinity produced over ten million dollars up to 1868. Town an important trading post and famed for its beautiful forests.

Placed by California Centennial Commission and Placer County Historical Society, 1950.

FOREST HILL (Placer Co.)   *3 mi. NE, SE corner Springs Garden and*
Colfax Foresthill rds.

Yankee Jim's

Gold was discovered here in 1850 by "Yankee Jim," a reputed lawless character, and by 1857 town was one of the most important in Placer County. The first mining ditch in the county was constructed here by H. Starr and Eugene Phelps. Colonel William McClure introduced hydraulic mining to this area in June of 1853.

Placed by California Centennial Commission and Placer County Historical Society, 1950.

FORT BIDWELL (Modoc Co.)   *Fandango Pass Rd.,*
10.8 mi. E of US 395,
9.2 mi. W of Fort Bidwell

Applegate-Lassen Emigrant Trail
(Fandango Pass)

This spot marks the convergence of two pioneer trails widely used by emigrants during the years 1846–50. The Applegate Trail, established in 1846, led from the Humboldt River in Nevada to the Willamette Valley in Oregon. The Lassen cut-off, established by Peter Lassen in 1848, turned south at Goose Lake to the northern mines and settlements of California.

Placed by California State Park Commission in cooperation with Modoc County Supervisors and Alturas Parlor No. 159 of Native Daughters of the Golden West, 1956.

FORT BRAGG (Mendocino Co.)

321 Main St.

Fort Bragg

Established in this vicinity June 11, 1857, by 1st Lt. Horatio Gates Gibson, 3rd Artillery, later Brig. Gen. U.S. Army. Named by Gibson in honor of his former company commander, Braxton Bragg, later General. CSA abandoned in October, 1864.

Placed by California State Park Commission in cooperation with citizens of Fort Bragg and Union Lumber Company, 1957.

FORT JONES (Siskiyou Co.)

On E. Side Rd., .5 mi. SE of
E. Side Rd. and SH 3 intersection

Fort Jones 1852–1858

On this ground there was established Oct. 16, 1852, a military post by Companies A and B, First United States Dragoons from Apr. 23, 1853 until June 23, 1853. The date of its abandonment, this fort was garrisoned by Company E, 4th U.S. Infantry. Named in honor of Col. Rodger Jones, brevet major general. The adjutant general of the army 1825–52 dedicated this 14th day of July 1946 to the officers and men who served here, among whom were Sgts. James Bryan and John Griffin and Pvt. Gundor Salverson who, upon their discharge, became pioneer settlers of the valley erected in their memory by the County of Siskiyou.

Private plaque placed 1946.

FORT TEJON (Kern Co.)

Fort Tejon State Historic Park,
on Lebec Rd., 2.8 mi. N of Lebec

Fort Tejon

This military post was established by the United States Army on June 24, 1854, to suppress stock rustling and for the protection of Indians in the San Joaquin Valley. As regimental headquarters of the First Dragoons, Fort Tejon was an important military, social, and political center. Camels for transportation were introduced here in 1858. The fort was abandoned Sept. 11, 1864.

Placed by California State Park Commission in cooperation with Kern County Historical Society, El Tejon Parlor No. 239 of Native Daughters of the Golden West, Bakersfield Parlor No. 42 of Native Sons of the Golden West, and Kern County Museum, 1954.

FOUNTAIN SPRINGS (Tulare Co.)

SW corner CH J22
and CH M109

Fountain Springs

One and one-half miles northwest of this point the settlement of Fountain Springs was established before 1855. It was at the junction of the Stockton-Los Angeles road and the one to the Kern River gold mines. From 1858 to 1861 Fountain Springs was a station on the Butterfield Overland Mail route.

Placed by California State Park Commission in cooperation with Tulare County Historical Society, 1958.

FOUNTAIN SPRINGS (Tulare Co.)

8 mi. S, SW corner CH
M109 and CH M12

Tailholt

Tailholt began as a gold mining camp about 1856 during the Kern River gold rush. Gold was obtained from placer and shaft operations. Mining has been carried on intermittently since the time of discovery. During periods of activity there has been a considerable settlement here. The name was changed to White River about 1870.

Placed by California Centennial Commission and Tulare County Historical Society, 1949.

FRANKLIN (Sacramento Co.)

NE corner of Franklin Cemetery

Grave of Alexander Hamilton Willard

Alexander Hamilton Willard—born Charlestown, N.H., Aug. 24, 1778; died Franklin, Mar. 6, 1865. Last surviving member of the Lewis and Clark Expedition. He kept a journal and gave valuable service as a gunsmith.

Placed by State Society Daughters of Founders and Patriots of America, 1957.

FREEMAN JUNCTION (Kern Co.)

On SH 178, .2 mi. W
of SH 14 junction

Freeman Junction

In 1834 explorer Joseph R. Walker passed this junction of Indian trails after discovering nearby Walker Pass. Death Valley '49er parties here diverged west and south after their escape from Death Valley en route to the California gold fields. Later this became a junction point where the bandit Tiburcio Vasquez preyed on stages and freighters traveling between the Kern River mines and Los Angeles and the mines of Bodie and the Panamints.

Placed by California State Park Commission in cooperation with Death Valley '49ers, Inc., and Kern County Historical Society, 1961.

FREMONT (Alameda Co.)

1250 Stanford Ave., off I-680 at
Mission Blvd., N .5 mi. to
Stanford Ave., E to winery

Leland Stanford Winery

This winery was founded in 1869 by Leland Stanford, railroad builder, Governor of California, United States Senator, and founder of Stanford University. The vineyard, planted by his brother, Josiah Stanford, helped to prove that wines equal to any in the world could be produced in California. The restored buildings and winery are now occupied and operated by Weibel Champagne Vineyards.

Placed by California State Park Commission in cooperation with R. E. and F. E. Weibel and Weibel, Inc., 1958.

FREMONT (Alameda Co.) *Vallejo Mill Historical Park, NE corner Niles Canyon Rd. and Mission Blvd.*

Vallejo Flour Mill

(S plaque at NE corner Orchard Dr. and Mission Blvd.;
N plaque at SW corner Mayhew Rd. and Mission Blvd.)

Site of flour mill, Niles, built 1853 by Don Jose de Vallejo, brother of Gen. Vallejo, on his Rancho Arroyo de la Alameda. Niles was once called "Vallejo Mills." Stone aqueduct carrying water for mill parallels Niles Canyon Road.

Placed by Department of Public Works, Division of Highways.

FRENCH CAMP (San Joaquin Co.) *1672 W. Bowman Rd., 2.2 mi. W. of I-5*

California Chicory Works

The partnership of C. A. Bachmann and Charles H. W. Brandt, formed in 1885, was the largest chicory supplier in America while operating at this site during the 1890s. Chicory roots are roasted, ground, and used as a mixture with or substitute for coffee. Using its own ship, *The Dora,* and the finest German equipment to process the chicory, the company shipped its product to market until about 1911.

Placed in cooperation with San Joaquin County Historical Society, 1981.

FRENCH CAMP (San Joaquin Co.) *On Elm St. at French Camp School*

French Camp

Here was the terminus of the Oregon-California Trail used by the French-Canadian trappers employed by the Hudson's Bay Company from about 1832 to 1845. Michel la Framboise, among others, met fur hunters here annually, where they camped with their families. In 1844 Charles M. Weber and William Gulnac promoted the first white settlers' colony on Rancho del Campo de los Franceses, which included French Camp and the site of Stockton.

Placed by California State Park Commission in cooperation with the Reynolds family, Native Daughters of the Golden West, Ladies Auxiliary to California Pioneers, and French Camp District Chamber of Commerce, 1959.

FRENCH CORRAL (Nevada Co.) *2.7 mi. S, W side Pleasant Valley Rd. at S fork of Yuba River*

Bridgeport (Nyes Crossing) Covered Bridge

Built in 1862 by David Isaac Johnwood with lumber from his mill in Sierra County, this bridge was part of the Virginia Turnpike Company toll road which served the northern mines and the busy Nevada Comstock Lode. Utilizing a combination truss and arch construction, it is one of the oldest housed spans in the west and the longest single-span, wood-covered bridge in the United States.

Placed by California State Park Commission in cooperation with Nevada County Historical Society and Wm. B. Meek-Wm. M. Stewart Chapter No. 10 of E Clampus Vitus, 1964.

FRENCH CORRAL (Nevada Co.)
On Pleasant Valley Rd.,
in center of community
The World's First Long Distance Telephone Line
Commemorating the first long distance telephone in the world. Built in 1877 by the Ridge Telephone Co., it connected French Corral with French Lake 58 miles away. It was operated by the Milton Mining Co. from this building which was built about 1853.

Placed by Columbia Parlor No. 70 of Native Daughters of the Golden West, 1940.

FRENCH GULCH (Shasta Co.)
On Trinity Hill Rd., 3 mi. E of SH 299
French Gulch
Founded nearby by French miners in 1849, the town of Morrowville, relocated here, was the center of one of the state's richest gold producing areas. Total production was over $20,000,000. One of California's first stamp mills operated at the nearby Franklin Mine. From 1856 to 1858, French Gulch was the trailhead on the western branch of the California-Oregon trail. St. Rose Catholic Church was founded in 1856. As a supply and stopping place the town rivaled Shasta.

Placed in cooperation with Gertrude Moss Historical Fund, Shasta Historical Society, and Trinitarianus Chapter No. 62 of E Clampus Vitus, 1993.

FRESNO (Fresno Co.)
5021 W. Shaw Ave.
Forestiere Underground Gardens
Here, beneath the hot, arid surface of the San Joaquin Valley, Baldasare Forestiere (1879–1946) began in the early 1900s to sculpt a fantastic retreat. Excavating the hardpan by hand, he created a unique complex of underground rooms, passages, and gardens which rambled throughout a ten-acre parcel. His work is being preserved as a living monument to a creative and individualistic spirit unbounded by conventionality.

Placed in cooperation with the Rick Forestiere family, 1979.

FRESNO (Fresno Co.)
NE corner Stanislaus and O sts.
Fresno Junior College—1910
Historical landmark commemorating Fresno Technical School, constructed 1895. Known as the Fresno High School from 1895–1921, established as the first junior college of California 1910, normal school-forerunner to Fresno State College 1911, Fresno Technical High School 1921–48, Fresno Junior College 1948–59, and Fresno Tech Alumni Association.

Placed by Paul Easterbrook Fresno Technical High School Alumni, Fresno City College Associated Students, and Frontier Chevrolet Company.

FRESNO (Fresno Co.)
At Fresno Fairgrounds
Fresno Assembly Center
This memorial is dedicated to over 5,000 Americans of Japanese ancestry who were confined at the Fresno Fairgrounds from May to October 1942. This was an early phase of the mass incarceration of over 120,000 Japanese Americans during World War II pursuant to Executive Order 9066. They were detained without charges, trial, or establishment of guilt. May such injustice and suffering never recur.

Placed in cooperation with Fresno District Fair, Japanese American Citizens League, and Central California Nikkei Foundation, 1992.

FRESNO (Fresno Co.) *Fulton and Mariposa Mall, in planter, 100 ft. SW of clock tower*

Site of the Fresno Free Speech Fight

At the corner of Mariposa and I streets, from October 1910 to March 1911, the Industrial Workers of the World fought for the right of free speech in their efforts to organize Fresno's unskilled labor force. This was the first attempt at organizing the valley's unskilled workers.

Placed in cooperation with Fresno Parlor No. 25 of Native Sons of the Golden West, 1974.

FRIANT (Fresno Co.) *S shore, Millerton Lake Recreation Area*

Millerton

Due north of here, now covered by the waters of the lake, was the site of Millerton, first county seat of Fresno County 1856–74.

Placed by Jim Savage Chapter 1852 of E Clampus Vitus.

GAVIOTA (Santa Barbara Co.) *1.5 mi. NW, US 101 N, at rest stop*

Gaviota Pass
Fremont-Foxen Memorial

Here, on Christmas Day 1846, natives and soldiers from the Presidio of Santa Barbara lay in ambush for Lt. Col. John C. Fremont, U.S.A. and his battalion. Advised of the plot, Fremont was guided over the San Marcos Pass by Benjamin Foxen and his son, William, and captured Santa Barbara without bloodshed.

Placed by Santa Barbara Parlor No. 116 of Native Sons of the Golden West and Lions Club of Santa Maria.

GEORGETOWN (El Dorado Co.) *Main St., on wall in front of fire station*

Georgetown

Founded Aug. 7, 1849, by George Phipps and party, nicknamed Growlersburg from the heavy nuggets that "growled" in the miners' pans. Georgetown was the hub of an immensely rich gold area. After the disastrous fire of 1852, the old town was moved from the canyon in lower Main Street to its present site. Unique in early day planning, Main Street was laid out 100 feet wide and side streets 60 feet. Population was 3,000 in 1854–56.

Placed by California Centennial Commission, Georgetown Divide Rotary Club, and James W. Marshall Chapter of E Clampus Vitus, 1951.

GLEN ELLEN (Sonoma Co.) *1 mi. S, 2400 London Ranch Rd.*

Jack London State Historic Park

This is the "House of Happy Walls," built in 1919 by Charmian K. London in memory of her husband, Jack London, renowned author. Here are housed many of his works and the collection gathered in their travels throughout the world. Charmian's house, the ruins of Jack's "Wolf House," and his grave were presented in 1960 to the State of California by his nephew, Irving Shepard.

Placed by California State Park Commission in cooperation with the citizens of Sonoma County, 1960.

GLENBURN (Shasta Co.)
2 mi. NW, SE corner McArthur Rd. and Soldier Mountain Dr.

In Commemoration of Fort Crook

Established July 1, 1857, by Lt. George Crook and command for the protection of the immigrants and settlers. Later occupied by Capt. John W. Gardner and Capt. McGregor. The boundaries of the fort were designed as one mile in every direction from the flag pole.

Placed by Fort Crook Historical Society, Fall River Valley, 1934.

GLENDALE (Los Angeles Co.)
1330 Dorothy Dr.

Casa Adobe de San Rafael

Built by Tomas and Maria Sanchez
1865–1871
Restored by the City of Glendale 1932

Placed by Verdugo Parlor No. 240 of Glendale Native Daughters of the Golden West, and Glendale Beautiful, 1973.

GLENDALE (Los Angeles Co.)
2211 Bonita Dr.

San Rafael Rancho

First granted to Jose Maria Verdugo, Oct. 20, 1784. Catalina adobe built about 1828, and Gen. Andres Pico oak tree campsite before he surrendered to Gen. John C. Fremont, 1847.

Placed by California Parlor No. 247 of Native Daughters of the Golden West, 1947.

GLENDORA (Los Angeles Co.)
400 block E. Bennet Ave., at Minnesota Ave.

Glendora Bougainvillea

Planted in 1901 by the R. H. Hamlins, early citrus growers, the Glendora bougainvillea is the largest growth of this exotic plant in the United States. The parent stock was brought to California by a whaling ship about 1870, and the vines survive as one of the best examples remaining of the early 20th-century promotional image of California as paradise.

Placed in cooperation with the L. J. Pittman family, 1978.

GLENNVILLE (Kern Co.)
Kern County Fire Dept., Glennville Substation, on SH 155

Glennville Adobe

Kern County's oldest residence. Built before Civil War by Thomas Fitzgerald as trading post at junction of two Indian trails. Present Greenhorn Road follows east-west trail (later McFarlane Toll Road) to Kern River mining districts. Town named in 1857 after James Madison Glenn, an early settler.

Placed by California State Division of Beaches and Parks in cooperation with Kern County Historical Society, El Tejon Parlor No. 239 of Native Daughters of the Golden West, and Kern County Museum, 1952.

GLENNVILLE (Kern Co.)

1.1 mi. W, NE corner Jack Ranch and White River rds.

Lavers Crossing

In 1854 John C. Reid filed a squatter's claim on this spot, the same year Kern County's first school class was held here. In 1859 David Lavers, with his father and brother, John, built a hotel and stage barn on the old Bull Road. The crossing was the principal community in Linn's Valley until about 1870.

Placed by Kern County Historical Society, El Tejon Parlor No. 239 of Native Daughters of the Golden West, and Kern County Museum, 1959.

GLENWOOD (Santa Cruz Co.)

4171 Glenwood Dr., .4 mi. N of Glenwood cut-off rd.

Glenwood

Historic town founded by Charles C. Martin, who came around Horn 1847, and his wife, Hannah Carver Martin, who crossed the Isthmus. First homesteaded area in 1851 and operated tollgate and station for stagecoaches crossing mountains. Later Martin developed lumber mill, winery, store, and Glenwood Resort Hotel.

Placed by California Centennial Commission, Santa Cruz Parlor No. 26 of Native Daughters of the Golden West, Santa Cruz Parlor No. 90 of Native Sons of the Golden West, and decendants of Martin family, 1950.

GOLD HILL (El Dorado Co.)

Gold Trails Elementary School, 1336 Cold Springs Rd.

Wakamatsu Tea and Silk Farm Colony

Site of the only tea and silk farm established in California. First agricultural settlement of pioneer Japanese immigrants who arrived at Gold Hill on June 8, 1869. Despite the initial success, it failed to prosper. It marked the beginning of Japanese influence on the agricultural economy of California.

Placed in cooperation with Japanese American Citizen League, El Dorado County Historical Society, and Friends of the Centennial Observance, 1969.

GOLD RUN (Placer Co.)

NW corner I-80 and Magra Rd.

Gold Run

(Plaque in front of post office)

Founded in 1854 by O.W. Hollenbeck and originally called Mountain Springs. Famed for its hydraulic mines which from 1865 to 1878 shipped $6,125,000 in gold. Five large water ditches passed through the town serving the mining companies, which had to cease operations in 1882 when state law was passed prohibiting hydraulic mining.

Placed by California Centennial Commission and Placer County Historical Society, 1950.

GRASS VALLEY (Nevada Co.)   *1.2 mi. E, Empire Mine State Historical Park, 10791 Empire St.*

Empire Mine

This plaque marks the site of the Empire Mine, noted for its continuous operation 1850–1957 producing over $120,000,000 in gold.

Placed by Manzanita Parlor No. 29 of Native Daughters of the Golden West, 1963.

GRASS VALLEY (Nevada City)   *212 W. Main St.*

The Holbrooke Hotel

The present bar of the hotel has been in continuous operation since 1852, when it was known as the Golden Gate Saloon. The wooden building had a rear extension called the Exchange Hotel and offered food and lodging by January 1853. The saloon was destroyed in the fire of 1855 and rebuilt out of fieldstone with a brick front. The Holbrooke, built in 1862, had the adjacent Golden Gate Saloon incorporated in the hotel building.

Placed in cooperation with Historical Landmarks Commission of Nevada County, 1978.

GRASS VALLEY (Nevada Co.)   *S. Church St., between Dalton and Chapel sts.*

Mount Saint Mary's Convent and Academy

Built by the Rev. Thomas J. Dalton and dedicated May 2, 1865, by Bishop Eugene O'Connell as Sacred Heart Convent and Holy Angels Orphanage. Under the Sisters of Mercy it served from 1866 to 1932 as the first orphanage of the northern mines. It functioned as an academy (1868–1965) and a convent (1866–1968).

Placed in cooperation with Mount Saint Mary's Historic Preservation Committee and the Sisters of Mercy, 1972.

GRASS VALLEY (Nevada Co.)   *Mining and Pelton Wheel Museum, S. Mill at Allison Ranch Rd.*

North Star Mine Powerhouse

The North Star Powerhouse, built by A. D. Foote in 1895, was the first complete water-powered, compressed air transmission plant of its kind. Compressed air, generated by Pelton water wheels, furnished power for the entire mine operation. The 30-foot Pelton Wheel was the largest in the world, and was in continuous use for over 30 years.

Placed in cooperation with Nevada County Historical Society, 1971.

GRASS VALLEY (Nevada Co.)   *10 mi. S, SH 49, on SE side of Wolf Creek Bridge*

Overland Emigrant Trail

At this point the Overland Emigrant Trail approaches the present highway. More than 100 years ago the trail resounded to the creaking wheels of pioneer wagons and the cry of hardy but footsore travelers buoyed by the realization their long trip to the gold fields was about over.

Placed in cooperation with Nevada County Historical Landmarks Commission, 1976.

GRASS VALLEY (Nevada Co.)   *SW corner Hocking Ave.*
and Jenkins St.

Site of One of the First Discoveries
of Quartz Gold In California

This tablet commemorates the discovery of gold-bearing quartz and the beginning of quartz mining in California. The discovery was made on Gold Hill by George Knight, October 1850. The occurrence of gold-bearing quartz was undoubtedly noted here and elsewhere about the same time, or previously, but the above discovery created the great excitement that started the development of quartz mining into a great industry. The Gold Hill Mine, from 1850 to 1857, is credited with a total production of $4,000,000.

Placed by Quartz Parlor No. 58 of Native Sons of the Golden West and Manzanita Parlor No. 29 of Native Daughters of the Golden West, 1929.

GREENVILLE (Plumas Co.)   *4.4 mi. E, on Beckwourth-Greenville Rd.*

Peter Lassen
Site of
trading post
1851

Placed by Plumas Pioneer Parlor No. 219 of Native Daughters of the Golden West and Plumas Parlor No. 228 of Native Sons of the Golden West, 1930.

GREENWOOD (El Dorado Co.)   *SW corner SH 193 and Greenwood St.*
intersection

Greenwood

John Greenwood, a trapper and guide who came to California in 1844, established here a trading post in 1849. The mining town of Greenwood, which developed during the gold rush, boasted a theater, four hotels, 14 stores, a brewery, and four saloons. Among its illustrious citizens was John A. Stone, California songwriter, who was buried here in 1863.

Placed by California State Park Commission in cooperation with the Golden Key, 1955.

GROVELAND (Tuolumne Co.)   *NE corner Main and Back sts.*

Groveland

Formerly called "First Garrote," traced to hanging of Mexican for stealing horse. Adobe buildings still standing (1949) built in 1849, as shown by dated adobe brick taken from partition. Gold discovered here 1849. Thousands in placer gold taken from mines in Garrote Creek, Big Creek, and other diggings. Deer Flat, Noisy Flat, and the Rancheria well-known nearby places in heyday.

Placed by California Centennial Commission and Big Oak Flat Highway 120 Association, 1949.

GROVELAND (Tuolumne Co.)   *2.4 mi. SE, on SH 120*

Second Garrote

Sizable settlement was established at this rich placer location in 1849 by miners spreading east from Big Oak Flat and Groveland. Famous hangman's tree, part of which still stands (1950), reported to have been instrumental in death of a number of lawbreakers during heyday of this locality, hence its name.

Placed by California Centennial Commission and Charles G. Nall Post No. 3668 of Veterans of Foreign Wars, 1950.

HALF MOON BAY (San Mateo Co.)
10.8 mi. S, San Gregorio State Beach, SH 1, .1 mi. S of SH 84

Portola Camp

Captain Gaspar de Portola and his party of Spanish explorers, journeying overland from San Diego in a fruitless search for Monterey Bay, camped here by San Gregorio Creek for a three-day rest and treatment of their sick, Oct. 24–27, 1769. Having missed Monterey, they later discovered San Francisco Bay instead.

Placed by California Centennial Commission in cooperation with County Board of Supervisors and San Mateo County Historical Association, 1949.

HAMILTON CITY (Glenn Co.)
3.7 mi. N, NE corner 1st and Cutler aves.

William Semple Green, 1832–1905

Arrived, via Panama route, San Francisco, Oct. 10, 1849. Arrived Colusa County, July 6, 1850. Ferry boat captain, mail carrier, surveyor, editor, writer, legislator, Surveyor General of the United States, California State Treasurer, irrigationist, friend of man. On Dec. 18, 1883, posted the first water notice on an oak tree on the west bank of the Sacramento River immediately east of this spot for the diversion of 500,000 miner's inches of water for the irrigation of lands on the west side of the Sacramento Valley.

Placed by Glenn-Colusa Irrigation District and Colusa County Historical Society, 1954.

HARDWICK (Kings Co.)
1.5 mi. SE, 5833 14th Ave.

Mussel Slough Tragedy

Here on May 11, 1880, during a dispute over land titles between settlers and railroad, a fight broke out in which seven men lost lives—two deputy U.S. marshals and five ranchers. Legal struggle over titles finally compromised.

Placed by California Centennial Commission and Kings County Centennial Committee, 1950.

HAVILAH (Kern Co.)
Caliente-Bodfish Rd., south side of county courthouse

Havilah

Gold deposits at Havilah were discovered in 1864. After Kern County was organized in 1866, Havilah was the county seat until 1872, when the government was moved to Bakersfield. Havilah was an active mining center for more than twenty years. There are still some active mines in this vicinity.

Placed by Bakersfield Parlor No. 42 of Native Sons of the Golden West, El Tejon Parlor No. 239 of Native Daughters of the Golden West, Kern County Historical Society, and Kern County Chamber of Commerce, 1938.

HEALDSBURG (Sonoma Co.)   6050 Westside Rd.
Walters Ranch Hop Kiln
This structure served the important hop industry of California's north coast region, once the major hop-growing area in the west. Built in 1905 by a crew of Italian stonemasons, it represents the finest existing example of its type, consisting of three stone kilns for drying hops, a wooden cooler, and a two-story press for baling hops for shipment.

Placed in cooperation with Griffin Vineyard, 1977.

HEMET (Riverside Co.)   *Maze Stone Park, N 3.2 mi.*
                                           on California Ave. from SH 74
Maze Stone
This pictograph, representing a maze, is an outstanding example of the work of prehistoric peoples. It, with 5.75 acres of land, was donated to Riverside County as a county park on Apr. 16, 1956, by Mr. and Mrs. Rodger E. Miller.

Placed by California State Park Commission in cooperation with Riverside County Board of Supervisors, and Hemet Woman's Club, 1957.

HEMET (Riverside Co.)   *Ramona Bowl, 27400 S. Girard St.*
Pochea Indian Village Site
(Plaque located near restrooms)
Pochea was one of a cluster of Indian villages forming the very large settlement of Pahsitnah, which extended along the ridge east and west of Ramona Bowl. Pahsitnah was thriving when the Spanish first passed by in 1774. A tragic story tells of the natives contracting smallpox from Europeans, a terrible epidemic spreading, and some survivors fleeing to the area of the present Soboba Reservation.

Placed in cooperation with San Jacinto Valley Museum, Hemet Area Museum Association, Ramona Pageant Association, and Billy Holcomb Chapter of E Clampus Vitus, 1983.

HEMET (Riverside Co.)   *Ramona Bowl, 27400 S. Girard St.*
Ramona
(Plaque located inside entrance)
Within this valley was laid part of the scene, and here resided a number of the characters portrayed in Helen Hunt Jackson's historical novel *Ramona*, which depicted life and presented the status of the Indian on many great ranchos in early California beginning around the 1850s. This story, dramatized by the late Garnet Holme, was first presented on this site Apr. 13, 1923, becoming an annual event.

Placed by California Centennial Commission in cooperation with Ramona Pageant Association, Inc., 1950.

HOLY CITY (Santa Clara Co.)   *1.2 mi. SE, Old Santa Cruz Hwy. and*
                                    Mtn. Charlie Rd. intersection
Patchen
"Mountain Charley" McKiernan, one of the earliest residents of the Santa Cruz Mountains, settled near here in 1850. John Martin Schultheis and his wife homesteaded land about a mile from here in 1852. Their home is still standing (1950). The

Patchen Post Office, named for a famous racehorse, was located in this vicinity 1872–1920.

Placed by California Centennial Commission and Los Gatos Lions Club, 1950.

IMPERIAL (Imperial Co.)   *6.5 mi. W, on west bank of New River,*
S of Worthington Rd.

Site of Fort Romualdo Pacheco
(1825–1826)

In 1774, Spain opened an overland route from Sonora to California, but it was closed by Yuma Indians in 1781. In 1822, Mexico attempted to reopen this route. Lt. Romualdo Pacheco and soldiers built an adobe fort at this site in 1825–26, the only Mexican fort in Alta California. On Apr. 26, 1826, Kumeyaay Indians attacked the fort, killing three soldiers and wounding three others. Pacheco abandoned the fort, removing soldiers to San Diego.

Placed in cooperation with Imperial Valley College Barker Museum, Imperial Valley Pioneer Society, and Squibob Chapter of E Clampus Vitus, 1981.

IMPERIAL (Imperial Co.)   *6 mi. SW of I-8 and Dunaway Rd.*
intersection

Yuha Well

Known as Santa Rosa de Las Lajas (Flat Rocks), this site was used on Mar. 8, 1774, by the Anza exploring expedition, opening the land route from Sonora, Mexico, to Alta California. On December 11 to 15, 1775, the three divisions of Anza's colonizing expedition used this first good watering spot beyond the Colorado River on the way from Sonora to San Francisco.

Placed in cooperation with U.S. Department of the Interior and Squibob Chapter of E Clampus Vitus, 1993.

INDEPENDENCE (Inyo Co.)   *2.6 mi. N, .3 mi. NE US 395, between*
Schabell Ln. and Fort Rd.

1862—Camp Independence—1877

Near this spot on July 4, 1862, a troop of U.S. Calvary, under command of Col. George S. Evans, raised the American flag and named the place Camp Independence. The soldiers had been sent to protect the settlers from threatened Indian outbreaks. Before barracks could be erected, some of the soldiers provided shelter for themselves in the caves which may be seen in the nearby ravine. Camp abandoned July 1877.

Private wooden sign on Indian reservation property.

INDEPENDENCE (Inyo Co.)   *3 mi. NE, 500 ft. SW of Miller*
and Schabell lanes intersection

Camp Independence

At the request of settlers, Col. George Evans led a military expedition to this site on July 4, 1862. Hence its name "Independence." Indian hostilities ceased and the camp closed. War again broke out in 1865 and the camp was reoccupied as Fort Independence until its abandonment in 1877. This fort made possible the early settlements in the Owens Valley.

Placed by Slim Princess Chapter of E Clampus Vitus, 1981.

INDEPENDENCE (Inyo Co.)   *253 Market St.*
Mary Austin's Home
1868–1934

"But if ever you come beyond the borders as far as the town that lies in a hill dimple at the foot of Kearsarge, never leave it until you have knocked at the door of the brown house under the willow tree at the end of the village street, and there you shall have such news of the land, of its trails and what is astir in them, as one lover of it can give to another . . ."—*The Land of Little Rain.*
Placed by California State Park Commission.

INDEPENDENCE (Inyo Co.)   *139 Edwards St.*
Putnam's Stone Cabin

One hundred thirty feet west of this site, Charles Putnam built the first cabin of permanent habitation in what is now Inyo County in August 1861. The building served as a home, trading post, hospital, and "fort" for early settlers, as well as a survival point for travelers. It became the center of the settlement of "Putnam's," which five years later took the name "Independence."
Placed by California State Park Commission in cooperation with Eastern California Museum Association, Inc., 1964.

INDIAN WELLS (Kern Co.)   *Indian Wells Lodge, on SH 14,*
                                   4.9 mi. N of Freeman Junction
Indian Wells

Indian water hole on Joseph R. Walker Trail of 1834 where Manly-Jayhawker parties of 1849 found their first water after five days of travel from Argus Range. During 1860s was site of stage and freight station from Los Angeles to Coso and Cerro Gordo mines.
Placed by California Centennial Commission and Kern County Historical Society, 1950.

INDIO (Riverside Co.)   *28 mi. E, General Patton Memorial Museum,*
                                 N on Chiriaco Summit exit from I-10
Desert Training Center,
California-Arizona Maneuver Area

The D.T.C. was established by Maj. Gen. George S. Patton, Jr., in response to a need to train American combat troops for battle in North Africa during World War II. The camp, which began operation in 1942, covered 18,000 square miles. It was the largest military training ground ever to exist. Over one million men were trained at the 11 sub-camps (seven in California).
Placed in cooperation with General Patton Memorial Museum, 1989.

INGLEWOOD (Los Angeles Co.)   *Centinela Park, 700 Warren Ln.*
Aguaje de la Centinela
(Centinela Springs)

On this site bubbling springs once flowed here from their source in a deep water basin that has existed continuously since the Pleistocene era. Prehistoric animals,

Indians, and early Inglewood settlers were attracted here by the pure artesian water. The springs and valley were named after sentinels guarding cattle in the area.

Placed in cooperation with Historical Society of Centinela Valley, 1970.

IONE (Amador Co.) *150 W. Marlette*
Methodist Episcopal Church

The cornerstone was laid in 1862. Constructed of locally fired brick, the church was completed in 1866. Dedicated as "Ione City Centenary Church" and later known as the "Cathedral of the Mother Lode." The church was the first to serve the religious needs of the people in the area.

Placed in cooperation with Amador County Historical Society and Ione Community Methodist Church, 1970.

IONE (Amador Co.) *1 mi. N, Preston School of Industry, Waterman Rd.*
Preston Castle
(Plaque located .9 mi. N on SH 104)

The "Castle," built in 1890–94, is the most significant example of Romanesque Revival architecture in the Mother Lode. It was built to house the Preston School of Industry, established by the State Legislature as a progressive action toward rehabilitating, rather than simply imprisoning, juvenile offenders. Doors of the 120-room "castle" closed in 1960 after new facilities were completed.

Placed in cooperation with Amador County Historical Society, 1974.

IONE (Amador Co.) *18 E. Main St.*
Daniel Stewart Co. Store

General merchandise store built by Daniel Stewart in 1856. First brick building erected in Ione Valley from nearby Muletown brick. Ione, once known as "Bed-bug" and "Freeze-Out," was an important supply center on the main road to the Mother Lode and southern mines.

Placed by California State Park Commission in cooperation with Chispa Parlor No. 40 of Native Daughters of the Golden West and Ione Parlor No. 33 of Native Sons of the Golden West, 1964.

IOWA HILL (Placer Co.) *On Iowa Hill Rd., .1 mi. SW of post office*
Iowa Hill

Gold was discovered here in 1853, and by 1856 weekly production was estimated at one hundred thousand dollars. Total value of gold produced up to 1880 placed at twenty million dollars. Town was destroyed by fire in 1857 and again in 1862 but each time was rebuilt with more substantial buildings. Last big fire 1920 destroyed most of town.

Placed by California Centennial Commission, Placer County Historical Society, and Iowa Hill Community Club, 1950 and 1976.

JACKSON (Amador Co.) *1.6 mi. N, SH 49, W roadside rest area*
Argonaut and Kennedy Mines

Argonaut Mine, discovered 1850, and Kennedy Mine, discovered 1856, played dramatic roles in the economic development of California. They produced

$105,268,760 in gold. Kennedy Mine has a vertical shaft of 5,912 feet, the deepest in the United States, and changed mining methods in the Mother Lode. Argonaut Mine was the scene of the Mother Lode's most tragic mine disaster. Forty-eight miners were trapped in a fire at the 3,500-foot level on Aug. 27, 1922—a few survived. Both mines closed in 1942.

Placed in cooperation with Amador County Board of Supervisors, Amador County Chamber of Commerce, and Amador County Landmark Advisory Committee, 1968.

JACKSON (Amador Co.) 113 Main St.
Pioneer Hall
The Order of Native Daughters of the Golden West was organized on these premises, the site of the Pioneer Hall, on Sept. 11, 1886.

Placed by Upsula Parlor No. 1 of Native Daughters of the Golden West, 1932.

JACKSON (Amador Co.) SE corner Main and Church sts.
Site of Pioneer Jewish Synagogue
On Sept. 18, 1857, Congregation B'nai Israel of Jackson dedicated on this site the first synagogue in the Mother Lode. High holy day worship continued until 1869 when the larger Masonic Hall was used to accommodate the congregation. The wooden structure then served as a schoolhouse until 1888. Relocated onto a nearby lot, it became a private dwelling, and was razed in 1948.

Placed in cooperation with Commission for the Preservation of Pioneer Jewish Cemeteries, and Landmarks of the Judah L. Magnes Memorial Museum, 1976.

JACUMBA (Imperial Co.) 7 mi. NE, 1 mi. N of I-8 and In-Ko-Pah
Park Rd. interchange, on old SH 80
Desert Tower
Bert Vaughn of Jacumba built the stone tower in 1922–23 to commemorate the pioneers and road and railroad builders who opened the area. In the 1930s, W. T. Ratcliffe carved the stone animal figures which lurk in the rocks surrounding the tower, creating a fantasy world of surprise and strange beauty. This remarkable sculptural assemblage is one of California's exceptional Folk Art Environments.

Placed in cooperation with Imperial Valley Pioneers and Squibob Chapter of E Clampus Vitus, 1984.

JAMESTOWN (Tuolumne Co.) NE corner Main and Donovan sts.
Mark Twain Bret Harte Trail
Jamestown (also called Jimtown)
Known as gateway of Mother Lode and to southern mines. Gold first discovered in Tuolumne County west of this point on Woods Creek by James Woods shortly before town was founded by Col. George James, Aug. 8, 1848. Large quantities of gold recovered from stream beds and gulches during "gold rush." Surrounded by famous mines from which millions were extracted in later years. First mercantile business in southern mines said to have been in Butterfield Building built in 1850, still standing (1948).

Placed by California Centennial Commission and Jamestown Promotion Club, 1948.

JANESVILLE (Lassen Co.)   *On Main St., .1 mi. N of Janesville*
                                              Elementary School

Fort Janesville
Built in 1859 during
Piute War

Placed by Nataqua Parlor No. 152 of Native Daughters of the Golden West, 1961.

JENNER (Sonoma Co.)   *12 mi. N, 19005 Coast Hwy. (SH 1)*

Fort Ross

Founded in 1812 by Russians from Sitka. When Russians withdrew to Alaska, 1841, Capt. Sutter bought the improvements and supplies. Acquired by the state in 1906 and remaining buildings restored—Greek Orthodox chapel, commandant's quarters, and stockade. Now a state historical monument.

Placed by Department of Public Works, Division of Highways.

JULIAN (San Diego Co.)   *Julian Memorial Park,*
                                          Washington and Fourth sts.

Julian

Historic gold mining town founded by Drury D. Bailey
February 1870.

Placed by Native Sons and Daughters of the Golden West, San Diego Historical Society, and San Diego County Board of Supervisors, 1948.

JULIAN (San Diego Co.)   *8 mi. SE, 1.7 mi. SE on Sunrise*
                                          Hwy. from SH 79 intersection

Pedro Fages Trail

On Oct. 29, 1772, Col. Pedro Fages headed east from San Diego searching for army deserters. It was the first entry by Europeans into Oriflamme Canyon. From there, Fages and his men traveled on through Cajon Pass, around the Mojave and the Central Valley, and eventually reached Mission San Luis Obispo. As a result, he discovered the Colorado Desert and the San Joaquin Valley.

Placed in cooperation with San Diego Historical Society, Congress of History, and Native Sons of the Golden West, 1973.

KAWEAH (Tulare Co.)   *43795 N. Fork Dr.*

Kaweah Post Office, Kaweah Colony

The Kaweah cooperative colony was a utopian project started in 1886. For several years it attracted international attention, and many settlers came here and actually did much to further their ideals. Unable to secure title to the land, and because of internal difficulties, the organization ceased to exist after 1892, leaving as one of its tangible reminders the Kaweah Post Office.

Placed by California Centennial Commission and Tulare County Historical Society, 1948.

KEELER (Inyo Co.)   *3.1 mi. NW, 300 ft. W of SH 136*
Owens Lake Silver-Lead Furnace
The Owens Lake Silver-Lead Furnace and Mill was built here by Col. Sherman Stevens in 1869 and used until March 1874. James Brady assumed its operation in 1870 for the Silver-Lead Company and built the town of Swansea. During the next few years the output of this furnace and one at Cerro Gordo was around 150 bars of silver every 24 hours, each weighing 83 pounds.

Placed by California State Park Commission in cooperation with Eastern California Museum Association, 1961.

KELSEYVILLE (Lake Co.)   *Main St. and Bell Hill Rd. intersection*
Site of First Adobe Home, Lake County
Built by Charles Stone and Andy Kelsey on land purchased from Salvador Vallejo. Constructed by forced Indian labor, causing much resentment and culminating in murder by Indians of both Stone and Kelsey in the fall of 1849. Their remains are beneath this monument.

Placed by California Centennial Commission and County of Lake, 1950.

KERNVILLE (Kern Co.)   *2.7 mi. SE, Old Kernville Cemetery, Wofford Rd.*
Kernville
Kernville, called Whiskey Flat until 1864, was founded in 1860 when Adam Hamilton, whiskey dealer, moved shop here from more temperate Quartsburg, founded earlier that year. Both camps resulted from the discovery of the Big Blue Ledge by "Lovely" Rogers while tracking a stray mule from the earlier camp of Keyesville.

Placed by Kern River Chamber of Commerce, 1937.

KING CITY (Monterey Co.)   *23 mi. W, US 101 to Jolon Rd., 26.5 mi. to Hunter-Ligget Military Reservation*
Misión San Antonio de Padua
(Turn off 5 miles north)
(Plaque located N bound roadside rest, US 101)
Located in the valley of the San Antonio River within the Santa Lucia range, Misión San Antonio de Padua, established on July 14, 1771, was the third in a series of missions founded in Alta California by Father Junipero Serra. Its picturesque setting makes it one of today's most outstanding examples of early mission life.

Placed in cooperation with California Historical Landmarks Advisory Committee and the Department of Public Works.

KING CITY (Monterey Co.)   *23 mi. W, .2 mi. W of US 101 on Jolon Rd.*
Mission San Antonio de Padua
Founded by Father Junipero Serra, July 14, 1771. Most picturesque setting. First mass was celebrated in presence of one Indian, later congregation grew to a thousand neophytes. Famous for its fine horses and expert vaqueros.

Placed by Department of Public Works, Division of Highways.

KIRKWOOD (Amador Co.)   *On SH 88*
Kirkwood's
This building has been the pioneer home of the Kirkwood and Taylor families since it was built by Zachary Kirkwood in 1864. This building was one of the first resorts operated in the Sierra Nevada Mountains.
Placed by James W. Marshall Chapter No. 49 of E Clampus Vitus, 1966.

KIRKWOOD (Amador Co.)   *10.5 mi. W, on SH 88*
Rachael Melton
died
Oct. 4, 1850
Native of Iowa
Erected by guests
at Kirkwood
1905

KIRKWOOD (Amador Co.)   *8.7 mi. W, on SH 88 at Mud Lake Rd.*
Old Emigrant Road
At this place the highway crosses the site of the Old Emigrant Road which here began a long loop around the Silver Lake basin, taking it to an elevation of 9,640 feet at one place. This difficult portion of the road was used by thousands of vehicles from 1848 to 1863, when it was superseded by a route approximating the present highway.
Placed by California State Park Commission in cooperation with the Silver Lake Camper's Association, 1959.

KLAMATH (Del Norte Co.)   *US 101 to Ter-Wer Valley exit,*
3.4 mi. to Ter-Wer Riffle Rd.,
turn right to Ter-Wer Riffle
and Klamath Glen rds. intersection
Fort Ter-Wer
Site of Fort Ter-Wer, United States military post, established Oct. 12, 1857, by 1st Lt. George Crook and men of Company D to keep peace between the Indians and whites. The fort was destroyed by a flood in December 1861, and abandoned June 10, 1862.
Placed by California State Park Commission in cooperation with Del Norte Historical Society, 1961.

KNIGHT'S FERRY (Stanislaus Co.)   *1.4 mi. W of SH 120, on Sonora Rd.*
1 Mile
Knight's Ferry
Picturesque mining center and trading post, 1849, once called Dentville. Early ferry to the southern mines; county seat 1862–72; rare wooden covered bridge reputedly designed by U. S. Grant, brother-in-law of Dent brothers, 1854; old flour mill, 1854.
Placed by Department of Transportation, Division of Highways.

KYBURZ (El Dorado Co.) *9 mi. W, at US 50 and Ice House Rd.*
intersection

Moore's (Riverton)

This was the site of a change station of the Pioneer Stage Company in the 1850s and 1860s. During 1860–61, the California Overland Pony Express maintained here the first pony remount station east of Sportsman's Hall.

Placed by California State Park Commission in cooperation with James W. Marshall Chapter No. 49 of E Clampus Vitus, and California Overland Pony Express Trail Association, 1960.

KYBURZ (El Dorado Co.) *8.7 mi. E, on US 50*

Strawberry Valley House

This popular resort and stopping place for stages and teams of the Comstock, established by Swift and Watson in 1856, became a remount station of the California Overland Pony Express on Apr. 4, 1860. Here on that date, Division Superintendent Bolivar Roberts waited with a string of mules to help pony rider Warren Upson through the snowstorm on Echo Summit.

Placed by California State Park Commission in cooperation with Highway 50 Association and California Overland Pony Express Trail Association, 1960.

KYBURZ (El Dorado Co.) *1 mi. W, on US 50*

Webster's
(Sugar Loaf House)

This was the site of Webster's Sugar Loaf House, well-known stopping place during the Comstock rush. Beginning in April 1860, it was used as a remount station of the California Overland Pony Express. In 1861 it became a horse change station for pioneer stage companies and overland mail.

Placed by California State Park Commission in cooperation with Highway 50 Association and California Overland Pony Express Trail Association, 1960.

LA CAÑADA (Los Angeles Co.) *8.3 mi. N of I-210,*
at Clear Creek Vista Point, on SH 2

The Angeles National Forest

This was the first national forest in the State of California, second in the United States, created by proclamation, Dec. 20, 1892, by President Benjamin Harrison.

The first name given to the forest was "San Gabriel Timberland Reserve." It was changed to "San Gabriel National Forest," Mar. 4, 1907, and then "Angeles National Forest," July 1, 1908.

Placed in cooperation with History and Landmarks Association of San Fernando, Antelope Valley Parlors of Native Sons and Daughters of the Golden West, and Rancho San Fernando Parlor No. 285 of Native Sons of the Golden West, 1960.

LA GRANGE (Stanislaus Co.) *30173 Yosemite Blvd.*

La Grange

This area has seen four phases of mining—placer, tunneling, hydraulic, and dredging. This bucket, one of a chain of 100, holds 12 C.F. and is from one of the world's largest dredges. The Tuolumne Gold Dredging Co. started operation of this dredge on

June 15, 1938, and continued until 1949 when it was abandoned about three miles south of here. Other and smaller dredges operated on the river west of La Grange.

Placed by Estanislao Chapter No. 58 of E Clampus Vitus, 1977.

LA PORTE (Plumas Co.)   *SW corner Main and Church sts.*
Emigrant Trail 1850
Gold discovered Rabbit Creek—1850
Renamed La Porte—1857

Placed by Plumas Pioneer Parlor No. 219 of Native Daughters of the Golden West, Quincy Parlor No. 131 of Native Sons of the Golden West, and Golden Anchor Parlor No. 182 of Native Sons of the Golden West, 1928.

LA VERNE (Los Angeles Co.)   *919 Puddingstone Dr.*
La Casa de Carrion

This house, built in 1868 by Saturnio Carrion, was restored in 1951 by Paul E. Traweek.

Placed by California State Park Commission in cooperation with Rancho San Jose Parlor No. 307 of Native Daughters of the Golden West, 1959.

LAGUNA NIGUEL (Orange Co.)   *On Coast Hwy., .3 mi. SW of SH 1*
intersection, also on SW corner
Coast Hwy. and Crown Valley
2 Miles
Dana Point

Named for Richard Henry Dana. Described in his book *Two Years Before the Mast* as the most romantic California spot. In the glamorous days of the ranchos, 1830–40, Yankee vessels traded supplies for hides here.

Placed by Department of Public Works, Division of Highways.

LAGUNITAS (Marin Co.)   *18 mi. W of US 101, off Sir Francis Drake*
Blvd., 1.3 mi. inside Samuel P. Taylor State Park
Pioneer Paper Mill

The first paper mill on the Pacific Coast was built here in November 1856 by Samuel Penfield Taylor. Using water power and later steam, it was replaced in 1884 by a larger steam-powered mill nearby, which was closed by the Depression of 1893 and destroyed by fire in 1915.

Placed in cooperation with Native Sons and Daughters of the Golden West of Marin County, 1956.

LAKE ISABELLA (Kern Co.)   *2 mi. N, on SH 178, at entrance to Old*
Isabella Rd. Recreation Area
Campsite of Edward M. Kern

Near this spot at the confluence of the north and south forks of the Kern River, the Theodore Talbot party of Capt. John C. Fremont's third expedition to the West camped for several weeks during December 1845 and January 1846. The river was named by Fremont in honor of Edward M. Kern, topographer for the expedition. Kern County was established in 1866 and derived its name from that of the river.

Placed in cooperation with Kern County Historical Society, El Tejon Parlor No. 239 of Native Daughters of the Golden West, and Kern County Museum, 1962.

LAKE ISABELLA (Kern Co.)　　　*3.3 mi. W, 2 mi. S of SH 155, on Black Gulch Rd.*
Keysville
From 1853 until 1870, Keysville was a center of both placer and quartz gold mining. On the knoll just below the townsite may still be seen the outlines of an earthworks fort, built to meet a possible Indian attack in 1863. The original Keys Mine is still active.

Placed by Bakersfield Parlor No. 42 of Native Sons of the Golden West, El Tejon Parlor No. 239 of Native Daughters of the Golden West, and Kern County Chamber of Commerce, 1937.

LAKEPORT (Lake Co.)　　　*255 N. Main St.*
Lake County Courthouse
Lake County's century-old classic courthouse, designed by A. P. Pettit in 1871, served as the seat of county government from 1871 until 1968 when it was replaced by the new courthouse. Among the court's landmark cases were the White Cap Murders, a notorious episode in vigilantism held here in 1890, and several water right cases which set precedent still in effect.

Placed in cooperation with Lake County Bicentennial Committee and the Old Courthouse Committee, 1978.

LAKESIDE (San Diego Co.)　　　*13468 Old Hwy. 8*
Mexican Grant
Commemorating Canada de Los Coches Rancho, smallest Mexican grant in California, granted in 1843 to Apolinaria Lorenzana by Governor Manuel Micheltorena—site of old gristmill.

Placed by Cuyamaca Parlor of Native Sons of the Golden West, 1948.

LARKSPUR (Marin Co.)　　　*125 E. Sir Francis Drake Blvd.*
Green Brae Brick Kiln
The Remillard Brick Company, of which the Green Brae brick kiln is the only surviving structure, was by 1900 the largest brickmaking firm on the Pacific Coast. The kiln is one of the few remaining examples of the Hoffman type kiln in the U.S. and is an engineering landmark of statewide significance. The kiln supplied much of the brick required to rebuild San Francisco after the 1906 earthquake, and the Remillard Brick Company served as a chief supplier of bricks for the entire Pacific Coast. It was closed in 1915.

Placed in cooperation with Intermark Interests Inc., 1989.

LANCASTER (Los Angeles Co.)　　　*557 W. Lancaster Blvd.*
Western Hotel
This building, erected by the Gilroy family in 1874, was purchased in 1902 by George T. Webber, who operated it as the Western Hotel. The Lancaster Chamber of Commerce was organized in its dining room. Between 1905 and 1913, construction

crews of the Los Angeles-Owens River Aqueduct were housed here; it became a center of commercial and social activity in the early life of the community.

Placed by California State Park Commission in cooperation with History and Landmarks Association of the Antelope Valley and San Fernando Parlors of Native Sons and Daughters of the Golden West, Lancaster Chamber of Commerce, and Joshua Tree Parlor No. 288 of Native Daughters of the Golden West, 1958.

LASSEN VOLCANIC NATIONAL PARK (Shasta Co.)

3.7 mi. from NW entrance on SH 44, .2 mi. E of park marker No. 60 on Park Hwy.

Mt. Lassen—10,451 Feet

This tablet marks the route of those early pioneers who, in 1852, first went over the Noble Pass linking the Humboldt-Nevada road with Shasta and Northern California, and their road is followed at this locality by the Park Highway.

Placed by Mr. and Mrs. Loomis and Shasta Historical Society, 1931.

LATON (Kings Co.)

1.1 mi. SW, Kingston Park, Douglas Ave.

Kingston

Founded in 1856 by L. A. Whitmore who operated the first Kings River ferry crossing. After 1858 town became stopping place for Butterfield Stages. Toll bridge superseded ferry in 1873. On Dec. 26, 1873, Tiburicio Vasquez and bandit gang made bold raid on town, robbing entire village.

Placed by California Centennial Commission and Kings County Centennial Committee, 1950.

LEBEC (Kern Co.)

.6 mi. N, on Lebec Rd.

Don Pedro Fages

In 1772 Don Pedro Fages, leaving the first written record of explorations in the south San Joaquin Valley, passed this site traveling from San Diego to San Luis Obispo via Cajon Pass, Mojave Desert, Hughes Lake, Antelope Valley, Tejon Pass, Canada de Las Uvas (Grapevine Canyon), and Buena Vista Lake.

Placed by Bakersfield Parlor No. 42 of Native Sons of the Golden West, El Tejon Parlor No. 39 of Native Daughters of the Golden West, Kern County Historical Society, and Kern County Chamber of Commerce, 1938.

LEMOORE (Kings Co.)

3 mi. N, SW corner SH 41 and Lacy Blvd.

El Adobe de Los Robles Rancho

This restored adobe, second oldest in San Joaquin Valley, was built by Daniel Rhoades, who came to California in 1846 by overland caravan. Rhoades and his brother, John, among organizers of first expedition to rescue Donner party at Donner Lake. Adobe built in 1856, has had continued occupancy since.

Placed by California Centennial Commission and Kings County Centennial Committee, 1950.

LIKELY (Modoc Co.) *6.5 mi. NW, 1 mi. SW of Ferry Ranch on CR 60*
Infernal Caverns Battleground
Charles Brachet, 1st Sergt., 1 Cav., September 26, 1867
Carl Brauss, New York, Pvt., 23 Inf., September 16, 1867
David Rusler, Sergt., 23 Inf., September 26, 1867
James Lyons, Pvt., 1 Cav., September 26, 1867
Michael Meara, Sergt., 1 Cav., September 26, 1867
Byron Carey, Pvt., 1 Cav., September 26, 1867

LINDSAY (Tulare Co.) *1 mi. W, SW corner SH 65 and Hermosa St.*
Butterfield Overland Mail Route
This route, following an earlier emigrant trail, was laid out in the 1850s as part of the Stockton-Los Angeles Road. It was used by the Butterfield Overland Mail stages between St. Louis and San Francisco from 1858 to 1861. This was the first overland mail operated on a regular schedule.
Placed by California State Park Commission in cooperation with Tulare County Historical Society, 1958.

LITCHFIELD (Lassen Co.) *7.6 mi. N, on US 395*
Noble Emigrant Trail
This route was first used in 1852 by emigrants to Northern California seeking to avoid the hardships of the Lassen Trail. It crossed the desert from the Humboldt River in Nevada, passed this point, and proceeded over the mountains to the town of Shasta. Later, 1859–61, it was known as the Fort Kearney, South Pass, and Honey Lake Wagon Road. From this point Peter Lassen and J. G. Bruff, on Oct. 4, 1850, saw Honey Lake while on an expedition hunting for Gold Lake.
Placed in cooperation with Lassen County Historical Society, 1959.

LIVERMORE (Alameda Co.) *2 mi. SE, 4590 Tesla Rd., at S. Livermore Ave.*
Concannon Vineyard
Here, in 1883, James Concannon founded the Concannon Vineyard. The quality it achieved in sacramental and commercial wines helped establish Livermore Valley as one of America's select winegrowing districts. Grape cuttings from this vineyard were introduced to Mexico between 1889 and 1904 for the improvement of its commercial viticulture.
Placed by California State Park Commission in cooperation with Livermore Chamber of Commerce and Las Positas Parlor No. 96 of Native Sons of the Golden West, 1958.

LIVERMORE (Alameda Co.) *5050 Arroyo Rd., across from Veterans Hospital, south of Livermore*
Cresta Blanca Winery
Here Charles A. Wetmore planted his vineyard in 1882. The Cresta Blanca wine he made from its fruit won for California the first International Award, the highest honor at the 1889 Paris Exposition, first bringing assurance to California winegrowers that they could grow wines comparable to the finest in the world.

Placed by California State Park Commission in cooperation with Livermore Chamber of Commerce, 1957.

LIVERMORE (Alameda Co.)   *Livermore Memorial Park, Portola Ave., between N. L St. and Livermore Ave.*
Robert Livermore

First settler of Livermore Valley. Born in England 1799—died Rancho Las Positas 1858. Arrived in Monterey 1822. Married Josefa Higuera y Fuentes 1830. Settled on Rancho Las Positas 1835. "Next to the mission fathers he was the first man to engage himself in the culture of grapes, fruits, and grain." The Livermore hacienda was a short distance north of this spot.

Placed by Las Politas Parlor No. 96 of Native Sons of the Golden West and Historic Landmarks Committee of Native Sons of the Golden West, 1935.

LIVERMORE (Alameda Co.)   *5565 Tesla Rd.*
Wente Bros. Winery

Here the first Wente vineyard of 47 acres was established by C. H. Wente in 1883. In 1935 his sons, Ernest and Herman, introduced California's first varietal wine label, Sauvignon Blanc. The efforts of the Wente family have helped establish the Livermore Valley as one of the premier winegrowing areas of California. In their centennial year, Wente Bros. is the oldest continuously operating, family-owned winery in California.

Placed in cooperation with Joaquin Murietta Chapter 13 of E Clampus Vitus and Livermore Heritage Guild, 1983.

LOCKEFORD (San Joaquin Co.)   *.6 mi. N on Elliott Rd.*
Pioneer Hill

It was on this hill that Dr. Dean Jewett Locke and his brother Elmer H. Locke built the first cabin on this section in 1851. Disturbed by grizzly bears, they spent their first nights in the oak trees. Dr. Locke, physician for the Boston and Newton Joint Stock Company, left Boston on Apr. 16, 1849, crossing the plains. Arriving at Sacramento, Sept. 16, 1849, he built and maintained a ford across the Mokelumne River, and because of this fact his wife, Delia Hammond Locke, in 1859 named the town he laid out on his ranch Lockeford. Luther Locke, his father, was postmaster of the first post office established in 1861. Dr. Locke was born in Langdon, New Hampshire, Apr. 16, 1825, and died in Lockeford May 4, 1887.

Placed by Stockton Parlor No. 256 of Native Daughters of the Golden West, 1936.

LODI (San Joaquin Co.)   *SE corner S. Sacramento and E. Pine sts.*
Lodi Arch

Designed by architect E. B. Brown and built in 1907 for the Lodi Tokay Carnival, the arch served as an entrance into Lodi and a symbol of agricultural and commercial growth. Essentially unaltered since construction, the structure is one of few remaining Mission Revival ceremonial arches left within California.

Placed in cooperation with City of Lodi, 1981.

LOMPOC (Santa Barbara Co.) *3 mi. E, La Purisima Mission State Historic Park, on SH 246, north side of Mission Gate and Purisima rds. intersection*

3 Miles
La Purisima Mission

(Second plaque located 1 mi. from site)

Established Dec. 8, 1787, by Father Lasuen. Damaged by earthquake 1812. Removed from control of Franciscans, abandoned 1834. State and National Park Service restoring major and many small structures, and water system. Only example in California of complete mission. State historical monument.

Placed by Department of Public Works, Division of Highways.

LOMPOC (Santa Barbara Co.) *508 S. F St. at E. Locust Ave.*

Original Site of Mission de La Purisima Concepcion de Maria Santisima

The ruins at this site are part of the original Mission La Purisima, founded by Padre Fermin de Lasuen on Dec. 8, 1787, as the 11th in the chain of Spanish Missions in California. The mission was destroyed by earthquake on Dec. 21, 1812; the present Mision (mission) La Purisima was then established several miles away.

Placed in cooperation with La Purisima Parlor No. 327 of Native Daughters of the Golden West, 1979.

LOMPOC (Santa Barbara Co.) *5 mi. NE, Mission Hills District*

First Successful Cement Job

(Plaque located 1.6 mi. N of Union Oil Co.
Production Office, off Rucker Road)

This well, Hill No. 4, studded Sept. 26, 1906, and completed Apr. 30, 1906, is the first oil well in which a water shutoff was attained by pumping cement through the tubing and behind the casing—forerunner of the modern cementing technique. It was drilled by Union Oil Company to a total depth of 2,507 feet, and 1,872 feet of ten-inch casing and 2,237 feet of eight-inch casing were so securely cemented off that the well subsequently produced for over 45 years. The development of oil well cementing was one of the most significant events in the history of petroleum technology. It has increased the productive life of thousands of oil wells, and has thereby made available for the good of humanity millions of barrels of oil that might otherwise have remained in subterranean storage. This monument is also a tribute to a worthy pioneer, Frank F. Hill, under whose direction Hill No. 4 was drilled, and to whom the petroleum industry is indebted for initiating the oil well cementing process.

Placed by Union Oil Company of California Petroleum Production Pioneers, Inc., 1952.

LONE PINE (Inyo Co.) *.9 mi. N, 200 ft. W of US 395*

Disaster in 1872

On the date of Mar. 26, 1872, an earthquake of major proportions shook Owens Valley and nearly destroyed the town of Lone Pine. Twenty-seven persons were killed. In addition to single burials, 16 of the victims were interred in a common grave enclosed by this fence.

Private plaque.

LONE PINE (Inyo Co.)   *9.6 mi. N, 200 ft. W of US 395*
Manzanar
In the early part of World War II, 110,000 persons of Japanese ancestry were interned in relocation centers by Executive Order No. 9066, issued on Feb. 19, 1942. Manzanar, the first of ten such concentration camps, was bounded by barbed wire and guard towers, confining 10,000 persons, the majority being American citizens. May the injustices and humiliation suffered here as a result of hysteria, racism, and economic exploitation never emerge again.

Placed in cooperation with Manzanar Committee and Japanese American Citizens League, 1973.

LONG BEACH (Los Angeles Co.)   *4600 Virginia Rd.*
Rancho Los Cerritos
The 27,000-acre rancho was once part of an 18th-century Spanish land grant to soldier Manuel Nieto. The Monterey-style adobe was constructed in 1844 and served the Temple and Bixby families as headquarters for large-scale cattle and sheep ranching operations in the 19th century. In the 1880s the land was subdivided for farming and city development.

Placed in cooperation with the City of Long Beach and Friends of Rancho Los Cerritos, 1989.

LOS ANGELES (Los Angeles Co.)   *Fletcher Bowron Square, 300 block N. Main St.*
Bella Union Hotel Site
Near this spot stood the Bella Union Hotel, long a social and political center. Here, on Oct. 7, 1858, the first Butterfield Overland Mail stage from the east arrived 21 days after leaving St. Louis. Warren Hall was the driver, and Waterman Ormsby, reporter, the only through passenger.

Placed by California State Park Commission in cooperation with Los Angeles County board of Supervisors, 1958.

LOS ANGELES (Los Angeles Co.)   *2100 N. Highland Ave., Hollywood*
Hollywood's First Major Film Company Studio
One-half of this structure, then in use as a barn, was rented by Cecil B. DeMille as the studio in which was made the first feature-length motion picture in Hollywood, *The Squaw Man,* in 1913. It was originally located at the corner of Selma and Vine streets, and in 1927 was transferred to Paramount Studios. Associated with Mr. DeMille in making *The Squaw Man* were Samuel Goldwyn and Jesse Lasky, Sr.

Placed by California State Park Commission and Historical Landmarks Committee of Los Angeles County in cooperation with Paramount Pictures Corporation, 1956.

LOS ANGELES (Los Angeles Co.)   *800 W. Lilac Terr., near Lookout Dr., behind U.S. Naval and Marine Corps Reserve Center*
First Jewish Site in Los Angeles
The Hebrew Benevolent society of Los Angeles (1854), first charitable organization in the city, acquired this site by deed on Apr. 9, 1855, from the city council for

a sacred burial ground. This property represented the first organized community effort by the pioneer Jewish settlers.

Placed in cooperation with Jewish Federation Council of Greater Los Angeles, 1968.

LOS ANGELES (Los Angeles Co.)   *Hancock Park, 5801 Wilshire Blvd., between Curson and Ogden sts.*

Hancock Park

La Brea Pits presented to the citizens of Los Angeles County in December 1916 by Capt. Allan Hancock with a request that the scientific features be preserved.

First historic reference to the tar pools recorded in the diary of Gaspar de Portola on Aug. 3, 1769.

Originally a portion of the Rancho La Brea granted by Governor Alvarado, 1840.

Placed by California Parlor No. 247 of Native Daughters of the Golden West, 1940.

LOS ANGELES (Los Angeles Co.)   *1911 S. Figueroa St., S end University of Southern California*

Los Angeles Memorial Coliseum

This stadium was originally completed in 1923. It was partially redesigned and enlarged for the 1932 Olympic Games. Both designs were by architects John and Donald B. Parkinson. The coliseum has witnessed many important sports, political, and historical events. When the games of the XXIIIrd Olympiad began here on July 28, 1984, the coliseum became the first stadium in the world to host the Olympic Games twice.

Placed in cooperation with American Insitute of Architects, Los Angeles Memorial Coliseum Commission, and University of Southern California, 1984.

LOS ANGELES (Los Angeles Co.)   *El Pueblo de Los Angeles State Historic Park, 500 block N. Main St.*

Los Angeles Plaza

A part of the original Pueblo lands of El Pueblo de Nuestra Senora La Reina de Los Angeles de Porciuncula founded in 1781 under the Spanish "Laws of the Indies" during the reign of Carlos III, King of Spain. This plaza is southeast of and adjoining the site of the original plaza, center of the settlement established by Gov. Felipe de Neve in 1781. When the plaza church was completed in the 1820s this site was reserved as a public plaza. It was officially dedicated as a public park 1869.

Placed by California Parlor No. 247 of Native Daughters of the Golden West, 1950.

LOS ANGELES (Los Angeles Co.)   *200 E. Ave 43, at Pasadena Fwy. No. 11*

Charles Fletcher Lummis

March 1, 1859, to Nov. 25, 1928, he founded the Southwest Museum. He built his house. He saved four old missions. He studied and recorded Spanish America. "He tried to do his share."

Private plaque.

LOS ANGELES (Los Angeles Co.)   *The Mirror Bldg., 145 S. Spring St.*
Historical Site

This block is the site of first brick schoolhouse in Los Angeles known as School No. 1, built 1854–55.

Butterfield Overland Mail Company office and corral 1858–61, office of U.S. Quartermaster 1861, corral for camels from Fort Tejon 1861, and Los Angeles City Hall built 1884.

Placed by California Parlor No. 247 of Native Daughters of the Golden West, 1949.

LOS ANGELES (Los Angeles Co.)   *1700 Stadium Way*
Navy and Marine Corps Reserve Center—Los Angeles

Designed as the largest enclosed structure without walls in the world by noted California architects Robert Clements and Associates, this art deco building, constructed between 1938 and 1941 by the WPA, is the largest and second-oldest Navy Reserve Center in the United States. It has served as the induction, separation, and training center for more than 100,000 sailors since World War II as well as the filming site for countless motion pictures and television shows.

Placed in cooperation with United States Navy, 1987.

LOS ANGELES (Los Angeles Co.)   *535 N. Main St.*
La Iglesia de Nuestra Senora
La Reina de Los Angeles
The oldest church in the City of Los Angeles
Placed by California Parlor of Native Daughters of the Golden West, 1937.

LOS ANGELES (Los Angeles Co.)   *El Pueblo de Los Angeles State*
Historical Park, 501 N. Los Angeles St.
Plaza Firehouse

Dedicated to the firemen of Los Angeles Fire Department—past, present, and future—who, since 1871, by their courage and faithful devotions to duty, have protected the lives and property of the citizens of Los Angeles from the ravages of fire.

Placed by California State Park Commission in cooperation with Box 15 Club of Los Angeles, 1960.

LOS ANGELES (Los Angeles Co.)   *Rustic Canyon Recreation Center,*
NW corner Hilltree and Latimer rds.
Santa Monica Forestry Station

In 1887 the State Board of Forestry established the nation's first experimental forestry station. Located in Rustic Canyon, the station tested exotic trees for planting in California, established plantations for management studies, and produced planting stock for scientific and conservation purposes. The station was operated by the Board of Forestry until 1893 and by the University of California until 1923.

Placed in cooperation with California Division of Forestry and the City and County of Los Angeles, 1971.

LOS ANGELES (Los Angeles Co.) *University of Southern California,*
Widney Hall Alumni House,
Childs Way, between Hoover Blvd.
and University Ave.

The Oldest University Building in Southern California

Dedicated on Sept. 4, 1880, this original building of the University of Southern California has been in use continuously for educational purposes since its doors were first opened to students on Oct. 6, 1880, by the university's first president, Marion McKinley Bovard. The building was constructed on land donated by Ozro W. Childs, John G. Downey, and Isaias W. Hellman, under the guiding hand of Judge Robert M. Widney, the University's leading founder.

Placed by California State Park Commission, 1955.

LOS ANGELES (Los Angeles Co.) *El Pueblo de Los Angeles State*
Historic Park, 400 block of Main St.

Pico House
1869
Built by Gov. Pio Pico

Placed by Los Angeles Parlor No. 124 of Native Daughters of the Golden West, 1934, and El Pueblo de Los Angeles State Historic Park Commission, 1971.

LOS ANGELES (Los Angeles Co.) *Elysian Park entrance, NW corner*
Elysian Park Dr. and N. Broadway

Portola Trail
1769

Spanish colonization of California began in 1769 with the expedition of Don Gaspar de Portola from Mexico. With Capt. Don Fernando Rivera y Moncada, Lt. Don Pedro Fages, Sgt. Jose Francisco Ortega, and Frs. Juan Crespi and Francisco Gomez, he and his party camped near this spot on Aug. 2, 1769, en route to Monterey.

Placed by California State Park Commission in cooperation with Los Angeles Recreation and Park Commission and California Parlor No. 247 of Native Daughters of the Golden West, 1958.

LOS ANGELES (Los Angeles Co.) *St. Vincent Court, in alley between*
6th and 7th sts. and Broadway and Hill

St. Vincent's Place

Named for St. Vincent's College, the oldest institution of higher learning in Southern California, which was succeeded by Loyola University. The college was founded in 1865 by the Vincentian Fathers in the old adobe Lugo house on the east side of the Los Angeles Plaza. From 1868 to 1887 the college occupied this site as its second campus.

Placed by Bullock's, Inc., and Board of Supervisors of the County of Los Angeles, 1957.

LOS ANGELES (Los Angeles Co.) *Horticulture Area, University High*
School, 11800 Texas Ave.

Fr. Junipero Serra Spring

Placed by San Vicente Chapter of Daughters of the American Revolution, 1954.

LOS ANGELES (Los Angeles Co.)
Fletcher Bowron Square,
300 block of N. Main St.

Los Angeles Star

Southern California's first newspaper, *The Los Angeles Star,* was founded in this block on May 17, 1851, and for many years exerted a major influence upon this part of the state. Suspended temporarily from 1864 to 1868, it continued later as an effective voice of the people until its final termination date in 1879.

Placed in cooperation with Los Angeles County Board of Supervisors and Historical Society of Southern California, 1964.

LOS BAÑOS (Merced Co.)
1460 E. Pacheco Blvd.

Canal Farm Inn

This original San Joaquin Valley ranch headquarters of California pioneer and cattle baron Henry Miller (1827–1916) was established in 1873. His farsighted planning, development in the 1870s of a vast gravity irrigation system, and the founding of Los Baños (1889) provided the basis for the present stability and wealth of this area.

Placed by California State Park Commission in cooperation with Los Baños Parlor No. 206 of Native Sons of the Golden West, 1956.

LOS BAÑOS (Merced Co.)
Los Baños Park, 803 E. Pacheco Blvd.

Los Baños

Los Baños (the baths) del Padre Arroyo was a favorite bathing place for padres from San Juan Bautista Mission during their travels to the San Joaquin Valley. Visited as early as 1805 by Spanish explorers, its name was changed to Los Baños Creek by later American emigrants. The town of Los Baños was established at its present site in 1889 after the location of the post office of Los Baños near the creek in 1874.

Placed by California State Park Commission in cooperation with Los Baños Parlor No. 206 of Native Sons of the Golden West, and City of Los Baños, 1957.

LOS BAÑOS (Merced Co.)
15 mi. W, Romero Overlook, San Luis
Reservoir, 31770 W. SH 152

Pacheco Pass

On June 21, 1805, Lt. Gabriel Moraga, on his first exploratory journey into the San Joaquin Valley, traversed this pass and recorded it. Since then it has been trail, toll road, stagecoach road, and freeway—the principal route between the coastal areas to the west and the great valley and mountains to the east.

Placed in cooperation with Merced County Historical Advisory Committee and Native Daughters of the Golden West, 1969.

LOS GATOS (Santa Clara Co.)
Forbes Mill Museum, 75 Church St.

Forbes Flour Mill

This is all that remains of the four-story stone flour mill built in 1854 by James Alexander Forbes. The town which grew around this building was first called Forbes Mill, then Forbestown, and finally Los Gatos.

Placed by California Centennial Commission in cooperation with Los Gatos Lions Club, 1950.

LOS GATOS (Santa Clara Co.)   *15891 Ravine Rd.*
Kotani-En

Kotani-En is a classical Japanese residence in the formal style of a 13th-century estate with tile roofed walls surrounding a tea house, shrine, gardens, and ponds. Constructed for Max M. Cohen in 1918–24 of mahogany, cedar, bamboo, and ceramic tile by master artisan Takashima and 11 craftsmen from Japan, Kotani-En represents a harmonious union of art and nature in a two-acre rustic environment. Kotani-En is a prominent example of Japanese landscape architecture in America.

Placed in cooperation with Mountain Charlie Chapter No. 1850 of E Clampus Vitus, 1984.

LOWER LAKE (Lake Co.)   *16118 Main St.*
Lower Lake Stone Jail

Built in 1876 at the height of the quicksilver mining boom, the Lower Lake stone jail was a response to rapid town growth and urgent need for civil order. Stephen Nicolai, one of the first stonemasons in Lower Lake, built the jail from local materials and with the help of Theodore and John Copsey. The jail is one of the smallest in the United States.

Placed in cooperation with Yerba Buena Chapter No. 1 of E Clampus Vitus, 1982.

LUCERNE VALLEY (San Bernardino Co.)   *3.2 mi. W, on SH 18 at*
Rabbit Springs Rd.
Chimney Rock

Conflicts between Indians and white settlers over the rich lands of the San Bernardino Mountains culminated in the Battle at Chimney Rock on Feb. 16, 1867. Although the Indians defended themselves fiercely, they were forced to retreat into the desert. In the years following, the Indians' traditional mountain food-gathering areas were lost to white encroachment.

Placed in cooperation with Billy Holcomb Chapter of E Clampus Vitus, Lucerne Valley Museum Association, and Lucerne Valley Chamber of Commerce, 1986.

MAGALIA (Butte Co.)   *On Skyway, .3 mi. N of Pentz-Magalia Rd.*
The Dogtown Nugget

This marker symbolizes the discovery of the first large gold nugget in California. It was found across this canyon in Willard Gulch Apr. 12, 1859. Weight 54 pounds.
Placed by Centennial Parlor No. 295 of Native Daughters of the Golden West, 1955.

MALIBU (Los Angeles Co.)   *23200 Pacific Coast Hwy. (SH1)*
The Adamson House

Designed by Stiles O. Clements in 1929, this Spanish Colonial Revival home contains the best surviving examples of decorative ceramic tile produced by Malibu Potteries. During its short existence from 1926 to 1932, Malibu Potteries made an outstanding contribution to ceramic art in California through its development and production of a wide range of artistic and colorful decorative tile. The home was built for Merritt Huntley Adamson and Rhoda Rindge Adamson, daughter of Frederick Hastings Rindge and May Knight Rindge, last owners of the Rancho Malibu Spanish land grant.

Placed in cooperation with Malibu Historical Society and Malibu Lagoon Museum, 1989.

MALIBU (Los Angeles Co.)
Point Dume State Beach,
corner Birdview Ave. and Cliffside Dr.
Point Dume (Dume)
On Nov. 24, 1793, English explorer George Vancouver, commander of an expedition to determine the extent of settlement of the northwest coast of America, named this rocky promontory Point Dume, after his Franciscan friend, Father Francisco Dumetz, at Mission San Buenaventura. Point Dume is the western terminus of Santa Monica Bay and has been an important landmark for navigators since Vancouver's voyage in 1793.

Placed in cooperation with Malibu Historical Society and Malibu Lagoon Museum, 1988.

MANTECA (San Joaquin Co.)
10 mi. S, Caswell Memorial Park,
200 ft. behind display shelter in picnic area
Estaneslao's Stronghold
Near here in May 1829, Estaneslao, the Indian chief for whom the river and county were named, defeated Sgt. Sanchez in a battle. Later the same month, Gen. Vallejo returned with infantry, cavalry, and artillery, burned the woods, and routed the Indians. Estaneslao escaped to Mission San Jose and Fr. Duran's protection and was later pardoned by Gov. Echeandia.

Placed by Tuleburgh Chapter No. 69 of E Clampus Vitus, 1974.

MARICOPA (Kern Co.)
1.5 mi. N, SH 33 to Petroleum Club Rd.,
between Kerto and Cadet rds.
Lakeview Gusher No. 1
America's most spectacular gusher "blew in" here on Mar. 14, 1910. Initial flow was 18,000 barrels per day, and later reached uncontrolled peak of 100,000 barrels per day, completely destroying the derrick. This Union Oil well, between Taft and Maricopa, produced nine million barrels of oil in 18 months.

Placed by Miocene Parlor No. 228 of Native Daughters of the Golden West, Kern County Historical Society, and Kern County Museum, 1952.

MARIPOSA (Mariposa Co.)
3.2 mi. W, 4189 SH 140
Agua Fria
One-fourth mile north of Carson Creek, tributary of Agua Fria, was located Agua Fria, first county seat of Mariposa County in 1850–51, one of original 27 counties in California until 1852, while mining was main industry of region. Mariposa County comprised one-sixth of state and included all of what is now Merced, Madera, Fresno, Tulare, Kings, and Kern counties. Town of Mariposa became seat of government in 1852. The courthouse was completed in 1854.

Placed by Mariposa Parlor No. 63 of Native Daughters of the Golden West, 1954.

MARIPOSA (Mariposa Co.)
10th and Bullion sts.
Mariposa County Courthouse
Erected 1854
In continuous use since erection
Placed by Yosemite Parlor No. 24 of Native Sons of the Golden West, 1929.

MARKLEEVILLE (Alpine Co.)   *18 Mi. SW, on SH 4*
Historical Landmark
—Ebbetts Pass—

Named after Maj. John Ebbetts and pointed out in 1853 to surveyor G. H. Goddard who referred to it as a "route of great promise—probably the best one for a transcontinental railway."

No emigrant train used this route, but a stage road was completed here in 1864 to serve the mining region of Silver City.

Placed by U.S. Forest Service, Stanislaus National Forest.

MARKLEEVILLE (Alpine Co.)   *14 mi. W of SH 4 and SH 88S junction*
Ebbets Pass Route
Historical Landmark No. 318

Placed by Department of Public Works, Division of Highways.

MARTINEZ (Contra Costa Co.)   *John Muir National Historic Site,*
4202 Alhambra Ave.
Vicente Martinez Adobe

In 1849 Vicente Martinez built a two-story adobe ranch house on this portion of the Rancho Pinole. This land was inherited from his father, Don Ignacio Martinez, a Spanish officer who became comandante of the San Francisco Presidio and later alcalde of San Francisco. In 1966 the National Park Service acquired the adobe, and it is now open to the public.

Placed in cooperation with National Park Service and Joaquin Murietta Chapter No. 13 of E Clampus Vitus, 1983.

MARTINEZ (Contra Costa Co.)   *John Muir National Historic Site,*
4202 Alhambra Ave.
John Muir Home

Ranch home of John Muir 1838–1914, explorer, naturalist, author, and foremost advocate of forest protection and of national parks. The John Muir Trail through the High Sierra, Muir Woods National Monument, and Muir Glacier in Alaska are named for him.

Placed by Department of Public Works, Division of Highways.

MARTINEZ (Contra Costa Co.)   *Across street from 4575 Pacheco Blvd.*
Dr. John Marsh
California pioneer
murdered here
September 24, 1856

Placed in cooperation with Martinez Horsemen's Association, 1960.

MARYSVILLE (Yuba Co.)   *SW corner First and D sts.*
Bok Kai Temple

Dedicated Mar. 21, 1880, this building replaced the first temple built nearby in the early 1850s. It has been a Chinese community project since 1866, serving as a meeting hall, court, school, and place of worship. In this "Palace of Many Saints," Bok

Eye, the water god, is the central deity and has been celebrated in Marysville on Bomb Day since Chinese settled here.

Placed in cooperation with Yuba County Historical Commission, 1976.

McARTHUR (Shasta Co.) *3.6 mi. E, on SH 299*
Site of First School in Fall River Valley

In 1868, near this spot, the first school in Fall River Valley was built. The building was of log construction, 20 feet by 30 feet, with no floor or windows. About 1870, the first sawmill in the valley was built at Dana where lumber was obtained to floor the schoolhouse and build school desks.

Placed by California State Park Commission in cooperation with Fall River Teachers' Association and Fort Crook Historical Society, 1961.

McKITTRICK (Kern Co.) *1 mi. N, NE corner SH 22 and LoKern Rd.*
Buena Vista Refinery

Eight miles due west of this marker stood one of California's first commercial oil refineries. Between August 1864 and April 1867, approximately 4,000 gallons of illuminating oil produced there was shipped to San Francisco by the Buena Vista Petroleum Company. Refining operations terminated due to excessive transportation rates.

Placed by Kern County Historical Society, Miocene Parlor No. 228 of Native Daughters of the Golden West, Petroleum Production Pioneers, and Kern County Museum, 1954.

McKITTRICK (Kern Co.) *.5 mi. S, SW corner SH 33 and SH 58*
McKittrick Brea Pit

Located one-eighth mile west of here is an ancient asphaltum seepage in which hundreds of Pleistocene (15,000–50,000 years ago) birds and animals were trapped. Site first explored in 1928 by the University of California, with excavation completed in 1949 by Los Angeles and Kern County museums.

Placed by Kern County Historical Society, Miocene Parlor No. 228 of Native Daughters of the Golden West, El Tejon Parlor No. 239 of Native Daughters of the Golden West, and Kern County Museum, 1952.

MENDOCINO (Mendocino Co.) *44831 Main St.*
Mendocino Presbyterian Church

This is one of the oldest Protestant churches in continuous use in California. Organized as the Presbyterian Church on Nov. 6, 1859, the building, constructed of redwood, was dedicated on July 5, 1868.

Placed by California State Park Commission in cooperation with Native Sons of the Golden West, 1959.

MENLO PARK (San Mateo Co.) *1100 Merrill Ave.*
Menlo Park Railroad Station

This building, constructed in 1867 by the San Francisco and San Jose Railroad Company, is the oldest railroad passenger station in California. The Victorian ornamentation was added in the 1890s when the station was remodeled to serve the newly opened Stanford University. The extension on the northwest was added to accommodate increased traffic generated by the establishment of Camp Fremont nearby during World War I.

Placed in cooperation with City of Menlo Park, 1983.

MENLO PARK (San Mateo Co.)   *E. Creek Dr. and Alma St. intersection*
Portola Journey's End,
November 6–10, 1769

Near "El Palo Alto," the tall tree, the Portola expedition of 63 men and 200 horses and mules camped. They had traveled from San Diego in search of Monterey, but discovered instead the Bay of San Francisco. Finding the bay too large to go around, and deciding that Monterey had been bypassed, they ended the search and returned to San Diego.

Placed in cooperation with Portola Expedition Bicentennial Foundation, 1968.

MERCED (Merced Co.)   *Merced County Fairgrounds, J at 7th sts.,*
adjacent to parking lot at entrance
Merced Assembly Center

This was one of 15 temporary detention camps established during World War II to incarcerate persons of Japanese ancestry, a majority of whom were American citizens, without specific charges or trial. From May to September 1942, 4,669 residents of Northern California were detained until permanent relocation camps were built. May the injustices and humiliation suffered here as a result of hysteria, racism, and economic exploitation never recur.

Placed in cooperation with Livingston-Merced Chapter of Japanese American Citizens League, 1982.

METTLER (Kern Co.)   *5.5 mi. W, on SH 166*
Fages-Zalvidea Trails

In 1772 Don Pedro Fages, first recorded white man to visit the southern San Joaquin Valley, crossed this spot on his way from San Diego to San Luis Obispo. Near this point crossed Fr. Jose Maria de Zalvidea in 1806, while accompanying the Ruiz expedition in search of mission sites.

Placed by Bakersfield Parlor No. 42 of Native Sons of the Golden West, El Tejon Parlor No. 239 of Native Daughters of the Golden West, Kern County Historical Society, and Kern County Chamber of Commerce, 1941.

METTLER (Kern Co.)   *7 mi. S, NE corner D St. and Grapevine Rd.*
Rose Station

Wm. B. Rose, in 1875, a mile east, built an adobe stage station on the site of the Overland Mail way station, established 1858. From 1853 to 1875 site was known as Rancho Canoa (trough), originally vaquero camp of Sebastian Indian Reservation. Rose Station was a stockmen's headquarters, post office, and polling place.

Placed by Bakersfield Parlor No. 42 of Native Sons of the Golden West, El Tejon Parlor No. 239 of Native Daughters of the Golden West, Kern County Historical Society, and Kern County Chamber of Commerce, 1941.

METTLER (Kern Co.)   *7 mi. S, NE corner D St. and Grapevine Rd.*
The Sebastian or Tejon Indian Reservation

The Sebastian or Tejon Indian Reservation (headquarters ten miles east of here) was established in 1853 by Gen. Edward Fitzgerald Beale as one of several California reservations. The number of Indians quartered here varied from 500 to 2,000. General Beale acquired title to this area under Mexican Land Grant of 1843. In 1864 the U.S. government transferred the Indians to other reservations.

Placed by Bakersfield Parlor No. 42 of Native Sons of the Golden West, El Tejon Parlor No. 239 of Native Daughters of the Golden West, Kern County Historical Society, Kern County Chamber of Commerce, and Kern County Museum, 1937.

METTLER (Kern Co.)
6 mi. NE, SW corner David and Wheeler Ridge rds.

Sinks of the Tejon

Six miles east of this point was the site of the Butterfield Stage Line station called "Sinks of Tejon." Operating through present Kern County during 1858–61, this famous line ran from St. Louis, Missouri, to San Francisco until the outbreak of the Civil War.

Placed by California State Park Commission in cooperation with Kern County Historical Society, El Tejon Parlor No. 239 of Native Daughters of the Golden West, and Kern County Museum, 1956.

MEYERS (El Dorado Co.)
Yank's Station Shopping Center, SW corner SH 50 and Apache Ave.

Yank's Station

This was the site of the most eastern remount station of the Central Overland Pony Express in California. Established as a trading post in 1851 by Martin Smith, it became a popular hostelry and stage stop operated by Ephraim "Yank" Clement. Pony rider Warren Upson first arrived here on the evening of Apr. 28, 1860. Changing ponies, he galloped on to Friday's in Nevada to deliver his mochela to Bob Haslam for the ride to Genoa. Used as a pony remount station until Oct. 26, 1861, it was sold to George D. H. Meyers in 1873, and the name changed to Meyers.

Placed by California State Park Commission in cooperation with James W. Marshall Chapter No. 49 of E Clampus Vitus, Lake Tahoe South Shore Chamber of Commerce, and California Overland Pony Express Trail Association, 1960.

MICHIGAN BLUFF (Placer Co.)
Auburn-Foresthill and Gorman Ranch rds. intersection

Michigan Bluff

Founded in 1850 and first known as Michigan City which was located on slope one-half mile from here. In 1858, town became undermined and unsafe so was moved to this location and renamed Michigan Bluff. Leland Stanford, who gained wealth and fame in California, operated a store in Michigan City from 1853 to 1855.

Placed by California Centennial Commission and Placer County Historical Society, 1950.

MIDDLETOWN (Lake Co.)
NW corner SH 29 and Hill Ave.

Old Bull Trail Road
and St. Helena Toll Road

The Old Bull Trail Road ran from Napa Valley to Middletown. It was built by volunteers in the 1850s. A number of the grades were 35 percent. It was an official road in 1861 and abandoned in 1868. St. Helena Toll Road also ran from same points.

Was completed in 1868. The grades ran to 12 percent. State of California purchased from John Lawley heirs in 1925.

Placed by California Centennial Commission and County of Lake, 1950.

MIDDLETOWN (Lake Co.)   *5.3 mi. N, NE corner SH 29 and Hidden Valley Rd.*

Stone House

Oldest building in Lake County. Erected of stone in 1853–54 by Robert Sterling, whose wife was the first white woman in Coyote Valley. Rebuilt in 1894. Headquarters of Guenoc Land Grant and first store in valley.

Placed by California Centennial Commission and County of Lake, 1950.

MILL VALLEY (Marin Co.)   *Old Mill Park, Throckmorton and Cascade Dr.*

John Reed's Saw Mill

(Plaque located at NW corner
Blithedale Ave. and Tower Dr.)

Two miles west is the old saw mill, from which the city of Mill Valley acquired its name. It was constructed in the 1830s by John Reed, grantee of the Rancho Corte de Madera del Presidio. The creek waters furnished the motive power for the mill, which was the first in the San Francisco Bay region to supply lumber.

Placed by California Centennial Commission in cooperation with Marin County Historical Society, 1950.

MILL VALLEY (Marin Co.)   *1 W. Blithedale Ave.*

Outdoor Art Club

The Outdoor Art Club was designed in 1904 by Bernard Maybeck, internationally known American architect. Particularly notable for its unusual roof truss system, the building exemplifies Maybeck's creative use of natural materials. The club, founded in 1902 by 35 Mill Valley women, is dedicated to preserving the area's natural environment.

Placed in cooperation with the Outdoor Art Club, 1979.

MILLBRAE (San Mateo Co.)   *Skyline and Hillcrest blvds. intersection*

First Camp after Discovery of San Francisco Bay

(Plaque located 500 ft. W on Hillcrest Blvd.)

On Nov. 4, 1769, the expedition of Capt. Gaspar de Portola, after crossing Sweeney Ridge, beheld the bay of San Francisco for the first time. That night they camped at a small lagoon, now covered by San Andreas Lake. Finding the bay too large to go around and thinking they had bypassed Monterey Bay, the expedition camped here again on Nov. 12, 1769, on their return to San Diego. First made a state registered Historical Landmark No. 27, June 15, 1932, this site was rededicated as a U.S.A. bicentennial project of San Andreas Lake Chapter, Daughters of the American Revolution, and the City of Millbrae, California, on Nov. 6, 1976.

Placed in cooperation with State of California and San Francisco Water Department.

MISSION HILLS (Los Angeles Co.) *15151 San Fernando Mission Blvd.*
Mission San Fernando Rey de Espana
Founded by
Father Fermin Francisco de Lasuen
September 8, 1797
Placed by Los Angeles Parlor No. 124 of Native Daughters of the Golden West, 1939.

MISSION HILLS (Los Angeles Co.) *10940 N. Sepulveda Blvd.*
Ranchito Romulo
Oldest portion built about 1834 by ex-mission Indians
Enlarged by Eulogio de Celis in 1846
Upper story added by Romulo Pico in 1874
Restored by Mr. and Mrs. M. R. Harrington in 1930
Placed by California Parlor No. 247 of Native Daughters of the Golden West, 1936.

MOJAVE (Kern Co.) *16246 Sierra Hwy.*
Mojave 20-Mule-Team Borax Terminus
Just west of this point was the Southern Pacific terminus for the 20-mule-team borax wagons that operated between Death Valley and Mojave from 1884 to 1889. The route ran from the Harmony Borax Mining Works, later acquired by the Pacific Coast Borax Company, to the railroad loading dock in Mojave—over 165 miles of mountain and desert trail. A round trip required 20 days. The ore wagons hauled a payload of 24 tons. They were designed by J. W. W. Perry, Borax Company superintendent in Death Valley, and were built in Mojave at a cost of $900 each. New borax discoveries near Barstow ended the Mojave shipments in 1889.

Placed by California State Park Commission in cooperation with Kern County Historical Society, El Tejon Parlor No. 239 of Native Daughters of the Golden West, and Kern County Museum, 1958.

MOKELUMNE HILL (Calaveras Co.) *SE corner Main and Lafayette sts.*
Calaveras County Courthouse and Leger Hotel
A portion of this building served as the Calaveras County Courthouse from 1852 to 1866, when the county seat was removed to San Andreas. George W. Leger then acquired the court building and made it a part of his adjoining hotel, which has been operated since early gold mining days. It was known as the Grand Hotel in 1874 when fire damaged it and destroyed its dance hall. Restored in 1879, it has since been known as the Leger Hotel.

Placed by California State Park Commission in cooperation with Mokelumne Hill Lions Club, 1959.

MOKELUMNE HILL (Calaveras Co.) *SW corner Main and Center sts.*
Mokelumne Hill
Mokelumne is an Indian word, first applied to the nearby river. Earliest settlement at Happy Valley by French trappers. Gold discovered by discharged members of Stevenson's regiment in 1848. Center of richest placer mining section of Calaveras County and one of the principal mining towns of California. Corral Flat produced over thirty million in gold. Sixteen feet square constituted a claim. So-called French

War for possession of gold mines occurred in 1851. *Calaveras Chronicle* established in 1850. Fights between grizzly bear and bulls amused early residents. At one time headquarters of Joaquin Murietta. Town destroyed by fires in 1854, 1864, and 1874. County seat of Calaveras County from 1853 to 1866.

Placed by Calaveras County Chamber of Commerce and Native Daughters of the Golden West, 1937.

MOKELUMNE HILL (Calaveras Co.)   *5 mi. SW, at Paloma Rd. and Edster St. intersection*

Paloma (Fosteria)

Gwin Mine, Paloma, Lower Rich Gulch, was mined for placer in 1849. Quartz was discovered by J. Alexander in 1851. Property acquired by William M. Gwin, California's first U.S. senator, in 1851. The Gwin Mine, closed in 1908, yielded millions.

Placed by California Centennial Commission and Paloma Community Club, 1949.

MONTEBELLO (Los Angeles Co.)   *NE corner Washington Blvd. and Bluff Rd.*

Rio San Gabriel Battlefield

Near this site, on Jan. 8, 1847, was fought the Battle of the Rio San Gabriel between American forces commanded by Capt. Robert F. Stockton, U.S. Navy Commander-in-Chief, Brig. Gen. Stephen W. Kearny, U.S. Army, and Californians commanded by Gen. Jose Maria Flores.

Placed by Board of Supervisors of the County of Los Angeles, 1944.

MONTEBELLO (Los Angeles Co.)   *SW corner N. Lincoln Ave. and N. San Gabriel Blvd.*

Site of Mission Vieja

This tablet was erected by Walter P. Temple and blessed by Right-Reverend John J. Cantwell, Bishop of Monterey and Los Angeles, July 31, 1921, to commemorate the founding of Mission San Gabriel Archangel, on this ground, at Old Mission by Reverend Fathers Angel Somero and Pedro B. Gambon, Sept. 8, 1771.

Private plaque.

MONTEREY (Monterey Co.)   *Civic Center, Pacific St. between Jefferson and Madison sts.*

Colton Hall

In this building, from Sept. 1 to Oct. 13, 1849, assembled the convention which drafted the consitution under which California was admitted to statehood, Sept. 9, 1850. The 48 delegates met on the upper floor which ran the length of the main building. Robert Semple was chairman and William G. March, secretary. The stairway leading to the convention hall was in the rear of the building. Reverend Walter Colton, first American alcalde in Monterey, erected this building which bears his name as a public hall and schoolhouse. Colton and Robert Semple established in Monterey, on Aug. 15, 1846, the first American newspaper in California.

Placed by Historic Landmark Committee of Native Sons of the Golden West, 1931.

MONTEREY (Monterey Co.) *Monterey State Historic Park, Custom House Plaza, between Scott and Decatur sts.*

Monterey Custom House

It was over this building that the American flag was raised by Commodore John Drake Sloat, July 7, 1846, signaling the passing of California from Mexican rule.

Private plaque, restored by Native Sons of the Golden West and the people of California.

MONTEREY (Monterey Co.) *494–498 Alvarado St.*

Home of Juan Bautista Alvarado

Native of Monterey, Governor of California under Mexican rule Dec. 20, 1836–Dec. 20, 1842. During his administration, the increasing influx of Americans, and the Russian settlement at Fort Ross, began to be regarded as serious problems. Russians withdrew in 1841.

Placed by California Centennial Commission in cooperation with Monterey Parlor No. 75 of Native Sons of the Golden West, 1949.

MONTEREY (Monterey Co.) *Monterey State Historic Park, SW corner Artillery and Pacific sts.*

Junipero Serra

(Landing Place of Sebastian Vizcaino
and Fray Junipero Serra)

MONTEREY (Monterey Co.) *Monterey State Historic Park, SW corner Jefferson and Calle Principal sts.*

Built in 1835

by
Thomas Oliver Larkin,
only U.S. consul to California
under Mexican rule,
American Consulate from 1844–46

Private plaque.

MONTEREY (Monterey Co.) *530 Houston St.*

In this house

in the year 1879 lived
Robert Louis Stevenson
essayist, storyteller, and poet
whose contributions to literature
delighted the world.
This memorial unveiled
November 13, 1932, the 82nd
anniversary of his birth,
is presented by
the Literary Anniversary Club

MONTEREY (Monterey Co.)   *550 Church St.*
Royal Presidio Chapel of San Carlos Borromeo
John Graham of Boston, Mass. (site of the burial on Sept. 13, 1791), the first known U.S.A. citizen buried in California. He joined Alejandro Malaspina's global expedition in Cadiz, Spain, in 1789 as a gunner-of-the-sea on the cornette *Atrevida;* died aboard ship and was brought ashore in Monterey for burial in the English cemetery of the Royal Presidio Chapel.

Placed by California State Society of Daughters of the American Revolution, 1973.

MONUMENT PEAK (San Bernardino Co.)   *2.2 mi. W of Cedar Pines*
Park, 1 mi. on Doyle Rd. to
Bailey Cyn. Rd., then 1.2 mi. to site
The Mohave Indian Trail
Traveled by Father Francisco Garces, March 1776, and Jedediah S. Smith, November 1826.

Placed by San Bernardino County Historical Society, 1931.

MORGAN HILL (Santa Clara Co.)   *NW corner Tennant Ave.*
and old Hwy. 101
Site of 21-Mile House
This famous tavern and stage stop was located 21 miles from San Jose on the road to Monterey. The 21-Mile House was built in 1852 by William Host beneath a spreading oak that later was called the Vasquez Tree. The house was sold to William Tennant in November 1852. Now destroyed, this stopping station was a place where horses could be changed, fed, and stabled, and where tired and hungry passengers could refresh themselves.

Placed in cooperation with California Pioneers of Santa Clara County and Mountain Charlie Chapter No. 1850 of E Clampus Vitus, 1982.

MORRO BAY (San Luis Obispo Co.)   *.4 mi. NW, at City Park on*
Embarcadero Rd.
Morro Rock
An important mariner's navigational landfall for over 300 years. Chronicled in the diaries of Portola, Fr. Crespi, and Costanso in 1769 when they camped near this area on their trek to find Monterey. Sometimes called the "Gibraltar of the Pacific," it is the last in the famous chain of nine peaks which start in the city of San Luis Obispo.

Placed in cooperation with Morro Bay Chamber of Commerce and San Luis Obispo Historical Society, 1968.

MT. SHASTA (Siskiyou Co.)   *1 mi. W, SW corner W. Jessie St.*
and Old Stage Rd.
Strawberry Valley Stage Station
1857–1886
Across the road from this marker stood the Strawberry Valley Stage Station which served the patrons of the line from its completion in 1857 until 1886, when railroad construction reached the valley. The small building across the road was the Berryvale Post Office, which operated from 1870 to 1887. The first postmaster was Justin

Hinckley Sisson. Behind the marker stood the famous Sisson Hotel, well known to mountain climbers, fishermen, hunters, and vacationers throughout California. It was built about 1865 by J. H. Sisson and in 1916 was destroyed by fire. The Shasta Trout Hatchery was founded in 1888 but prior to this, in 1877, J. H. Sisson reared trout to stock the streams in this vicinity. When the business center was moved to its present location on the railroad in 1886, its name was changed from Strawberry Valley to Sisson, and in 1923 the town was renamed Mount Shasta City.

Placed by Sikiyou County Historical Society, 1947.

MOUNTAIN SPRINGS (Imperial Co.) *200 ft. W of I-8 westbound lane, just N of Mountain Springs Rd.*
Mountain Springs Station Site

In 1862–70, about a mile north of here, Peter Larkin and Joe Stancliff used a stone house as a store from which ox teams pulled wagons up a 30 percent grade. The San Diego & Fort Yuma Turnpike Co. used the site as a toll road station until 1876. The crumbling house was replaced in 1917 by another still visible to its east. But road changes, beginning in 1878 and culminating in today's highway, have left the older stone house ruins inaccessible.

Placed in cooperation with Squibob Chapter of E Clampus Vitus, 1991.

MURPHYS (Calaveras Co.) *457 Main St.*
Old Sperry Hotel

This hostelry originally built in 1855 by J. L. Sperry of Sperry Flour fame and his partner, John Perry. Among early guests whose names appear on old register are Mark Twain, Horatio Alger, Thomas H. Lipton, Henry Ward Beecher, the Rothchilds, Gen. U. S. Grant, and C. E. Bolton (Black Bart). The quaint old hotel, according to tradition, is the one referred to in Bret Harte's *A Night in Wingdam.* Murphys camp founded in early '49 by John and Daniel Murphy, brothers. Millions of gold taken from camp and vicinity.

Placed by Chispa Parlor No. 139 of Native Sons of the Golden West and Ruby Parlor No. 46 of Native Daughters of the Golden West, 1980.

MURPHYS (Calaveras Co.) *457 Main St.*
Murphys Hotel

James L. Sperry and John Perry opened the Sperry and Perry Hotel Aug. 20, 1856. In 1881 Henry Atwood and then Harvey Blood owned it. In 1822 the Mitchler family renamed it the Mitchler Hotel. In 1945 the McKimins changed its name to Murphys Hotel. In 1963 a College of the Pacific group purchased it. One of the oldest operating hotels in California.

Placed in cooperation with Murphys A & Q, Inc., 1980.

MURPHYS (Calaveras Co.) *Main and Jones sts. intersection*
Murphys

One of the principal mining communities in Calaveras County, named for the discoverer of gold on the flat in 1849. The objective of many immigrants coming over the Sierras by Ebbetts Pass. Murphys Flat and surrounding mines produced 20,000,000 dollars in gold. Early regulations restricted claims to eight ft. square.

Suspension flume conveying water across Murphys Creek and drainage race draining the flat were two outstanding accomplishments of early-day miners. Business portion of town destroyed by fire Aug. 20, 1859. Joaquin Murietta, bandit, began his murderous career here. Calaveras light guards, recruiting for Civil War, organized here May 4, 1861.

Placed by Ruby Parlor No. 46 of Native Daughters of the Golden West and Chispa Parlor No. 139 of Native Sons of the Golden West, 1937.

MURPHYS (Calaveras Co.) .9 mi. SW, on Pennsylvania Gulch Rd.
Site of Brownsville
A thriving mining camp on rich Pennsylvania Gulch in the 1850s and 1860s. Named for Alfred Brown, former owner of Table Mountain Ranch. Laws of the Brownsville mining district provided that each miner could own one wet and one dry claim, not to exceed 150 square feet.

Placed by California State Park Commission in cooperation with Chispa Parlor No. 139 of Native Sons of the Golden West and Ruby Parlor No. 46 of Native Daughters of the Golden West, 1953.

MURPHYS (Calaveras Co.) 470 Main St.
Peter L. Traver Building
Constructed by Peter L. Traver in 1856. Oldest stone building in Murphys. Iron shutters and sand on roof protected it from fires of 1859, 1874, and 1893. It served as general store, Wells Fargo office, and later, garage.

Placed by California State Park Commission in cooperation with Chispa Parlor No. 139 of Native Sons of the Golden West and Ruby Parlor No. 46 of Native Daughters of the Golden West, 1953.

NAPA (Napa Co.) 1333 3rd St.
First Presbyterian Church Building
Designed by pioneer architects R. H. Daley and Theodore Eisen, this church is an outstanding example of late Victorian Gothic architectural styling. It is the best surviving example in this region of the early works associated with Eisen, who later became an important Southern California architect. The First Presbyterian Church has been in continuous use since its construction in 1874. Longest early pastorates are Richard Wylie and Erwin Bollinger.

Placed in cooperation with Napa County Historical Society, 1975.

NEEDLES (San Bernardino Co.) N. K St., on shoulder NW corner of Colorado River Bridge
National Old Trails
This bridge marks the site where the National Old Trails Highway, later Highway 66, crossed the Colorado River. It links the Mohave Indian lands visited by Father Garces in 1776. Near this location the American explorer Jedediah Smith and his band of Rocky Mountain men crossed the river in 1826 and opened the pioneer trail into Southern California.

Placed in cooperation with Fort Mohave Indian Tribe, City of Needles, County of San Bernardino, and Arizona County of Mohave, 1978.

NEEDLES (San Bernardino Co.)
14 mi. N, on east side of Pew Rd.,
2.6 mi. S of State Line
Von Schmidt State Boundary Monument

This boundary monument, a cast iron column erected in 1873, marks the southern terminus of the California-Nevada state boundary established by A. W. Von Schmidt's 1872–73 survey. Von Schmidt's line, the first officially recognized oblique state line between California and Nevada, erred slightly; the boundary was later corrected to the present line, three-quarters mile to the north.

Placed in cooperation with Needles Chapter of San Bernardino County Museum Association and the California, Arizona, and Nevada Development Association-Can-Do, 1974.

NEVADA CITY (Nevada Co.)
211 Broad St.
The National Hotel

This hotel, one of the oldest in continuous operation west of the Rockies, opened for business in August 1856. Originally known as the "Bicknell Block," the structure consists of three common-walled buildings of simple brick construction embellished with classic revival and wrought iron railing ornamentation.

Placed in cooperation with Nevada County Landmarks Commission, 1976.

NEVADA CITY (Nevada Co.)
401 Broad St.
Nevada Theatre

California's oldest theatre building, the Nevada, opened Sept. 9, 1865. Celebrities such as Mark Twain, Jack London, and Emma Nevada have appeared on its stage. Closed in 1957, the theatre was later purchased through public donations and reopened May 17, 1968, to again serve the cultural needs of the community.

Placed in cooperation with Historical Landmarks and Liberal Arts Commission of Nevada County, 1974.

NEVADA CITY (Nevada Co.)
28 mi. N, Malakoff Diggins State Historic
Park, 16 mi. E of SH 49
on Tyler Foote Crossing Rd.
North Bloomfield Mining and Gravel Company
(Plaque located in Park Diggins Overlook)

This was a major hydraulic operation in California. Its vast system of canals and flumes using a drainage tunnel 7,800 feet long was termed a feat of engineering skill. It was the principal defendant in an anti-debris lawsuit settled by the Sawyer Decision in 1884. Judge Lorenzo Sawyer's famous decision created control that virtually ended hydraulic mining in California.

Placed in cooperation with Malakoff Citizen's Advisory Committee and Chapter No. 10 of E Clampus Vitus, 1972.

NEVADA CITY (Nevada Co.)
325 Spring St.
Pelton Wheel Manufacturing Site

The Pelton water wheel, first commercially manufactured here at George Allan's Foundry & Machine Works in 1879, was a major advancement in water power utilization and greatly advanced hard-rock mining. Its unique feature was a series of paired buckets, shaped like bowls of spoons and separated by a splitter, that divided the incoming water jets into two parts. By the late 1800s, Pelton wheels were providing energy to operate industrial machinery throughout the world. In 1888 Lester Pelton moved his business to San Francisco but granted continuing manufacturing rights to Allan's Foundry where the wheels were manufactured into the early 1900s, when most local mines shifted to electric power.

Placed in cooperation with Nevada County Cultural Preservation Trust and Pacific Gas & Electric Company, 1994.

NEVADA CITY (Nevada Co.)   *132 Main St.*
South Yuba Canal Office

Headquarters for the largest network of water flumes and ditches in the state. The South Yuba Canal Water Company was the first incorporated to supply water for hydraulic mining. The original ditch was in use in May 1850, and this company office was in use from 1857 to 1880. The holdings later became part of the vast PG&E hydroelectric system.

Placed in cooperation with Nevada County Historical Landmarks Commission and California Heritage Council, 1970.

NEW ALMADEN (Santa Clara Co.)   *Biltmore Park, SW corner Almaden Rd. and Almaden Way*
Site of First Mining in California

Here along Arroyo de Los Alamitos Creek in 1824, Luis Chabolla and Antonio Sunol first worked New Almaden ore in an arrastra. In constant production since 1845, more than one million flasks of quicksilver valued in excess of 50 million dollars have been produced.

Placed in cooperation with California Pioneers of Santa Clara County and Mountain Charlie Chapter No. 1850 of E Clampus Vitus, 1979.

NEW IDRIA (San Benito Co.)   *NW corner SH 25 and Panoche Rd.*
54 Miles
New Idria Mine

Ranks among the most famous quicksilver mines of the world. Named for Idria Mine, then in Austria. Mission fathers, before American occupation, made assays and determined ore to be cinnabar. Work began in fifties. In 1881, between two and three hundred men were employed.

Placed by Department of Public Works, Division of Highways.

NEWBURY PARK (Ventura Co.)   *51 S. Ventu Park Rd.*
Stagecoach Inn

Originally located some 200 yards north, the Stagecoach Inn was built in 1876. Its redwood lumber came by sea and was freighted up the steep Conejo Grade by multi-team wagons. From 1887 to 1901 the hotel served as a regular depot for the Coast Stage Line, which carried both passengers and mail. In 1965 it was moved to its present location.

Placed by California State Park Commission in cooperation with Conejo Valley Historical Society and Mr. and Mrs. H. Allen Hays, 1966.

NEWCASTLE (Placer Co.)   *SW corner Main and Page sts.*
First Transcontinental Railroad—Newcastle

Regular freight and passenger trains began operating over the first 31 miles of Central Pacific's line to Newcastle June 10, 1864, when political opposition and lack of money stopped further construction during that mild winter. Construction was resumed in April 1865. At this point stagecoaches transferred passengers from the Dutch Flat Wagon Road.

Placed in cooperation with Conference of California Historical Societies and Placer County Historical Society, 1969.

NEWCASTLE (Placer Co.)   *7 mi. NW, 4725 Virginiatown Rd.*
Virginiatown

Founded June 1851—commonly called "Virginia." Over two thousand miners worked rich deposits. Captain John Bristow built California's first railroad, 1852, carrying pay dirt to Auburn Ravine, a distance of one mile. Site of Philip Armour's and George Aldrich's butcher shop, said to have led to founding of famous Chicago Armour Meat Packing Company.

Placed by California Department of Natural Resources in cooperation with Placer County Historical Society and the County of Placer, 1952.

NEWHALL (Los Angeles Co.)   *On W. Pico Canyon Rd., 3.3 mi. W of I-5*
First Commercial Oil Well in California

On this site stands CSO-4 (Pico #4), California's first commercially productive well. It was spudded in early 1876 under the direction of Demetrius G. Scofield, later to become first president of Standard Oil Company of California, and was completed at a depth of 300 feet on Sept. 26, 1876, for an initial flow of 30 barrels of oil a day.

Later in the same year the well was deepened to 600 feet, using what was perhaps the first steam rig employed in oil well drilling in California. Upon this second completion it produced at a rate of 150 barrels a day and is still producing after 77 years. The success of this well prompted formation of the Pacific Coast Oil Company, a predecessor of Standard Oil Company of California, and led to the construction of the state's first refinery nearby. It was not only the discovery well of the Newhall field but was indeed a powerful stimulus to the subsequent development of the California petroleum industry.

Placed by Standard Oil Company of California and Petroleum Production Engineers, Inc., 1953.

NEWHALL (Los Angeles Co.)   *Eternal Valley Memorial Park,*
     23287 N. Sierra Hwy.
Lyons Station

This site was the location of a combination store, post office, telegraph office, tavern, and stage depot accommodating travelers during the Kern River gold rush in the early 1850s. A regular stop for Butterfield and other early California stage lines, it was purchased by Sanford and Cyrus Lyons in 1855 and became known as Lyons Station. By 1868 at least twenty families lived here. Eternal Valley Memorial Park has memorialized their final resting place as "the garden of the pioneers."

Placed by California State Park Commission in cooperation with Eternal Valley Memorial Park, History and Landmarks Association of the San Fernando and

Antelope Valley Parlors of Native Sons and Native Daughters of the Golden West, and San Fernando Mission Parlor No. 280 of Native Daughters of the Golden West, 1959.

NEWHALL (Los Angeles Co.)   27201 W. Pico Canyon Rd.
Mentryville

Mentryville, named after Charles Alexander Mentry who drilled California's first successful commercial oil well in 1876, was one of the first oil towns in the state. Mentry's restored home, barn, and Felton School remain on the site where the California Star Oil Works Co., a predecessor of Standard Oil Co. of California, was founded.

Placed in cooperation with Santa Clarita Valley Historical Society and Newhall Woman's Club, C.F.W.C., 1976.

NEWHALL (Los Angeles Co.)   4.6 mi. NE, Placerita Canyon State and County Park, Placerita Canyon Rd.
3 Miles
Oak of the Golden Dream

(Additional plaques located
six and nine miles from site)

In Placeritas Canyon, March 1842, Francisco Lopez y Arballo, while gathering wild onions from around an old oak, discovered gold particles clinging to the roots of the bulbs. It is estimated that $80,000 in gold was recovered as a result of this discovery.

Placed by Department of Public Works, Division of Highways.

NEWHALL (Los Angeles Co.)   E corner I-5 and Lyons Ave.
3 Miles
Pioneer Oil Refinery

(Additional plaque located two miles from site)

In 1875, Star Oil Company, one of the predecessors of the Standard Oil Company of California, drilled its first well in Pico Canyon, 100 barrels per day. The discovery resulted the following year in the erection of the first commercial oil refinery in California.

Placed by Department of Public Works, Division of Highways.

NEWPORT BEACH (Orange Co.)   On Dover Dr., 500 ft. N of SH 1
Old Landing

In 1870 the first schooner, Capt. Abbot commanding, entered Newport Bay, unloading its cargo near what is now known as Old Landing. The landing was designated "Newport"—a new port—by James and Robert McFadden, Santa Ana pioneers, who established a regular shipping service here in the middle 1870s.

Placed by California State Park Commssion.

NEWPORT BEACH (Orange Co.)   Newport Pier, SE corner W. Ocean Front and McFadden Pl.
McFadden (Newport) Wharf

The original wharf at this site was completed in the winter of 1888–89 and was connected by railroad with the hinterland in the winter of 1890–91. It served as a shipping and distributing point for Orange, San Bernardino, and Riverside counties until 1907, and provided the nucleus from which developed the City of Newport Beach.

Placed by California State Park Commission in cooperation with the City of Newport Beach, 1965.

NEWPORT BEACH (Orange Co.)   *S end of Main St. at Ocean Front*
First Water-to-Water Flight

Glen L. Martin flew his own plane, built in Santa Ana, from the waters of the Pacific Ocean at Balboa to Catalina Island, May 10, 1912. This was the first water-to-water flight to that date. Martin, on his return to the mainland, carried the day's mail from Catalina—another first.

Placed by California State Park Commission in cooperation with the City of Newport Beach, 1963.

NORTH HOLLYWOOD (Los Angeles Co.)   *3919 Lankershim Blvd.*
Campo de Cahuenga

"Here was made the Treaty of Cahuenga by Gen. Andres Pico, commanding forces for Mexico, and Lt. Col. J. C. Fremont, U.S. Army, for the United States. By this treaty, agreed upon Jan. 13th, 1847, the United States acquired California; finally secured to us by the Treaty of Guadalupe Hidalgo, made Feb. 2nd, 1848."

The above legend was written Feb. 9th, 1898, by Mrs. Jessie Benton Fremont.

Placed by California History and Landmarks Club of Native Sons and Daughters of the Golden West, 1924.

OAK GROVE (San Diego Co.)   *SH 79*
Camp Wright
1861–1866

First established Oct. 18, 1861, on Warner's Ranch at "fork of the trail to San Diego," to guard the line of communications between California and Arizona. Moved to this site by Maj. Edwin A. Rigg, First California Volunteers, about Nov. 23, 1861. Named for Brig. Gen. George Wright, United States Army, who commanded the Pacific Department and California District from 1861 to 1865. Abandoned December, 1866.

Placed by San Diego County Board of Supervisors and Historical Markers Committee, 1953.

OAK GROVE (San Diego Co.)   *SH 79*
Oak Grove Stage Station

Occupied in 1858 by Warren Hall, Division Superintendent, Butterfield Overland Mail which operated between San Francisco and the eastern termini, St. Louis and Memphis, from Sept. 15, 1858, to Mar. 2, 1861. The first mail stage from the east driven from Fort Yuma by Warren Hall and Jacob Bergman passed here Oct. 6, 1858.

Placed by San Diego County Board of Supervisors and Historical Markers Committee, 1953.

OAKHURST (Madera Co.)
5.5 mi. N, Wassama Roundhouse State Historic Park, NE of SH 49 and SH 628 intersection

Wassama Roundhouse

Dating prior to the 1860s, the Wassama Roundhouse was reconstructed in 1985 on the location of the previous four houses. In 1903 the third roundhouse was built using portions of the center pole from the two earlier houses. The roundhouse served as the focal point of spiritual and ceremonial life for many Native Californians. The Wassama Roundhouse continues to serve this purpose.

Placed in cooperation with Grub Gulch Chapters 41–49 of E Clampus Vitus, 1992.

OAKLAND (Alameda Co.)
1540 12th Ave.

Church of St. James the Apostle

This church, founded under authority of Bishop Kip, first Episcopal Bishop for California, has given uninterrupted service to this community since June 27, 1858.

Placed by California State Park Commission in cooperation with Fruitvale Parlor No. 177 of Native Daughters of the Golden West, 1959.

OAKLAND (Alameda Co.)
685 14th St.

First Unitarian Church of Oakland

Designed in 1889 by Walter J. Mathews, this solid masonry Romanesque church departed radically from California's traditional Gothic wood frame construction. Noted for its world famous stained glass windows produced by Goodhue of Boston, and for arching redwood spans, the widest at that time west of the Rockies, the church remains a significant cultural and architectural landmark.

Placed in cooperation with First Unitarian Church of Oakland, 1977.

OAKLAND (Alameda Co.)
Joaquin Miller Park, NE corner Joaquin Miller Rd. and Sanborn Dr.

Joaquin Miller Home

Joaquin Miller, "Poet of the Sierras," resided on these acres, named by him "The Hights," from 1886 to 1913. In this building, known as the Abbey, he wrote *Columbus* and other poems. The surrounding trees were planted by him and he personally built, on the eminence to the north, the funeral pyre and the monuments dedicated to Moses, Gen. John C. Fremont, and Robert Browning. "The Hights" was purchased by the City of Oakland in 1919.

Placed by Historical Landmarks Committee of Native Sons of the Golden West, 1928.

OAKLAND (Alameda Co.)
2025 Broadway

Paramount Theatre
(Plaque at 475 21st St.)

This is a superior rendering of the "art deco" or "moderne" style of movie palace built during the rise of the motion picture industry. The Paramount, which opened on Dec. 16, 1931, is the most ambitious theatre design of architect Timothy L. Pflueger. Restored in 1973, it has retained an exceptional unity of style.

Placed in cooperation with Theatre Historical Society, 1976.

OAKLAND (Alameda Co.) *50 yds. past entrance kiosk, Redwood Gate, Redwood Regional Park*

Rainbow Trout Species Identified

The naming of the Rainbow Trout species was based on fish taken from the San Leandro Creek drainage. In 1855, Dr. W. P. Gibbons, founder of the California Academy of Sciences, was given three specimens obtained from the creek. He described and assigned them the scientific name *salmo iridia*. Rainbow Trout are now worldwide in distribution and are a highly prized game fish.

Placed in cooperation with East Bay Regional Park District, 1987.

OAKLAND (Alameda Co.) *Redwood Regional Park, Thomas J. Roberts Recreation Area, 11500 Skyline Blvd.*

Site of Blossom Rock Navigation Trees

Until at least 1851, redwood trees on this site were used as landmarks to avoid striking the treacherous submerged Blossom Rock, in San Francisco Bay, west of Yerba Buena Island. Although by 1855 the original stems had been logged, today's trees are sprouts from their stumps.

Placed in cooperation with East Bay Regional Park District, 1985.

OAKLAND (Alameda Co.) *NE corner 13th and Franklin sts.*

Site of College of California
Original Campus of University of California

University of California, chartered Mar. 23, 1868. Located between Franklin and Harrison, 12th and 14th streets, from 1869 to 1873, using buildings of former College of California, successor to Contra Costa Academy founded by Henry Durant, June 1853. He was elected first university president in June 1870. University moved to present Berkeley site September 1873.

Placed in cooperation with University of California, Alameda County Historical Society, and Oakland Chamber of Commerce, 1968.

OAKLAND (Alameda Co.) *3093 Broadway*

Site of Saint Mary's College

"The Old Brickpile"
1889–1928
Saint Mary's College Alumni
April 25, 1959
California Registered Historical Landmark
No. 676

Private plaque.

OCEANSIDE (San Diego Co.) *4050 Mission Ave. (SH 76)*

Mission San Luis Rey de Francia

Founded June 12, 1798, by Father Lasuen, then president of the California missions, and administered by Father Peyri. Notable for its impressive architecture—a composite of Spanish, Moorish, Mexican.

Placed by Department of Public Works, Division of Highways.

OCOTILLO WELLS (San Diego Co.) *1.6 mi. E, on SH 78*
Los Puertecitos

Juan Bautista de Anza's expedition marched through this little pass Dec. 19, 1775, on its way to strengthen Spanish colonization in California. Many of the 240 members of the party were recruited from Mexico to be the first residents of San Francisco. They had camped the preceding night somewhere in the wide flats just east of this monument.

Placed by California State Park Commission in cooperation with Cuyamaca Parlor No. 298 of Native Sons of the Golden West, 1959.

OGILBY (Imperial Co.) *On Gold Rock Ranch Rd., about 8 mi. N of I-8 and Ogilby Rd. intersection*
Tumco

(Plaque on grounds of Gold Rock Ranch)

Pete Walters of Ogilby discovered the first gold vein at Gold Rock on Jan. 6, 1884. From his Little Mary claim began a gold camp which reached its peak development between 1893 and 1899 as Hedges, with 3,200 residents. Nearly closed 1900–10, it was reopened as Tumco, 1910–13, and worked intermittently until 1941. Tumco has long been a California ghost town.

Placed in cooperation with Imperial Valley Pioneers Historical Society and Squibob Chapter of E Clampus Vitus, 1985.

OLANCHA (Inyo Co.) *.6 mi. S, on US 395 at Fall Rd.*
Farley's Olancha Mill

M. H. Farley, working for the Silver Mountain Mining Company in the Coso Mountains, conceived the idea in 1860 of building a processing mill on a creek flowing into Owens Lake. He explored and named Olancha Pass that year and completed the first mill and furnace in the Owens River Valley by December of 1862. It was located on Olancha Creek about one mile west of this marker.

Placed by California State Park Commission in cooperation with Southern Inyo Chamber of Commerce, 1965.

ORANGE (Orange Co.) *NW corner Lincoln Ave. and Orange Olive Rd.*
Old Santa Ana

Portola camped on bank of Santa Ana River in 1769. Jose Antonio Yorba, member of expedition, later returned to Rancho Santiago de Santa Ana. El Camino Real crossed river in this vicinity. Place was designated Santa Ana by travelers and known by that name until present town of Santa Ana was founded.

Placed by California State Park Commission.

ORINDA (Contra Costa Co.) *24 Adobe Ln.*
The Joaquin Moraga Adobe—1841

Jose Joaquin Moraga—member of the Juan Bautista de Anza 1776 expedition, founder and first commandante of the Presidio of San Francisco—was the grandfather of Don Joaquin Moraga who with his cousin Don Juan Bernal was awarded this grant in 1835, which they called Rancho Laguna de Los Palos Colorados. In August 1941 this property was acquired and restoration made by Katharine Brown

White Irvine of Oakland. Later ownership was bequeathed to her grandson, William Thornton White, III.

Placed by Contra Costa County Historical Society, 1954.

ORLAND (Glenn Co.) *1 mi. N, old Hwy. 99W at Hambright Creek*
The Swift Adobe

The first house in Glenn County. Built about 1848 by Granville P. Swift, a member of the Bear Flag Party, who came to California from Oregon in 1844. The site is 150 yards east on the bank of Hambright Creek. The house was built of clay by Indians. He soon had herds of cattle ranging up and down the valley tended by Indian vaqueros, and he made a fortune mining on the Feather River with his Indian laborers.

Placed by Orland Bicentennial Committee.

OROVILLE (Butte Co.) *Lake Oroville State Recreation Area, Bidwell Cyn, Bidwell Cyn Rd.*
Bidwell's Bar
1853–1856
Site of courthouse was 120 yds. west
of this point marked by small monument
1917

Placed by Argonaut Parlor No. 8 of Native Sons of the Golden West and Butte County Board of Supervisors, 1917.

OROVILLE (Butte Co.) *1500 Broderick St.*
Chinese Temple

Dedicated in the spring of 1863, this building served as a temple of worship for 10,000 Chinese then living here. Funds for its erection and furnishings were provided by the Emperor and Empress of China, and local Chinese labor built the structure. The building was deeded to the City of Oroville in 1935 by the Chinese residents.

Placed by California State Park Commission in cooperation with Oroville Woman's Community Club, 1962.

OROVILLE (Butte Co.) *2547 Oroville-Quincy Hwy. at Oak Ave.*
The Last Yahi Indian

For thousands of years the Yahi Indians roamed the foothills between Mt. Lassen and the Sacramento Valley. Settlement of this region by the white man brought death to the Yahi by gun, by disease, and by hunger. By the turn of the century only a few remained. Ishi, the last known survivor of these people, was discovered at this site in 1911. His death in 1916 brought an end to Stone Age California.

Placed by California State Park Commission in cooperation with Argonaut Parlor No. 8 of Native Sons of the Golden West and Ophir Parlor No. 190 of Native Daughters of the Golden West, 1966.

OROVILLE (Butte Co.) *Lake Oroville State Recreation Area, Bidwell Cyn, Bidwell Cyn Rd.*
Bidwell Bar Bridge and Toll House

Originally constructed on a site one and a half miles northeast of this location in 1856.

Rededicated on July 30, 1977, on this Kelly Ridge site to avoid inundation by the waters of Oroville Reservoir.
Placed by State of California, 1977.

OROVILLE (Butte Co.)   *6 mi. N, off SH 70, 5 mi. S on Cherokee Rd. to Oregon Gulch Rd.*
Oregon City
Entering California over the Applegate and Lassen Trails, a party of Oregonians, captained by Peter H. Burnett, arrived here in autumn of 1848 to establish the town of Oregon City. Burnett, little more than a year later, became the first civil governor of California. Oregon City, for a time, continued to prosper as a gold mining and supply center and then declined into virtual oblivion.
Placed by California State Park Commission in cooperation with California Heritage Council, Butte County Historical Society, Schoolmates Club, and Mr. James Lenhoff, 1966.

PACIFIC GROVE (Monterey Co.)   *SW corner 16th St. and Central Ave.*
Chautauqua Hall
The first Chautauqua in the West was organized at Pacific Grove in June 1879 for the presentation of "moral attractions" and "the highest grade of concerts and entertainment." Known worldwide as "Chautauqua-by-the-Sea," it made Pacific Grove an unequaled cultural center.
Placed in cooperation with City of Pacific Grove, 1970.

PACIFIC PALISADES (Los Angeles Co.)   *Will Rogers State Beach lifeguard headquarters, 15100 W. Pacific Coast Hwy. (SH 1)*
Port Los Angeles
"The Long Wharf"
In 1893 the Southern Pacific Railroad Company completed its 4,720-foot wharf, which served as a deep water port for the Los Angeles area. After San Pedro became Los Angeles's official harbor in 1897, shipping activity at Port Los Angeles declined. Ultimately abandoned and dismantled, no trace remained of what had been the longest wooden pier in the world.
Placed in cooperation with Pacific Palisades Historical Society, 1976.

PACIFICA (San Mateo Co.)   *SE corner SH 1 and Crespi Dr.*
Discovery of San Francisco Bay
Captain Gaspar de Portola camped Oct. 31, 1769, by the creek at the south side of this valley, and to that camp scouting parties brought news of a body of water to the east. On Nov. 4, the expedition advanced. Turning inland here, they climbed to the summit of Sweeney Ridge and beheld for the first time the Bay of San Francisco.
Placed by California Centennial Commission, County Board of Supervisors, and San Mateo County Historical Association, 1949.

PACIFICA (San Mateo Co.)   *SH 1 to Fassler Ave.,*
trail to top of Sweeney Ridge

**From this ridge the Portola expedition
discovered San Francisco Bay
November 4, 1769**

Private plaque.

PACIFICA (San Mateo Co.)   *Sanchez Adobe County Park, SW corner*
Linda Mar Blvd. and Seville Dr.

Sanchez Adobe

The home of Francisco Sanchez (born 1805, died 1862), alcalde of San Francisco and commandante of militia under the Mexican Republic, grantee of the 8,926-acre Rancho San Pedro, and later a respected American citizen. His house, built 1842–46, afterwards was owned and remodeled by Gen. Edward Kirkpatrick. It was purchased by the County of San Mateo in 1947 to be preserved as a public museum.

Placed by California State Park Commission in cooperation with San Mateo County Historical Association, 1953.

PALA (San Diego Co.)   *Pala Mission Rd.*

Asistencia de San Antonio

(Plaque on SH 76)

La Asistencia de San Antonio de Pala, notable for its bell tower, or campanile. The chapel was built by Father Peyri, 1816. Almost destroyed by earthquake and storm, but later restored. Indians are still at Pala.

Placed by Department of Public Works, Division of Highways.

PALO ALTO (Santa Clara Co.)   *367 Addison Ave.*

Birthplace of "Silicon Valley"

This garage is the birthplace of the world's first high-technology region, "Silicon Valley." The idea for such a region originated with Dr. Frederick Terman, a Stanford University professor who encouraged his students to start up their own electronics companies in the area instead of joining established firms in the East. The first two students to follow his advice were William R. Hewlett and David Packard, who in 1938 began developing their first product, an audio oscillator, in this garage.

Placed in cooperation with Hewlett Packard, 1989.

PALO ALTO (Santa Clara Co.)   *Stanford University, Campus Dr. W.,*
across from Stanford Driving Range

Development of Motion Pictures

In commemoration of the motion picture research conducted in 1878 and 1879 by Eadweard Muybridge at the Palo Alto Stock Farm, now the site of Stanford University. This extensive photographic experiment portraying the attitudes of animals in motion was conceived by and executed under the direction and patronage of Leland Stanford. Consecutive instantaneous exposures were provided for a battery of 24 cameras fitted with electroshutters.

Placed in cooperation with Stanford Historical Society, Stanford ECV Alumni, and Mountain Charlie Chapter No. 1850 of E Clampus Vitus, 1983.

PALO ALTO (Santa Clara Co.) 844 E. Charleston Rd.
First Commercially Practicable Integrated Circuit

At this site in 1959, Dr. Robert Noyce of Fairchild Semiconductor Corporation invented the first integrated circuit that could be produced commercially. Based on "planar" technology, an earlier Fairchild breakthrough, Noyce's invention consisted of a complete electronic circuit inside a small silicon chip. His innovation helped revolutionize "Silicon Valley's" semiconductor electronics industry and brought profound change to the lives of people everywhere.

Placed in cooperation with Intel Corporation, 1991.

PALO ALTO (Santa Clara Co.) South side La Selva Dr., between Military Way and Magnolia Dr.
Homesite of Sarah Wallis Mayfield Farm

Sarah Armstrong Wallis (1825–1905) was a pioneer in the campaign for women's voting rights. In 1870 she was elected president of California's first statewide suffrage organization, which in 1873 incorporated as the California State Woman Suffrage Education Association. The home she built on this site, Mayfield Farm, was a center of suffrage activities attracting state and national leaders such as Susan B. Anthony, Elizabeth Cady Stanton, and Ulysses S. Grant.

Placed in cooperation with Women's Heritage Museum of Palo Alto, 1986.

PALO ALTO (Santa Clara Co.) 27 Mitchell Ln., near NE corner El Camino Real and University Ave.
Hostess House

This building originally served Camp Fremont as a meeting place for servicemen and visitors. When moved from its original site to Palo Alto, it became the first municipally sponsored community center in the nation. It is the only remaining structure from California's World War I army training camps. Designed by Julia Morgan in 1918 for the YWCA, it was dedicated one year later to those who died in this war.

Placed in cooperation with City of Palo Alto, 1976.

PALO ALTO (Santa Clara Co.) 900 University Ave.
John Adams Squire House

Designed by T. Paterson Ross and constructed by builder George W. Mosher in 1904, this house is a notable example of California's interpretation of the Greco-Roman Classic Revival movement in America.

Placed in cooperation with Palo Alto Historical Association and City of Palo Alto, 1973.

PALO ALTO (Santa Clara Co.) 623 Mirada Rd.
Lou Henry Hoover House
(Plaque 100 ft. S of Cabrillo and Santa Ynez aves. intersection, Stanford University)

This 1919 residence of a developing international style of architecture embodied Mrs. Herbert Hoover's innovative architectural concepts. It was executed by architects Arthur B. Clark, Charles Davis, and Birge Clark, and was maintained as the

Hoover's family home. Here in 1928 Hoover received news of his election as President of the United States. Upon Mrs. Hoover's death the house was given to Stanford University.

Placed in cooperation with Stanford Historical Society and Stanford University, 1978.

PALO ALTO (Santa Clara Co.)
SE corner Channing Ave. and Emerson St.

Electronics Research Laboratory

Original site of the laboratory and factory of Federal Telegraph Company, founded in 1909 by Cyril F. Elwell. Here, with two assistants, Dr. Lee deForest, inventor of the three-element radio vacuum tube, devised in 1911–13 the first vacuum tube amplifier and oscillator. Worldwide developments based on this research led to modern radio communication, television, and the electronics age.

Placed in cooperation with City of Palo Alto and Palo Alto Historical Association, 1970.

PASADENA (Los Angeles Co.)
4 Westmoreland Pl.

The Gamble House

Built in 1908, the David B. Gamble House is a tribute to the genius of architects Charles Sumner Greene and Henry Mather Greene. Its design represents a unique California lifestyle and is a masterpiece of American craftsmanship. In 1966 it was made a gift by the Gamble family to the City of Pasadena in a joint agreement with the University of Southern California.

Placed in cooperation with City of Pasadena and University of Southern California, 1974.

PASADENA (Los Angeles Co.)
39 El Molino Ave.

Pasadena Playhouse

Considered Elmer Grey's outstanding design, the Pasadena Playhouse, an excellent example of Spanish Colonial Revival architecture, opened on May 18, 1925. The first in America to stage Shakespeare's 37 plays, the Playhouse has provided the theatre world with quality and excellence, and trained many of its stars. The legislature proclaimed it the State Theatre of California in 1937.

Placed in cooperation with Pasadena Playhouse Association, Pasadena Historical Society, and City of Pasadena, 1977.

PASO ROBLES (San Luis Obispo Co.)
2.5 mi. N of SH 46 on Airport Rd.

Estrella Adobe Church

The first Protestant church in northern San Luis Obispo County was built in 1879 by early settlers. This nondenominational church on the Estrella Plains prospered with the pioneer community, but by 1912 fell into disuse as the various denominations developed separate facilities. In 1952 this structure, then in ruins, was restored by the Paso Robles Women's Club History and Landmarks Committee.

Placed in cooperation with Friends of the Adobes, 1981.

PASO ROBLES (San Luis Obispo Co.)

2.5 mi. N of
SH 46 on Airport Rd.

Estrella Adobe Church
Built 1878 by Christian pioneers

Placed by History and Landmarks Section of Paso Robles Women's Club, and Paso Robles School for Boys, 1952.

PENRYN (Placer Co.)

SE corner Taylor and Rock Springs rds.

Griffith Quarry

In the fall of 1864, Mr. Griffith Griffith, a native of Wales, established the quarry located near this site which was later to supply high-quality granite for a number of the important buildings in San Francisco and Sacramento, including portions of the state capitol. This was also the site of the state's first commercially successful granite polishing mill, erected in 1874.

Placed in cooperation with Placer County Park and Historical Restoration Commission, 1976.

PESCADERO (San Mateo Co.)

San Gregorio St.

First Congregational Church of Pescadero

Built in May 1867, this is the oldest church building on its original site within the San Mateo-Santa Clara County region. Its Classical Revival style reflects the cultural background of pioneer Yankee settlers of the south San Francisco peninsula coast. The steeple was appended to the bell tower in 1890. During repairs caused by a minor fire in 1940, the social hall was added.

Placed in cooperation with First Congregational Church of Pescadero, 1984.

PESCADERO (San Mateo Co.)

14 mi. S, Ano Nuevo State Reserve,
NW corner SH 1 and New Years Creek Rd.

Steele Brothers' Dairy Ranches

Beginning in the 1850s, the Steele brothers pioneered one of the first large-scale commercial cheese and dairy businesses in California. They extended their operations from Point Reyes to Rancho Punta de Ano Nuevo in 1862. This 7,000-acre ranch consisted of five dairies extending from Gazos Creek to Point Ano Nuevo. For a century the Steele brothers' dairy ranches were of major importance in California's agricultural development.

Placed in cooperation with the Ano Nuevo Interpretive Association, 1982.

PETALUMA (Sonoma Co.)

3325 Adobe Rd.

6 Miles
Vallejo's Petaluma Adobe

(Plaque 300 ft. NW of Old Redwood Hwy.
and Adobe Rd. intersection)

Built by Gen. M. G. Vallejo, 1834–44, and known as "Casa Grande." According to Gen. Vallejo, "building was of immense proportions with different departments for factories and warehouses."

Placed by Department of Public Works, Division of Highways.

PETROLIA (Humboldt Co.)   *NE corner Mattole Rd. and Front St.*
California's First Drilled Oil Wells

California's first drilled oil wells producing crude to be refined and sold commercially were located on the north fork of the Mattole River, approximately three miles east of here. The old Union Mattole Oil Company made its first shipment of oil from here in June 1865 to a San Francisco refinery. Many old wellheads remain today.

Placed by California State Park Commission in cooperation with Eureka Oil Information Committee and Western Oil and Gas Association, 1955.

PILOT HILL (El Dorado Co.)   *.2 mi. N, on SH 49*
California's First Grange Hall

Pilot Hill Grange No. 1, with 29 charter members. Master, F. D. Brown; Secretary, A. J. Bayley; was organized Aug. 10, 1870. The Grange Hall, dedicated at this site Nov. 23, 1880, was built by Alcander A. Bayley.

Placed by Pilot Hill Grange No. 1 in cooperation with California State Park Commission, 1956 and 1982.

PIRU (Ventura Co.)   *2.2 mi. E, on SH 126*
Rancho Camulos

Governor Juan Alvarado granted the Rancho San Francisco on Jan. 22, 1839, to Antonio del Valle, including 48,815 square acres. Jacoba Feliz filed a claim against this grant which was dismissed June 8, 1857. The del Valle family chose Camulos as their home which later became known as the "Home of Ramona."

Placed by El Aliso Parlor No. 314 and Las Tres Vistas Parlor No. 302 of Native Daughters of the Golden West and Cabrillo Parlor No. 114 of Native Sons of the Golden West of Ventura County, 1955.

PIRU (Ventura Co.)   *Warring Park, 700 block Orchard St.*
Warring Park

On August 11, 1769, the explorers and priests accompanying Portola found a populous village of Piru Indians near this point. Carrying their bowstrings loose, they offered necklaces of stones in exchange for which the governor presented the Indians with beads.

Private plaque.

PLACERVILLE (El Dorado Co.)   *305 Main St.*
Hangman's Tree

This city, in the days of '49, was called "Hangtown." This was the site of Elstner's Hay Yard on which stood the "Hangman's Tree" where vigilantes executed many men for various crimes. The stump of the tree is under this building.

Placed by Marguerite Parlor No. 12 of Native Daughters of the Golden West and Placerville Parlor No. 9 of Native Sons of the Golden West, 1934.

PLACERVILLE (El Dorado Co.)   *1031 Thompson Way*
Methodist Episcopal Church

Erected in 1851. Oldest church building in El Dorado County. It originally stood on the corner of Cedar Ravine and Main Street. The Ponderosa pine beams are hand hewn. First church bell was purchased from the sailing ship *Staffordshire*. Restored by public contribution.

Placed by El Dorado County Chamber of Commerce.

PLACERVILLE (El Dorado Co.) *NE corner Main St. and Bedford Ave.*
Placerville
Originally Known as "Hangtown"
Incorporated May 13, 1854

Established on banks of "Hangtown" Creek as rich mining camp in spring of 1848. Millions in gold were taken from its ravines and hills. Supply center for surrounding mining camps and transportation terminus for the famous Comstock Lode. John M. Studebaker, Mark Hopkins, Leland Stanford, Phillip Armour, and Edwin Markham were among well-known men who contributed to Placerville's early history. Also, "Snowshoe" John A. Thompson, who carried from 60 to 80 pounds of mail on skis from Placerville over the Sierra to Carson Valley during winter months.

Placed by California Centennial Commission and James W. Marshall Chapter No. 49 of E Clampus Vitus.

PLACERVILLE (El Dorado Co.) *SW corner Main and Sacramento sts.*
Placerville Pony Express
Station and Terminus

Gold rush town and western terminus of the Placerville-Carson Road to the Comstock. Placerville was a relay station of the Central Overland Pony Express, Apr. 4, 1860–June 30, 1861. Here on Apr. 4, 1860, the first eastbound pony rider, William (Sam) Hamilton, changed horses, added one express letter to his mochela, and sped away for Sportsman's Hall. On July 1, 1861, Placerville became the western terminus of the Pony Express until its discontinuance on Oct. 26, 1861.

Placed by California State Park Commission in cooperation with El Dorado County Chamber of Commerce, James W. Marshall Chapter No. 49 of E Clampus Vitus, and Central Overland Pony Express Trail Association, 1960.

PLACERVILLE (El Dorado Co.) *543 Main St., parking lot opposite Chamber of Commerce*
John Mohler Studebaker
1833–1917
Pioneer blacksmith—soldier—inventor—builder
Placed by James Marshall Chapter 49 of E Clampus Vitus, 1939.

PLYMOUTH (Amador Co.) *7.2 mi. NE, on Plymouth-Shenandoah Rd.*
D'Agostini Winery

D'Agostini Winery was started in 1856 by Adam Uhlinger, a Swiss immigrant. The original wine cellar, with walls made from rock quarried from nearby hills, hand-hewn beams, and oak casks, is still in use and part of the present winery. Some original vines are still in production.

Placed by California State Park Commission in cooperation with James W. Marshall Chapter No. 49 of E Clampus Vitus, 1961.

POMONA (Los Angeles Co.) *491 Arrow Hwy.*
Adobe de Palomares
Completed about 1854 and restored in 1939, this was the family home of Don Ygnacio Palomares, who with Don Ricardo Vejar, was granted Rancho San Jose in 1837 by Gov. Juan B. Alvarado.
Placed by California State Park Commission in cooperation with Historical Society of Pomona Valley, 1957.

POMONA (Los Angeles Co.) *SW corner Mission Blvd. and White Ave.*
First Home of Pomona College
On this site, Sept. 12, 1888, was held the first session of Pomona College.
Placed by Historical Society of Pomona Valley, 1937.

POPE VALLEY (Napa Co.) *2.1 mi. NW, 6654 Pope Valley Rd.*
Litto's Hubcap Ranch
This is one of California's exceptional twentieth century folk art environments. Over a period of 30 years, Emanuele "Litto" Damonte (1892–1985), with the help of his neighbors, collected more than 2,000 hubcaps. All around Hubcap Ranch are constructions and arrangements of hubcaps, bottles, and pulltops which proclaim that "Litto, the Pope Valley Hubcap King," was here.
Placed in cooperation with Saving and Preserving Arts and Cultural Environments (SPACES), 1987.

PORTERVILLE (Tulare Co.) *Alta Vista School, 2293 E. Crabtree Ave.*
Tule River Indian Reservation
A reservation was originally established in 1857. Indians from a widespread area were brought here. The natives of this vicinity were the Koyeti tribe toward the west and the Yaudanchi tribe toward the east. Both were branches of the Yokuts Indians that occupied the San Joaquin Valley. This location not proving satisfactory, the Tule River Indian Reservation was moved to its present location, ten miles southeast, in 1873.
Placed by California Centennial Commission and Tulare County Historical Society, 1949.

PORTERVILLE (Tulare Co.) *Porterville Public Park, SW corner Main St. and W. Henderson Ave.*
Tule River Stage Station
Here Peter Goodhue operated an emigrant trail stopping place on the bank of the Tule River from 1854 until the river changed its course in 1862. This became a Butterfield Overland Mail stage station, 1858–61. It was kept in 1860 by R. Porter Putnam who in 1864 founded Porterville, named for him.
Placed by California State Park Commission in cooperation with Tulare County Historical Society and Grand Parlor of Native Daughters of the Golden West, 1953.

PORTOLA VALLEY (San Mateo Co.) *3915 Alpine Rd.*
Casa de Tableta
This structure, built by Felix Buelna in the 1850s, served as a gambling retreat and meeting place for Mexican-Californios. It was strategically located on the earliest trail used both by rancheros and American settlers crossing the peninsula to the

coast, and served this remote area. Acquired by an American in 1868, it has continued to serve under various names as a roadhouse and saloon.

Placed in cooperation with Town of Portola Valley, 1969.

PORTOLA VALLEY (San Mateo Co.)   *930 Portola Rd.*
Our Lady of the Wayside

Built in 1912, this country church was the first executed design of noted architect Timothy L. Pflueger, who had just begun work for James Miller. An awareness of the Spanish California missions inspired the style, which contrasts with the large commercial buildings and art deco theaters for which Pflueger later became notable. Construction of this Catholic church was initiated by a non-denominational club, The Family.

Placed in cooperation with town of Portola Valley, 1977.

PRAIRIE CITY (Sacramento Co.)   *NE corner US 50 and Prairie City Rd., 500 ft. N of US 50*
Prairie City

Site of Prairie City, mining town and center of trade in California gold rush days. In July 1853, Prairie City reached the height of its prosperity and included 15 stores and ten boarding houses and hotels. Two stagelines operated daily. A $50,000 quartz mill operated here in the fifties.

Placed by California Centennial Commission, Fern Parlor No. 123 of Native Daughters of the Golden West, and Granite Parlor No. 83 of Native Sons of the Golden West, 1950.

QUINCY (Plumas Co.)   *15.7 mi. W, Buck's Lake Lodge Marina, Buck's Lake Rd.*

Buck's Ranch
Hotel and Store

Original location one hundred yards northeast. Haven of pioneers, pack train division point for miners, to Feather River points. Stage Station, express, and post office. 1850–1852 emigrant trail. Destroyed by fire Jan. 13, 1928.

Placed by Plumas Pioneer Parlor No. 219 of Native Daughters of the Golden West and Quincy Parlor No. 131 of Native Sons of the Golden West, 1931.

QUINCY (Plumas Co.)   *1.8 mi. N, .4 mi. NW of SH 70, on dirt road*
Dedicated to
pioneers of Plumas County
to the
founders of Elizabethtown
and
Elizabeth Stark Blakeley
for whom this town was named
Sept. 1852

Placed by Plumas Pioneer Parlor No. 219 of Native Daughters of the Golden West and Quincy Parlor No. 131 of Native Sons of the Golden West, 1927.

QUINCY (Plumas Co.) *19.2 mi. W, 3.5 mi. W of Buck's Lake, on Buck's Lake Rd.*

P. Linthiouh
died Sept. 1852,
age 19.
O.H.
copied from tree,
carved by comrade, 1852.

Placed by Plumas Pioneer Parlor No. 219 of Native Daughters of the Golden West and Quincy Parlor No. 131 of Native Sons of the Golden West, 1931.

QUINCY (Plumas Co.) *2 mi. E, Plumas Co. Fairgrounds, E. Main St. and Fairgrounds Rd.*

Plumas County's First Schoolhouse
This is the original pioneer schoolhouse, erected in 1857. Trustees—J. W. Thompson & J. C. Church. Teacher—Mrs. S.A. Ballou. Nineteen scholars.

Placed by Plumas Pioneers Parlor 219 of Native Daughters of the Golden West, 1957.

QUINCY (Plumas Co.) *23.6 mi. NW, 4 mi. SE of Belden, on SH 70*

Rich Bar
Gold first found here July 1850 by miners coming over mountains from the Yuba diggings. Much production during early fifties along this east branch of the Feather River's north fork. Here "Dame Shirley" (Louise Amelia Knapp Smith Clappe) wrote her *Letters from the California Mines,* one of the foremost classics of the gold rush.

QUINCY (Plumas Co.) *5.8 mi. W, Buck's Lake Rd. to Spanish Ranch side road*

Spanish Ranch
Named for two
Mexicans who began
a horse ranch
here in 1850.

Private plaque.

RAILROAD FLAT (Calaveras Co.) *.5 mi. W of post office, NE of Railroad and Summit Level rds.*

Railroad Flat
This historic mining town, elevation 2,600 feet, was founded in 1849 and named after primitive mule-drawn ore cars used here. The center of rich placer and quartz mining, its largest producer was the Petticoat Mine. As a result of black fever, the town's population was decimated in 1880. The post office established in 1857, the Edwin Taylor store built in 1867, and the site of an Indian council house are among present-day attractions.

Placed by California State Park Commission in cooperation with Railroad Flat Community Club, 1957.

RANCHO CORDOVA (Sacramento Co.)

US 50 to Hazel Ave. exit, at Nimbus Dam, 300 ft. S of Lake Natoma boat ramp

The Coloma Road

Alder Springs, south of this point, marks the Old Coloma Road, running between Sutter's Fort and Cul-luh-mah (Coloma). Established in 1847, this road was used by James W. Marshall in January 1848 to bring the first gold from Sutter's Mill to the fort. Later, traveled by thousands to and from the diggings, it became the route of California's first stageline, established in 1849 by James E. Birch.

Placed by California State Park Commission in cooperation with Sacramento County Historical Society and the Grand Parlors of Native Sons and Native Daughters of the Golden West, 1960.

RANCHO CORDOVA (Sacramento Co.)

On White Rock Rd., .2 mi. E of Sunrise Blvd. and White Rock Rd. intersection

Fifteen-Mile House

Owned and operated from 1857 as a stage station by Henry F. W. Deterding, this was the site of the second remount station of the Central Overland Pony Express during Mar.–July 1860. Here on Apr. 4, 1860, Sam (Bill) Hamilton, with the first eastward mail of the Pony Express, changed ponies with Mormon Tavern as his next stop.

Placed by California State Park Commission in cooperation with Sacramento County Historical Society, Fern Parlor No. 123 of Native Daughters of the Golden West, and Central Overland Pony Express Trail Association, 1960.

RANCHO PALOS VERDES (Los Angeles Co.)

N side entrance to Portuguese Bend Club, Palos Verdes Dr. at Schooner Dr.

Portuguese Bend Whaling Station

On the slopes below and west of this plaque stood the quarters of Portuguese whalemen, who put out through the surf in boats under oars and sail to harpoon passing gray whales to be towed ashore where the blubber was stripped and "tried out" in large black iron try-pots to produce valuable whale oil for lamps and lubricants. Active from 1860 to 1885, this station began its decline with the advent of fossil oil; however, three of the original structures, the try-pots, and crumbling furnaces remained until about 1928. This site is registered as California Historical Landmark No. 381.

Private plaque, placed 1985.

RANCHO SANTA FE (San Diego Co.)

Village Green in front of The Inn

Rancho Santa Fe

Rancho Santa Fe began as Rancho San Dieguito, a land grant of nearly 9,000 acres made to Juan Maria Osuna in 1845. The Santa Fe Railway Company later used the land to plant thousands of eucalyptus trees for use as railroad ties. In the 1920s Rancho Santa Fe became one of the state's first planned communities unified by a single architectural theme, the Spanish Colonial Revival. Lilian Rice, one of California's first successful women architects, supervised the development and designed many of the buildings.

Placed in cooperation with Rancho Santa Fe Historical Society and Rancho Santa Fe Association, 1989.

RANDSBURG (Kern Co.)   *Kern County Desert Museum, Butte Ave.*
Rand Mining District

The Yellow Aster, or Rand, mine was discovered in April 1895 by Singleton, Burcham, and Mooers. The town of Randsburg quickly developed, followed by the supply town of Johannesburg in 1896. Both names were adopted from the profusion of minerals resembling those of the Rand mining district in South Africa. In 1907 Churchill discovered tungsten in Atolia, used in steel alloy during World War I. In June 1919, Williams and Nosser discovered the famous California Rand Silver Mine at Red Mountain.

Placed by Kern County Historical Society, El Tejon Parlor No. 239 of Native Daughters of the Golden West, Bakersfield Parlor No. 42 of Native Sons of the Golden West, and Kern County Museum, 1964.

RED BLUFF (Tehama Co.)   *1.5 mi. N, William B. Ide Adobe State Historical Park, 3040 Adobe Rd.*
William B. Ide Adobe
(Two additional plaques located
at Adobe Rd. and Main St.)

This adobe house, built by William B. Ide reputedly about 1850, represents a typical frontier structure of the American period. Ide, who came to California with his family in 1845, was the first and only president of the California Republic under the Bear Flag Party Proclamation of June 14, 1846.

Placed by California State Park Commission in cooperation with Berendos Parlor No. 23 of Native Daughters of the Golden West, 1960.

REDDING (Shasta Co.)   *SW corner old Hwy. 99 and Clear Creek Rd., on Westside Rd.*
Bell's Bridge

Twenty-two hundred feet south of here was located Bell's Bridge. Established by J. J. Bell in 1851, this was an important toll bridge on the road from Shasta City to Tehama. Bell's mansion, erected in 1859 on Clear Creek, was a favorite stopping place for miners on their way to the Shasta, Trinity, and Siskiyou gold fields.

Placed by California State Park Commission in cooperation with Santa Monica Chapter of Daughters of the American Revolution.

REDDING (Shasta Co.)   *Old Hwy. 99 and Canyon Rd.*
Clear Creek

In 1848 gold was first discovered on this creek by Maj. Pierson Barton Reading, early California pioneer.

Placed by California Highway Commission, 1931.

REDDING (Shasta Co.)   *Clear Creek Bridge, 6.9 mi. W of*
old Hwy. 99W, on Clear Creek Rd.

Reading Bar

Site of first gold discovery in Shasta County by Maj. P. B. Reading, March 1848.
Private plaque.

REDLANDS (San Bernardino Co.)   *25894 Mission Rd., SW of high*
powerline towers on N side of street

Guachama Rancheria

Guachama Rancheria, lying along this road, was named San Bernardino May 20,
1810, by Francisco Dumetz. In 1819 it became the San Bernardino Rancho of Mission San Gabriel. The adobe administration building stood about 70 yards north of
this spot, an enramada serving as chapel. The zanja was constructed to convey water
from the mountains for irrigation. Control by mission fathers ended in 1834.
Placed by Arrowhead Chapter of Daughters of the American Revolution, 1932.

REDLANDS (San Bernardino Co.)   *26930 Barton Rd.*

San Bernardino Asistencia

This branch of San Gabriel Mission was constructed about 1830 on the San
Bernardino Rancho. During the 1840s, its buildings were used by Jose del Carmen
Lugo as part of his rancho grant. Later, after its sale to the Mormons, it was occupied by Bishop Tenney in the 1850s and by Dr. Benjamin Barton in the 1860s. Its
restoration was completed in 1937 by the Works Progress Administration, assisted
by the San Bernardino County Historical Society.
*Placed by California State Park Commission in cooperation with San Bernardino
County Museum Association, 1960.*

REDLANDS (San Bernardino Co.)   *Sylvan Park, University St.*

Mill Creek Zanja

Spanish missionaries introduced the principle of irrigation in San Bernardino Valley, thus opening the way to settlement. Franciscan fathers engineered, and Indians
dug, this first ditch (or "zanja") in 1819–20. In historical sequence the zanja supported the San Bernardino Asistencia, Rancho San Bernardino, pioneer ranches,
orchards, and Redlands' domestic water supply.
*Placed by California State Park Commission in cooperation with Redlands
Kiwanis Club, City Park Department, and San Bernardino County Museum Association, 1965.*

REDLANDS (San Bernardino Co.)   *125 W. Vine St.*

A. K. Smiley Public Library

Albert K. Smiley, a leader of the city's library movement, donated this building
and park to the citizens of Redlands in 1898. Through his generosity, Redlands was
given one of California's few privately funded libraries of that era. In 1906 he also
contributed a wing, built to blend with the original design for this outstanding Mission Revival library.
*Placed in cooperation with Smiley Library Trustees, Friends of the Library, and
Redlands Area Historical Society, 1991.*

REDONDO BEACH (Los Angeles Co.)
SE corner Harbor Dr.
and Yacht Club Way

Old Salt Lake

This marker locates the site near which the Indians and early California settlers came to obtain their salt which at many times was more valuable than gold.

Placed by Tierra del Rey Parlor No. 300 of Native Daughters of the Golden West, 1955.

RESCUE (El Dorado Co.)
Green Valley and Deer Valley rds.
intersection

The Coloma Road

Past this point on the old Coloma Road, running between Sutter's Fort and his sawmill on the American River, James W. Marshall rode with the first gold discovered at Coloma on Jan. 24, 1848. Traveled by thousands to and from the diggings, this road became the route of California's earliest stageline, established in 1849 by James E. Birch.

Placed by California State Park Commission in cooperation with Golden Key of Greenwood, El Dorado Chamber of Commerce, and the Grand Parlors of Native Sons and Native Daughters of the Golden West, 1960.

RESCUE (El Dorado Co.)
3.9 mi. W, on Green Valley Rd.

Pleasant Grove House

This was the site of a popular roadhouse where the ponies of the Central Overland Pony Express were changed during July 1, 1860–June 30, 1861. From here the route of the pony riders continued westward to Folsom and eastward to Rescue, Dry Creek Crossing, and Missouri Flat to Placerville.

Placed by California State Park Commission in cooperation with Marguerite Parlor No. 12 of Native Daughters of the Golden West, and Central Overland Pony Express Trail Association, 1960.

RICHMOND (Contra Costa Co.)
Point Pinole Regional Shoreline,
Giant and Altas rds.

Site of Giant Powder Company

Point Pinole is the last site of the Giant Powder Company, the first company in America to produce dynamite. Following devastating explosions at their San Francisco and Berkeley sites, the business moved to this isolated location in 1892. Incorporating the established Croatian community of Sobrante, the company town of Giant quickly grew into one of the North Bay's industrial centers. Explosives were produced here until 1960 and were essential to mining, dam, and other construction projects throughout the western hemisphere.

Placed in cooperation with East Bay Regional Park District, 1992.

RIM FOREST (San Bernardino Co.) *.6 mi. E, on SH 18, at Daley Canyon Rd.*

The Daley Road
Built by Edward Daley & Company
1870
Placed by Arrowhead Parlor No. 110 of Native Sons of the Golden West and Lugonia Parlor No. 271 of Native Daughters of the Golden West, 1935.

RIPON (San Joaquin Co.) *Ripon City Park, Fourth and Locust sts.*

New Hope—1846—First Wheat
Approximately six miles west, 20 Mormon pioneers from the ship *Brooklyn* founded the first known agricultural colony in San Joaquin Valley; planted first wheat, also crops. They irrigated by pole and bucket method. Erected three log houses, operated sawmill and ferry across Stanislaus. Settlement later known as Stanislaus City.
Placed by California Centennial Commission and Daughters of Utah Pioneers, 1949.

RIVERSIDE (Riverside Co.) *Near Union Pacific Bridge, Jurupa Heights*

De Anza Crossing of the Santa Ana River, 1775 and 1776
(Plaque between clubhouse and No. 1 tee,
Jurupa Hills Country Club, 6161 Moraga Ave.)
On Jan. 1, 1776, the first party of colonists to come overland to the Pacific Coast crossed the Santa Ana River south of this marker and camped between here and the river. Recruited in the presidios of Sonora, Mexico, and led by Lt. Col. Juan Bautista de Anza, who had established the trail a year earlier, this humble and heroic band of 242 men, women, and children continued north to found San Francisco, thus setting a boundary to Russian expansion from the north. Prior to the opening of de Anza's trail, three precarious missions were maintained by uncertain ocean voyages; the flourishing missions and ranchos of Spanish California sprang from the droves of cattle, sheep, and horses brought over the trail.
Placed by Riverside Pioneer Historical Society, de Anza Caballeros, Jurupa Parlor No. 299 of Native Daughters of the Golden West, and Rubidoux Chapter of Daughters of the American Revolution, 1964.

RIVERSIDE (Riverside Co.) *3649 7th St.*

Mission Inn
Frank A. Miller (1857–1935) made adobe bricks for a small 12-room guest house which he opened in 1876. Over the years, by successive building additions, he fulfilled his dream by recreating this early California mission-style setting of a hotel.
Placed by California State Park Commission in cooperation with Mission Inn Garden Hotel, 1961.

RIVERSIDE (Riverside Co.) *City Park, SW corner Magnolia and Arlington sts.*

Parent Washington Navel Orange Tree
To honor Mrs. Eliza Tibbets and to commend her good work in planting at Riverside in 1873 the first Washington navel orange trees in California, native to Bahia,

Brazil. Proved the most valuable fruit introduction yet made by the United States Department of Agriculture.

Private plaque, placed 1920.

ROCKLIN (Placer Co.)   *SE corner Rocklin Rd. and First St.*
First Transcontinental Railroad—Rocklin

Central Pacific reached Rocklin, 22 miles from its Sacramento terminus, in May 1864, when the railroad established a major locomotive terminal here. Trains moving over the Sierra were generally cut in two sections at this point in order to ascend the grade. The first CP freight movement was three carloads of Rocklin granite pulled by the engine *Governor Stanford.* The terminal was moved to Roseville Apr. 18, 1908.

Placed in cooperation with Conference of California Historical Societies and Placer County Historical Society, 1969.

ROCKVILLE (Solano Co.)   *Rockville Cemetery, Suisun Valley Rd.*
Rockville Stone Chapel

Erected by pioneers of Methodist Episcopal Church South with volunteer labor and donated funds. Cornerstone laid Oct. 3, 1856. Dedicated February 1857. Site supplied by Landy and Sarah Alford. Chapel deteriorated by 1929 and deeded by the church to Rockville Public Cemetery District as a pioneer monument. Restored in 1940.

Placed by California State Park Commission in cooperation with Solano County Historical Society, 1963.

ROSAMOND (Kern Co.)   *Off SH 14, 6.8 mi. W on Rosamond Blvd.,*
.7 mi. N on Tehachapi-Willow Springs Rd.,
.6 mi. NW on Truman-Manly Rd.
Willow Springs

Willow Springs was a stage station on the Los Angeles-Havilah Stage Lines, 1864–72. From here light traffic went through Oak Creek Pass via Tehachapi Valley to Havilah and Kernville; heavy traffic went northeast to the Inyo mines, or via Jawbone Canyon to the south fork of the Kern, thence to the Kern mines.

Placed by Bakersfield Parlor No. 42 of Native Sons of the Golden West, El Tejon Parlor No. 239 of Native Daughters of the Golden West, Kern County Historical Society, Kern County Chamber of Commerce, and Department of Natural Resources, 1937.

ROSAMOND (Kern Co.)   *Off SH 14, 6.8 mi. W on Rosamond Blvd.,*
.7 mi. N on Tehachapi-Willow Springs Rd.,
.8 mi NW on Truman-Manly Rd.
Willow Springs

Visited by Padre Garces (1776) while following old horse-thief trace, later known as Jose Walker Trail. Fremont stopped here (1844). The famished Jayhawk Party (1850) found water here while struggling from Death Valley to Los Angeles. Still later was station on Los Angeles-Halilah and Inyo stagelines.

Placed by Kern County Historical Society and Kern County Museum, 1951.

ROSEVILLE (Placer Co.)

500 ft. W of Lincoln and Pacific sts. intersection

First Transcontinental Railroad—Roseville

Central Pacific graders reached Junction, now Roseville, Nov. 29, 1863, crossing the line of the California Central, which began building northward from Folsom in May 1858. That line was abandoned in 1868. CP's track reached junction Apr. 25, 1864, when trains began making daily runs 18 miles to and from Sacramento. Now Roseville is a major railroad distribution center.

Placed in cooperation with Conference of California Historical Societies and Placer County Historical Society, 1969.

ROUGH AND READY (Nevada Co.)

NE corner SH 20 and Mountain Rose Rd.

Rough and Ready

Established in 1849 and named after the Rough and Ready Company of miners from Wisconsin, in honor of Gen. Zachary Taylor, this was one of the principal towns of Nevada County. Here in 1850, articles of secession were drawn up establishing the "Republic of Rough and Ready." As a result of disastrous fire, only a few structures remain today of those built in the 1850s.

Placed by California State Park Commission in cooperation with Rough and Ready Chamber of Commerce, 1960.

RUBIDOUX (Riverside Co.)

4350 Riverview Dr.

Jensen-Alvarado Ranch

Danish sea captain Cornelius Jensen sailed into San Francisco during the gold rush to sell his cargo. In 1854 he settled in Agua Mansa, established a store, and married Mercedes Alvarado, a descendant of a pioneer California family. The Jensens purchased this ranch in 1865 and began planting vineyards and orchards. They used local materials to build their house which is of Danish vernacular design. The Jensens made this ranch an important civic, social, business, and agricultural center.

Placed in cooperation with Riverside County Historical Commission and E Clampus Vitus, 1987.

SAATATPA (Riverside Co.)

5.7 mi. W of I-10 near Beaumont, San Timoteo Cyn. Rd. along San Timoteo Creek, at mouth of Burn's Canyon

Saatatpa

Chief Juan Antonio and his band of Cahuilla Indians helped white settlers in the San Bernardino area defend their property and livestock against outlaws during the 1840s and 1850s. In late 1851, Juan Antonio, his warriors, and their families, settled at nearby Saatapta. During the winter of 1862–63 a smallpox epidemic swept through Southern California killing many Native Americans, including Juan Antonio. Cahuilla tradition asserts that the U.S. government sent army blankets that were contaminated with smallpox. After this disaster, Saatapta was abandoned.

Placed in cooperation with Riverside County Historical Commission and Billy Holcomb Chapter of E Clampus Vitus, 1987.

SACRAMENTO (Sacramento Co.)   *1809 C St.*
California Almond Growers Exchange
Almond Processing Facility

The California Almond Growers Exchange, founded in 1910, was the first successful grower-owned cooperative for marketing California almonds. It pioneered in many fields, including almond production, mechanization, and marketing. The first structure on this property was built in 1915 and was designed to merchanize almond processing. This shelling plant was one of the earliest structures of its type, and contained the world's first mechanical cracker.

Placed in cooperation with California Almond Growers Exchange, 1985.

SACRAMENTO (Sacramento Co.)   *W of 10th St. and Capitol Mall*
intersection
California's Historic Capitol

The historic capitol was designed by architects M. F. Butler and Ruben Clark. Its style is an adaption of Roman Corinthian architecture. Work began in 1860, and by late 1869 the capitol was partly occupied. In 1874, construction ended at a cost of $2.45 million. The west wing which once housed all branches of government is now a legislative facility. Its design and construction are tributes to California's pioneer architects, craftsmen, and builders.

Placed in cooperation with State Legislature, 1974.

SACRAMENTO (Sacramento Co.)   *SW corner 3rd and R sts.*
California's First Passenger Railroad

The Sacramento Valley Railroad, running from Sacramento to Folsom, was begun at this site on Feb. 12, 1855. Here, at Third and R streets, was located the Sacramento passenger terminal. The turntable and freight depot were at Third and Front streets. Completion of the railroad was celebrated at Folsom on Feb. 22, 1856.

Placed by California State Park Commission in cooperation with Sacramento County Historical Society, 1955.

SACRAMENTO (Sacramento Co.)   *NE corner Sutterville Rd.*
and Land Park Dr.

Camp Union, Sutterville

The 5th Infantry Regiment, California Volunteers, was organized here on 8 Oct. 1861 and trained by brevet Brig. Gen. George W. Bowie for duty in Arizona, New Mexico, and Texas against the Confederate forces. Since this was the year of the great flood, the troops aided the flood-stricken capitol. Company F (Sacramento Rangers), 2nd Cavalry Regiment, California Volunteers, was organized in Sacramento 29 Aug. 1861 and later served here. This company furnished a large number of officers for other units of the California Volunteers.

Placed by California State Park Commission in cooperation with Sacramento Historic Landmarks Commission and Lt. Lansdale Post No. 67 of Veterans of Foreign Wars of U.S., 1959.

SACRAMENTO (Sacramento Co.)   *Sutter's Fort State Historic Park,*
NE corner 28th and L sts.

The Coloma Road

Sutter's Fort, established by Capt. John A. Sutter in August 1839, marked the western end of the Coloma Road. Opened in 1847, this road ran from the fort to Sutter's sawmill at Coloma. Used by James W. Marshall in January 1848 to bring the news of the gold discovery to Sutter, it was traversed later by thousands of miners going to and from the diggings. In 1849 the Coloma road became the route of California's first stageline, established by James E. Birch.

Placed by California State Park Commission in cooperation with Sacramento County Historical Society and Grand Parlors of Native Sons and Native Daughters of the Golden West, 1960.

SACRAMENTO (Sacramento Co.)   *Haggin Oaks Muncipal*
Golf Course, 3645 Fulton Ave.,
N side of clubhouse

First Transcontinental Railroad—Western Base of the Sierra Nevada

On Jan. 12, 1864, President Abraham Lincoln decreed that where the Central Pacific Railroad crossed Arcade Creek, the western base of the Sierra Nevada began. The hardships of railroad construction through mountains resulted in increased government subsidies. These funds gave the company impetus to finish the transcontinental railroad.

Placed in cooperation with New Helvetia Chapter No. 5 of E Clampus Vitus, 1971.

SACRAMENTO (Sacramento Co.)   *California State University campus,*
on Jed Smith Dr., N side
of Guy West bridge

Five Mile Station

Departing at 2:45 a.m. from the Alta Telegraph Company in Sacramento, Pony Rider Sam (Bill) Hamilton carried the first mail eastward of the Central Overland Pony Express on Apr. 4, 1860. Here, quickly changing ponies, he sped on to the next stop at Fifteen Mile Station.

Placed by California State Park Commission in cooperation with Sacramento Historic Landmarks Commission, Sacramento Co. Historical Society, and Central Overland Pony Express Trail Association, 1960.

SACRAMENTO (Sacramento Co.)   *SW corner 16th and H sts.*

Governor's Mansion

This mansard-styled Victorian house was built for Albert Gallatin in 1877. It was acquired by the State of California and served as the first official governor's residence. Governor George C. Pardee and his family moved in during November 1903. It ultimately served as home for 13 governors over a span of 64 years.

Placed in cooperation with Sutter Parlor No. 111 of Native Daughters of the Golden West and Elk Grove Parlor No. 41 of Native Sons of the Golden West, 1968.

SACRAMENTO (Sacramento Co.)   *1000 2nd St., Old Sacramento*
B. F. Hastings Bank Building
(Western Terminus of the Pony Express)
(Plaque on wall at 2nd St., between J and I sts.)

This structure, erected in 1852–53, was occupied during the 1850s by the B. F. Hastings Bank, Wells Fargo & Company, various state officials, Sacramento Valley Railroad, and the Alta Telegraph Company and its successor, the California State Telegraph Company, who were the agents here for the Central Overland Pony Express, owned and operated by the firm of Russell, Majors, and Waddell. From this historic site the first overland journey eastward of the Pony Express was begun on Apr. 4, 1860.

Placed by California State Park Commission in cooperation with Sacramento Historic Landmarks Commission, Sacramento County Historical Society, California Historical Society, and Grand Parlors of Native Sons and Native Daughters of the Golden West, 1960.

SACRAMENTO (Sacramento Co.)   *117–119 K St., Old Sacramento*
The Lady Adams Building

Built in 1852 by the Lady Adams Mercantile Company, named after the brig which brought the partners around the Horn, she has survived fires, flood, and being lifted one story. She has served merchants, bankers, and as a "rooming house," and has been flat busted more than once. The only survivor of the fire of November 1852. She was named California Historical Landmark No. 603 on May 22, 1957, before we got around to it.

Placed by New Helvetia Chapter No. 5 of E Clampus Vitus, 1976.

SACRAMENTO (Sacramento Co.)   *NE corner Alhambra Blvd.*
and J St.

New Helvetia Cemetery

Established by John Sutter in 1849. Purchased in 1857 by J.W. Reeves who later deeded it to the City of Sacramento. 1,009 Chinese buried here were shipped to China by the Chinese societies who deeded their plots to the city.

Placed by Sutter Parlor No. 111 of Native Daughters of the Golden West, 1937.

SACRAMENTO (Sacramento Co.)   *NE corner 6th and H sts.*
Old Folsom Powerhouse—Sacramento Station

The first distribution point of electricity for a major city, Station A was constructed in 1894. Built by the Sacramento Electric Power and Light Company to receive power generated from Folsom Powerhouse. The first transmission of electricity was on July 13, 1895. This power distribution network resulted in the first overhead wire streetcar system in the Central Valley.

Placed 1970.

SACRAMENTO (Sacramento Co.)

Old Sacramento
State Historic Park

Old Sacramento

(Plaque located on wall at 2nd St.,
between J and I sts.)

Founded in December 1848 by John A. Sutter, Jr., Sacramento was an outgrowth of Sutter's Fort established by his father, Capt. John A. Sutter, in 1839. State Capitol since 1854, it was a major distribution point during the gold rush, a commercial and agricultural center, and terminus for wagon train, stagecoach, riverboat, telegraph, pony express, and the first transcontinental railroad.

Placed by California State Park Commission in cooperation with City and County of Sacramento, 1966.

SACRAMENTO (Sacramento Co.)   *SW corner Broadway and 10th sts.*

Sacramento City Cemetery

Resting place of California pioneers, this cemetery was established in 1850. Many of the victims of the cholera epidemic of that year are buried here. Included among the graves of illustrious Californians are those of governors John Bigler, Newton Booth, and William Irwin; Gen. George Wright, hero of the Mexican War; Mark Hopkins, co-builder of the Central Pacific Railroad; Gen. Albert M. Winn, founder of the Native Sons of the Golden West; Hardin Bigelow, first Mayor of Sacramento; William S. Hamilton, son of Alexander Hamilton; E. B. Crocker, founder of the Crocker Art Gallery; and Rev. O.C. Wheeler, organizer in 1850 of the First Baptist Church.

Placed by California State Park Commission in cooperation with Native Sons and Daughters of the Golden West, 1957.

SACRAMENTO (Sacramento Co.)

In sidewalk, between
Capitol and L sts.

First Synagogue Owned by Congregation B'nai Israel

This was the site of the first synagogue on the Pacific Coast, dedicated on Sept. 3, 1852. The building, prefabricated in Baltimore and shipped around Cape Horn in 1849, originally housed the Methodist Episcopal Church, whose trustees sold the edifice on June 4, 1852, to Alexander Myer, Joseph Levison, and Charles Friedman, officers of the Association of the Children of Israel (B'nai Israel). The congregation followed the orthodox tradition until 1880 when it became an adherent of reform Judaism.

Placed by California State Park Commission in cooperation with Congregation B'nai Israel and Sacramento Historic Landmarks Commission, 1958.

SACRAMENTO (Sacramento Co.)   *800 N St.*

"The children of California shall be my children."

This house built in the fifties was the birth place of Leland Stanford, Jr., and the home of his mother Jan Stanford, whose love for children was outstanding.

Placed by Rio Rita Parlor No. 253 of Native Daughters of the Golden West, 1934.

SACRAMENTO (Sacramento Co.)   *Sutter's Fort State Historic Park,*
27th and L sts.

Sutter's Fort

This memorial erected by the Native Sons and Native Daughters of the Golden West in honor of the first alcalde of New Helvetia; captain in the regular Mexican Army; good samaritan to the pioneers; one under whose regime gold was discovered; benefactor of the great State of California—
General John A. Sutter.

Fort restored as a result of movement inaugurated by Native Sons of the Golden West, the funds being originally provided by the Order, the State of California, and individuals. August 12, 1939.

SACRAMENTO (Sacramento Co.)   *N side of 29th and B sts.*

Captain John A. Sutter's Landing

Captain John A. Sutter, after coming up the Sacramento River from Yerba Buena in August 1839, landed approximately two hundred feet north of here, at what was then the south bank of the American River. A short time thereafter he established a permanent camp, and later built his fort. Sutter and his men were the first settlers within the present city limits of Sacramento.

Placed by California State Park Commission in cooperation with Native Sons and Native Daughters of the Golden West, and Sacramento Historic Landmarks Commission, 1958.

ST. HELENA (Napa Co.)   *2000 Main St.*

Beringer Brothers Winery

Built by Frederick and Jacob Beringer, natives of Mainz, Germany, this winery has the unique distinction of never having ceased operations since its founding in 1876. Here, in the European tradition, were dug underground wine tunnels hundreds of feet in length. These maintain a constant temperature of 58 degrees, a factor considered necessary in the maturing and aging of fine wines.

Placed in cooperation with La Junta Parlor No. 302 of Native Daughters of the Golden West, 1967.

ST. HELENA (Napa Co.)   *Krug Ranch, 2800 Main St.*

Charles Krug Winery

Founded in 1861 by Charles Krug (1825–92), this is the oldest operating winery in Napa Valley. The pioneer winemaker of this famous wine region, Krug made the first commercial wine in Napa County in 1858, at Napa.

Placed by California State Park Commission in cooperation with California Historical Society and Napa County Historical Society, 1957.

ST. HELENA (Napa Co.)   *3 mi. NW, Bale Grist Mill State*
Historic Park, 3369 N. St. Helena Hwy.

Old Bale Mill

This historic grist mill, known as the "Bale Mill," was erected by Dr. E. T. Bale, grantee Carne Humana Rancho, in 1846. The mill, with surrounding land, was deeded to the Native Sons of the Golden West by Mrs. W. W. Lyman. Restored through the efforts of the Native Son Parlors of Napa County, under the leadership of past Grand President Bismark Bruck, a grandson of Dr. Bale, and by the Historic Landmarks Committee of the Native Sons of the Golden West. The restored mill was dedicated June 21, 1925.

Placed by Historic Landmarks Committee of Native Sons of the Golden West.

SALINAS (Monterey Co.)   *3 mi. SW on old Hwy. 68, SW corner SH 68 and Spreckels Blvd.*

Hill Town Ferry
Historical Monument
1867–1889
marked by
San Jose de Guadalupe
Chapter
Daughters of the American
Colonists
1957

Private plaque.

SALINAS (Monterey Co.)   *Boronda Adobe Historic Center, 333 Boronda Rd.*

Jose Eusebio Boronda Adobe Casa

Built between 1844 and 1848 by Jose Eusebio Boronda, this is an outstanding example of a Mexican-era rancho adobe. Virtually unaltered since its construction, it shows many features of the "Monterey Colonial" style which resulted from the fusion of New England and California building traditions during California's Mexican period.

Placed in cooperation with Monterey County Historical Society, Inc., and Monterey Bay Chapter of A.I.A., 1974.

SALINAS (Monterey Co.)   *5 mi. NE, SE corner San Juan Grade and Crazy Horse Canyon Rd.*

Battle of Natividad

Combined American forces under Captains Charles D. Burrass (or Burroughs) and Bluford K. Thompson clashed with Comandante Manuel de Jesus Castro's Californians in this vicinity on Nov. 16, 1846. Casualties on each side consisted of several men killed and wounded. The Americans saved a large herd of horses for Lt. Col. John C. Fremont, who then later proceeded south to participate in the Armistice at Cahuenga in January 1847.

Placed by California State Park Commission in cooperation with Monterey County Historical Society, County of Monterey, and Monterey-Viejo No. 1846 of E Clampus Vitus, 1958 and 1983.

SALINAS (Monterey Co.)   *Sherwood Gardens Rodeo Grounds, Community Center, 940 N. Main St.*

Salinas Temporary Detention Center

This monument is dedicated to the 3,586 Monterey Bay area residents of Japanese ancestry, most of whom were American citizens, temporarily confined in the

Salinas Rodeo Grounds during World War II, from April to July 1942. They were detained without charges, trial, or establishment of guilt before being incarcerated in permanent camps, mostly at Poston, Arizona. May such injustice and humiliation never recur.

Placed in cooperation with Japanese American Citizens League chapters of Salinas Valley, Gilroy, Monterey Peninsula, San Benito County, and Watsonville, and the City of Salinas, 1984.

SAN ANDREAS (Calaveras Co.)

5 mi. S, on SH 49 at San Antonio Creek

Fourth Crossing

Located on the Stockton-Murphys road at the fourth crossing of the Calaveras River, this early mining settlement, once called "Foremans," was famous in the 1850s for its rich placer ores. Later it became an important stage and freighting depot and served the southern mines until after the turn of the century.

Placed by California State Park Commission in cooperation with Calaveras County Historical Society, 1965.

SAN ANDREAS (Calaveras Co.)

NW corner SH 49 and Main St.

San Andreas
Heart of the Southern Mines

Settled by Mexicans in 1848. Named after Catholic Parish of St. Andrew. First newspaper published here Sept. 24, 1856. Destroyed by fire June 4, 1858, and in 1863. County seat of Calaveras County since 1866. Rendezvous of Joaquin Murietta. Black Bart, notorious stage robber, tried and sent to prison from here. Noted mining camp since early days. Gold from the surrounding ancient river channels and placer mines contributed greatly to the success of the Union during the Civil War.

Placed by Calaveras County Chamber of Commerce, 1930.

SAN BERNARDINO (San Bernardino Co.)

N of softball field, Wildwood Park, Waterman and 40th sts. intersection

The Arrowhead Landmark

Located in the foothills of the San Bernardino Mountains directly above the City of San Bernardino, the arrowhead landmark can be seen for miles around. This important landmark has for centuries been a symbol of the San Bernardino Valley to the Native Indians and then to the pioneers and settlers that followed. It is believed to be a natural landmark. The face of the arrowhead consists of light quartz, supporting a growth of short white sage. This lighter vegetation shows in sharp contrast to the surrounding chaparral and greasewood. Indians who inhabited the San Bernardino Valley believed that the arrowhead pointed the way to the hot mineral springs below, with healing qualities, and thus considered it holy ground. Through the years, numerous forest fires have caused some erosion. But the arrowhead landmark continues to preserve its uniqueness and remains a symbol of the "pioneer spirit" of the San Bernardino Valley.

Placed by Friends of the Arrowhead, Inc., 1988.

SAN BERNARDINO (San Bernardino Co.) *20 mi. N, 3.6 mi. W of I-15,*
SH 138 in W. Cajon Canyon

Mormon Trail Monument

In June 1851, 500 Mormon pioneers came through this pass to enter the San Bernardino Valley where they colonized and established a prosperous community.
Placed by Sons of Mormon Pioneers, 1937.

SAN BERNARDINO (San Bernardino Co.) *17 mi. N,*
SE corner I-15 and SH 138

Santa Fe and Salt Lake Trail
1849

Erected in honor of the brave pioneers of California in 1917 by pioneers Sheldon Stoddard, Sydney P. Waite, John Brown, Jr., George Miller, George M. Cooley, Silas C. Cox, Richard Weir, Jasper N. Corbett.
Private plaque.

SAN BERNARDINO (San Bernardino Co.) *County Courthouse,*
corner of Court
and Arrowhead Ave.

Site of Mormon Stockade

On this site in 1893 was built the first house in San Bernardino, the home of Jose del Carmen Lugo, one of the grantees of the Rancho San Bernardino—also on this site, in 1851, a stockade of logs was built as a protection against Indians. In it more than a hundred pioneer families lived for over a year.
Placed by Arrowhead Parlor of Native Sons of the Golden West, 1927.

SAN BERNARDINO (San Bernardino Co.) *16 mi. N, NW corner I-15*
and Cleghorn Rd.

Santa Fe & Salt Lake Trail
Erected by Pioneer Society of San Bernardino, 1912

Sheldon Stoddard
Sydney P. Waite
came over this trail
1849
helped erect this monument, 1912
Private plaques.

SAN CLEMENTE (San Diego Co.) *San Clemente Civic Center,*
100 Avenida Presidio

La Cristianita

Two miles inland from this point, in Los Cristianitos Valley, the first Christian baptism in Alta California was performed by Padre Francisco Gomez, a member of the Portola expedition in 1769.
Placed by California State Park Commission in cooperation with Orange County, 1957.

SAN CLEMENTE (San Diego Co.)

*On Cristianita Rd.,
Camp Pendleton, 3 mi. E
of I-5 at San Clemente*

La Cristianita

Near this spring, the first Christian baptism in Alta California was performed by Padre Francisco Gomez, a member of the Portola expedition in 1769.

Placed by California State Park Commission in cooperation with San Diego County and U.S. Marine Corps, 1957.

SAN CLEMENTE (San Diego Co.)

*10 mi. S, .9 mi. SW of I-15,
.6 mi. SE of Las Pulgas Gate,
Camp Pendleton, on hill
1,000 ft. W of Boy Scouts adobe*

Las Flores (San Pedro) Asistencia

From 1823 to the 1840s the tile-roofed adobe chapel and hostel at Las Flores, built by Father Antonio Peyri, served as the asistencia to Mission San Luis Rey and provided comfort to travelers on El Camino Real. The adobe structure and adjacent corral were the site of the April 1838 battle between Juan Bautista Alvarado and Carlos Antonio Carrillo contesting the provincial governorship of Alta California.

Placed in cooperation with U.S. Marine Corps and Squibob Chapter of E Clampus Vitus, 1983.

SAN DIEGO (San Diego Co.)

3950 Conde St., Old Town

Adobe Chapel of the Immaculate Conception

Originally built as the home of San Diego's John Brown in 1850, the house was converted to a church by Don Jose Aguirre in 1858. Father Antonio D. Ubach, formerly a missionary among the Indians, was parish priest here from 1866 to 1907. It is said that he was the model for "Father Gaspara" in Helen Hunt Jackson's *Ramona*. In 1937 the WPA rebuilt the adobe chapel close to its original site.

Placed in cooperation with City of San Diego, San Diego County Historical Days Association, and Squibob Chapter of E Clampus Vitus, 1988.

SAN DIEGO (San Diego Co.)

*U.S.N. Submarine Support Fac.,
east side of Kephart and
Page rds., Point Loma*

Ballast Point Whaling Station Site

Late in 1857, the three Johnson brothers and the twin Packard brothers came to this site to survey possibilities for a station to "try out" or extract whale oil. Their operations began the next year. In 1869 the U.S. Government acquired the property for Fort Rosecrans, and in 1873 whaling operations at Ballast Point ended.

Placed in cooperation with U.S. Department of the Navy, Fort Guijarros Museum Foundation, and Squibob Chapter of E Clampus Vitus, 1987.

SAN DIEGO (San Diego Co.)
On Mason St., between San Diego Ave.
and Calhoun St., Old Town

Casa de Bandini

Dedicated to
Juan Bandini
1800–1859
Patriot and friend of the United States;
by San Diego Chapter, D.A.R.
and San Diego Chapter, S.A.R.
March 26, 1960.

SAN DIEGO (San Diego Co.)
4136 Wallace St., NW corner,
Presidio Hills Golf Course, Old Town

Casa de Carrillo

Presidio comandante Francisco Maria Ruiz built this house next to his 1808 pear garden late in 1821 for his close relative and fellow soldier, Joaquin Carrillo, and his large family. From this adobe dwelling, in April 1829, daughter Josefa Carrillo eloped to Chile with Henry Delano Fitch. When Ruiz died in 1839 and Joaquin soon afterwards, son Ramon Carrillo sold this property to Lorenzo Soto. It was transferred several times before 1932, deteriorating gradually, until George Marston and Associates restored the house and grounds and deeded them to the City of San Diego as a golf course.

Placed in cooperation with San Diego City Department of Parks and Recreation and Squibob Chapter of E Clampus Vitus, 1994.

SAN DIEGO (San Diego Co.)
3890 Twiggs St., Old Town

Casa de Lopez

Built by Juan Francisco Lopez, one of San Diego's early Spanish settlers, the casa larga, or long house, was among the first substantial houses built in the pueblo of San Diego, about 1835. In 1846 it was the home of Juan Matias Moreno, secretary to Pio Pico, California's last Mexican governor.

Placed by California State Park Commission.

SAN DIEGO (San Diego Co.)
2616 San Diego Ave., Old Town

Casa de Miguel Pedrorena

Don Miguel Elesforo Pedrorena arrived in San Diego in 1838. Married Maria Antonia Estudillo in 1842. In 1869 this adobe house was built by his son, Miguel Pedrorena.

Private plaque.

SAN DIEGO (San Diego Co.)
Presidio Park, SE corner
Presidio Dr. and Taylor St.

Derby Dike

Until 1853 the erratic San Diego River dumped tons of debris into the harbor or poured into False Bay, now Mission Bay. At times it threatened to destroy Old Town San Diego. Lieutenant George Horatio Derby, U.S. Topographical Corps, built a dike that diverted the waters into False Bay. This was the first effort to tame the river, and one of the first U.S. government projects in California. The river was not fully harnessed until the 1950s.

Placed in cooperation with San Diego Department of Parks and Recreation and Squibob Chapter of E Clampus Vitus, 1990.

SAN DIEGO (San Diego Co.)
Mission San Diego de Alcala, 10818 San Diego Mission Rd.

El Camino Real

This plaque is placed on the 250th anniversary of the birth of California's apostle, Padre Junipero Serra, O. F. M., to mark the southern terminus of El Camino Real as Padre Serra knew it and helped blaze it. 1713–November 24–1963.

Placed by California State Park Commission in cooperation with Committee for El Camino Real, 1963.

SAN DIEGO (San Diego Co.)
3966 Mason St., Old Town

Main Street School

First public schoolhouse in this county. Erected at this site in 1865 and known as "Mason Street School—District No. 1" when San Diego County covered an area larger than three New England states. Restored by popular subscription in 1955.

Placed by San Diego Board of Supervisors and Historical Markers Committee, 1955.

SAN DIEGO (San Diego Co.)
End of Rosecrans St., U.S.N. Submarine Support Fac., Point Loma

Fort Rosecrans

President Millard Fillmore's Executive Order of 1852 created a U.S. preserve on Point Loma. From 1870 to 1873 the Coast Artillery Corpsmen evicted whalers from the site in order to begin the military installation. In 1899 it was named for William S. Rosecrans, Civil War general and California congressman. Major fortifications were constructed in 1891–1903 and 1941–43. Transferred to the U.S. Navy in 1957, it became a submarine support facility.

Placed in cooperation with U.S. Department of the Navy and Squibob Chapter of E Clampus Vitus, 1993.

SAN DIEGO (San Diego Co.)
Cabrillo Memorial Dr., Point Loma

Fort Rosecrans National Cemetery

A burial ground before 1847, this graveyard became an Army post cemetery in the 1860s. It is the final resting place for most who fell at San Pasqual in 1846, and for the *USS Bennington* victims of 1905. It became Fort Rosecrans National Cemetery in 1934 and was placed under the Veterans Administration National Cemetery System in 1937. Over 50,000 who served the U.S. honorably in war and peace lie here.

Placed in cooperation with U.S. Department of Veterans Affairs and Squibob Chapter of E Clampus Vitus, 1990.

SAN DIEGO (San Diego Co.)
Presidio Park, Old Town

Erected in Honor of the 500 Volunteer Soldiers of the Mormon Battalion 1846–48

In the midst of preparations for their exodus to the valley of the Great Salt Lake, the Mormon pioneers were asked by the United States government to enlist a battalion of 500 volunteers for service in the war with Mexico. These troops started from western Iowa in July 1846 and arrived in San Diego Jan. 29, 1847, completing

135

the longest infantry march in history. This expedition helped with the war, prepared the way for colonization of the southwest, opened new trade routes, and strengthened distant national boundaries.

Placed by National Society of the Sons of Utah Pioneers, 1969.

SAN DIEGO (San Diego Co.)   *SE corner Market St. and Pacific Hwy.*
La Punta de Los Muertos
(Dead Men's Point)

Burial site of sailors and marines in 1782 when San Diego Bay was surveyed and charted by Don Juan Pantoja y Arriaga, pilot, and Don Jose Tovar, mate, of the royal frigates *La Princesa* and *La Favortia* under command of Don Agustin de Echeverria.

Placed by San Diego County Board of Supervisors and Historical Markers Committee, 1954.

SAN DIEGO (San Diego Co.)   *Old Mission Dam Park,*
1.9 mi. N of Mission Gorge Rd.,
on Fr. Junipero Serra Trail

Old Mission Dam

Built 1813–16. A part of the first permanent irrigation project by white men in California.

Placed by San Diego Chapter of Daughters of the American Revolution, 1941.

SAN DIEGO (San Diego Co.)   *Mission San Diego de Alcala,*
10818 San Diego Mission Rd.

California's first mission
founded July 16, 1769
by
Junipero Serra OFM
Placed by San Diego Chapters of Daughters and Sons of the American Revolution.

SAN DIEGO (San Diego Co.)   *Montgomery-Walker Park,*
NE corner Coronado Ave.
and Beyer Blvd., S. San Diego

Montgomery Memorial

John J. Montgomery made man's first controlled winged flights from this hilltop in August 1883. He opened for all mankind the "great highway of the sky."

Placed by San Diego Junior Chamber of Commerce Montgomery Memorial Committee, 1950.

SAN DIEGO (San Diego Co.)   *Base of Pier 160, Naval Oceans*
Systems Center, Point Loma

Near this site in 1829
the Stars and Stripes
were first (unofficially) raised
in what is now
the State of California
Placed by San Diego Girl Scouts, 1934.

SAN DIEGO (San Diego Co.)   *Cabrillo National Monument,*
Point Loma

Old Point Loma Lighthouse

This lighthouse, built in 1854, was one of the first eight lighthouses on the Pacific Coast. It continued in use until 1891, when the new Pelican Point Lighthouse began operating. The Point Loma Lighthouse became the site of the Cabrillo National Monument in 1913. During World War II the Navy used it as a signal tower. Today the lighthouse remains the central feature of the Point Loma Preserve.

Placed in cooperation with National Park Service and Squibob Chapter of E Clampus Vitus, 1988.

SAN DIEGO (San Diego Co.)   *Old Town State Historic Park*

Old Town San Diego

(Plaque located at 4016 Wallace St., W side of plaza)

Settled by pensioned soldiers and their families from the Presidio, Old Town grew in the early 1800s into a cluster of adobe houses and garden plots. By 1835 "it was composed of about 40 dark brown looking huts." The Stars and Stripes were first raised over the plaza in 1846 by Marines from the U.S.S. *Cyane.*

Placed in cooperation with local, civic, and historical organizations, 1969.

SAN DIEGO (San Diego Co.)   *Old Town Plaza, Old Town*

Plaza de San Diego Viejo
(Washington Square)

On this spot the United States flag was first raised in Southern California by Lt. Stephen C. Rowan U.S.N., commanding sailors and marines, July 29, 1846.

Private plaque.

SAN DIEGO (San Diego Co.)   *Parking lot on north side of Market St.,*
between Kettner Blvd. and California St.

San Diego Barracks
1850–1921

An army supply depot for Southern California was established on this site in 1850. Designated new San Diego post, it was garrisoned by troops from Dec. 2, 1858, to May, 1866. Reoccupied December, 1869. Name changed to San Diego Barracks Apr. 5, 1879. Abandoned Dec. 15, 1921. Acquired by City of San Diego July 13, 1938.

Placed by San Diego County Board of Supervisors and Historical Markers Committee, 1955.

SAN DIEGO (San Diego Co.)   *Presidio Park, Old Town*

San Diego Presidio Site

Soldiers, sailors, Indians, and Franciscan missionaries from New Spain occupied the land at Presidio Hill on May 17, 1769, as a military outpost. Two months later, Fr. Junipero Serra established the first San Diego mission on Presidio Hill. Officially proclaimed a Spanish presidio on Jan. 1, 1774, the fortress was later occupied by a succession of Mexican forces. The presidio was abandoned in 1837 after San Diego became a pueblo.

Placed in cooperation with San Diego Department of Parks and Recreation and Squibob Chapter of E Clampus Vitus, 1992.

SAN DIEGO (San Diego Co.)

San Diego State University, N end Aztec Bowl, at Scripps Terr. and Canyon Crest Dr. intersection

San Diego State University

In 1960 the state legislature authorized the California state colleges to grant honorary doctoral degrees to individuals who have made unusual contributions toward learning and civilization. On June 6, 1963, San Diego State College was the first of the California state colleges to award the doctorate when it conferred a Doctor of Laws degree on John F. Kennedy, President of the United States.

Placed in cooperation with San Diego State University and Squibob Chapter of E Clampus Vitus, 1983.

SAN DIEGO (San Diego Co.)

Presidio Park, SE corner Presidio Dr. and Taylor St.

Serra Palm

Traditionally the earliest planted tree in California. Directly in the rear, beneath the brow of the hill, lie the dead of the sacred expedition of 1769. Burial place of our first unknown soldiers.

Placed by California Centennial Commission in cooperation with San Diego County Historical Markers Committee, 1950.

SAN DIEGO (San Diego Co.)

U.S.N. Submarine Fac., at end of Rosecrans Ave., 500 ft. S of Kerricks Rd., Point Loma

Fort Guijarros Site

An outpost of Spain's far-flung empire at its greatest extent, this fort was completed before 1800 from plans drawn by Alberto de Cordoba in 1795. Its major action came under Corp. Jose Velasquez on Mar. 22, 1803, in the "Battle of San Diego Bay" with the American Brig *Lelia Byrd,* which was smuggling sea otter pelts.

Placed in cooperation with U.S. Department of the Navy, Casa de Espana, San Diego Cannoneers, San Diego Archaeological Society, and Squibob Chapter of E Clampus Vitus, 1981.

SAN DIEGO (San Diego Co.)   *NW corner Garnet Ave. and Pico St.*
Kate Olivia Sessions' Nursery Site
1857–1940

This plaque commemorates the life and influence of a woman who envisioned San Diego beautiful. On this site she operated a nursery and gained world renown as a horticulturist. She was the first woman to receive the International Meyer Medal in genetics.

Placed by California State Park Commission in cooperation with Pacific Beach Woman's Club, 1961.

SAN DIEGO (San Diego Co.)
Spanish Landing Park, Harbor Dr.
Spanish Landing

Near this point, sea and land parties of the Portola-Serra expedition met. Two ships, the *San Antonio* and *San Carlos,* anchored on May 4–5, 1769. The scurvy-weakened survivors of the voyage established a camp, where on May 14 and July 1 they greeted the overland parties from Baja California. Together they began the Spanish occupation of Alta California.

Placed in cooperation with San Diego Unified Port District and Squibob Chapter of E Clampus Vitus, 1976.

SAN DIEGO (San Diego Co.)
U.S. Coast Guard Station, end of Guijarros Rd., Point Loma
Cabrillo Landing

Seeking the mythical Strait of Anian (the Northwest Passage) for Spain, on Sept. 28, 1542, Iberian navigator Juan Rodriguez Cabrillo brought his three ships to Ballast Point, the first European landing on the coast of Alta California.

Placed in cooperation with U.S. Department of the Navy and Squibob Chapter of E Clampus Vitus, 1992.

SAN DIEGO (San Diego Co.)
2482 San Diego Ave., Old Town
The Whaley House

Built by Thomas Whaley in 1856–57, this is the oldest brick structure in Southern California. In addition to being the home of the Whaley family, it served variously as granary, store, courthouse and school, and as the town's first theater. Whaley's home was the cultural center of San Diego as well as its most luxurious residence.

Placed by San Diego County Board of Supervisors and Historical Markers Committee, 1959.

SAN FERNANDO (Los Angeles Co.)
4 mi. NW, .1 mi. N of Foothill and Balboa blvds. intersection
The Cascades

This is the terminus of the Los Angeles-Owens River Aqueduct, bringing water 338 miles from the eastern slopes of the Sierra Nevada to the City of Los Angeles. Begun in 1905, the great aqueduct was completed Nov. 5, 1913. The Mono Craters tunnel project, completed in 1940, extended the system 27 miles to its present northernmost intake near Tioga Pass.

Placed by California State Park Commission in cooperation with Los Angeles Department of Water and Power, History and Landmarks Association of San Fernando and Antelope Valley Parlors of Native Sons and Native Daughters of the Golden West, and San Fernando Mission Parlor No. 280 of Native Daughters of the Golden West, 1958.

SAN FERNANDO (Los Angeles Co.)
12685 Foothill Blvd.
The Griffith Ranch

Originally part of the San Fernando Mission lands, this ranch was purchased by David Wark Griffith, revered pioneer of silent motion pictures, in 1912. It provided the locale for many western thrillers, including *Custer's Last Stand,* and was the inspiration for the immortal production *Birth of a Nation*. It was acquired by Fritz B. Burns in 1948 who has perpetuated the Griffith name in memory of the great film pioneer.

Placed by California State Park Commission in cooperation with Mr. Fritz B. Burns, History and Landmarks Association of San Fernando and Antelope Valley Parlors of Native Sons and Native Daughters of the Golden West, and San Fernando Mission Parlor No. 280 of Native Daughters of the Golden West, 1959.

SAN FRANCISCO (San Francisco Co.) 430 Bush St.

On This Site
January 18, 1869

The California Theatre, built by William C. Ralston, opened with the following stock company: John McCullough, Lawrence Barrett, Henry Edwards, Willie Edouin, E. B. Holmes, William Mestayer, John T. Raymond, W. F. Burroughs, W. H. Sedley Smith, John Wilson, Edward J. Buckley, Mrs. Judah Emelie Melville, Elizabeth Saunders, Annette Ince, Marie E. Gordon, Sophie Edwin, Minnie Walton, Julia Buckley. This theatre remained a brilliant center of drama until Aug. 11, 1888. Among artists who played here were Charles W. Couldock, Edwin Adams, John Braoughan, Edwin Booth, Barton Hill, Walter Montgomery, Mrs. D. P. Bowers, Adelaide Neilson, Lotta Crabtree.

Placed by Commonwealth Club of California and Pacific Telephone and Telegraph Company, 1932.

SAN FRANCISCO (San Francisco Co.) SE corner of fort wall, Fort Point, below Golden Gate Bridge

Castillo de San Joaquin

The first ship to enter San Francisco Bay, the *San Carlos* (Capt. Ayala), dropped anchor off this point Aug. 5, 1775. Lieutenant-Col. Don Juan Bautista de Anza planted the cross on Cantil Blanco (White Cliff) Mar. 28, 1776. The first fortification, Castillo de San Joaquin, was completed Dec. 8, 1794, by Jose Joaquin de Arrillaga, sixth governor of California. In 1853 United States Army engineers cut down the cliff and built Fort Point, renamed Fort Winfield Scott in 1882. This fort, a partial replica of Fort Sumter, is the only brick fort west of the Mississippi; its seawall has stood undamaged for over a hundred years.

Placed by San Francisco Chapter of Daughters of the American Revolution.

SAN FRANCISCO (San Francisco Co.) Golden Gate Park, on J.F. Kennedy Dr., .5 mi. W of John McLearn Lodge

The Conservatory

California's first municipal greenhouse was completed in 1879. It was patterned after the Conservatory, Kew Gardens, England. A distinguished example of late Victorian style using early techniques of mass production and assembly of simple glass units. It was a gift to the City of San Francisco by public-spirited citizens.

Placed in cooperation with San Francisco Recreation and Park Commission and California Historical Society, 1970.

SAN FRANCISCO (San Francisco Co.)

*Portsmouth Plaza,
Clay and Kearny sts.*

Andrew Smith Hallidie
(Site of Eastern Terminus First Street Cars
in World Propelled by Cable)

Commenced operation Aug. 1, 1873. Ceased Feb. 15, 1942. Invented and installed by Andrew S. Hallidie, born London, England, Mar. 16, 1836. Died San Francisco, Apr. 24, 1900. Pioneer manufacturer of wire cables; regent, University of California; twice member Board of Freeholders for drafting proposed city charter; served on first Board of Trustees 1878, of the San Francisco Public Library.

Placed by California State Park Commission in cooperation with Friends of Andrew S. Hallidie.

SAN FRANCISCO (San Francisco Co.)

*Mission San Francisco de Asis,
Dolores St., between 16th and 17th sts.*

El Camino Real

This plaque is placed on the 250th anniversary of the birth of California's apostle, Padre Junipero Serra, OFM, to mark the northern terminus of El Camino Real as Padre Serra knew it and helped to blaze it.

1713–November 24–1963

Placed by California State Park Commission in cooperation with Committee for El Camino Real, 1963.

SAN FRANCISCO (San Francisco Co.)

750 Kearny St.

Site of the Jenny Lind Theatre
and San Francisco City Hall

The third Jenny Lind Theatre was opened by Tom Maguire on Oct. 4, 1851, on the same site as the two preceeding it which were destroyed in the fire of 1851. In 1852 the City of San Francisco purchased this theatre for use as the city hall.

Placed by California Centennial Commission of the Society of California Pioneers, 1949.

SAN FRANCISCO (San Francisco Co.)

*Aquatic Park, NW corner
Beach and Larkin sts.*

Entrance of the *San Carlos*
into San Francisco Bay

First ship into San Francisco Bay on Aug. 5, 1775, the Spanish packet *San Carlos,* under the command of Lt. Juan Manuel de Ayala, became the first ship to enter San Francisco Bay. A month and a half was spent in surveying the bay from its southernmost reaches to the northern end of present-day Suisun Bay. The *San Carlos* departed Sept. 18, 1775.

Placed in cooperation with San Francisco Twin Bicentennial, Inc., 1975.

SAN FRANCISCO (San Francisco Co.)

202 Green St.

Farnsworth's Green Street Lab

In a simple laboratory on this site, 202 Green Street, Philo Taylor Farnsworth, U.S. pioneer in electronics, invented and patented the first operational all-electronic "television system." On Sept. 7, 1927, the 21-year-old inventor and several dedicated assistants successfully transmitted the first all-electronic television image, the major breakthrough that brought the practical form of this invention to mankind. Further patents formulated here covered the basic concepts essential to modern television. The genius of Green Street, as he was known, died in 1971.

Placed in cooperaton with Philo T. Farnsworth Foundation, Inc., 1981.

SAN FRANCISCO (San Francisco Co.) *S side of Sacramento between Davis and Front*

Fort Gunnybags

Fort Gunnybags was situated on this spot. Headquarters of the Vigilance Committee during the year 1856.

Placed by California Historic Landmarks League, 1903, and Historic Landmarks Committee of Native Sons of the Golden West, 1918.

SAN FRANCISCO (San Francisco Co.) *505 Montgomery St.*

Hudson's Bay Company

On this block, then on Yerba Buena's waterfront, stood the California headquarters of the Hudson's Bay Company. In 1841, their chief trader, William G. Rae, purchased the property and started operations. This venture caused wide speculation about British intentions. Inadequate profits, a declining fur catch, and pressure of U.S. expansion caused Hudson's Bay Company to end California operations.

Placed in cooperation with Redwood Coast Outpost of the "Westerners," 1968.

SAN FRANCISCO (San Francisco Co.) *552 Montgomery St.*

Landing Place of Captain J. B. Montgomery

On July 9, 1846, in the early morning, in "the days when the water came up to Montgomery Street," Commander John B. Montgomery—for whom Montgomery Street was named—landed near this spot from the U.S. sloop-of-war *Portsmouth,* to raise the Stars and Stripes on the plaza, now Portsmouth Square, one block to the west.

Placed by Native Sons of the Golden West, 1915.

SAN FRANCISCO (San Francisco Co.) *NE corner Jackson and Montgomery sts.*

Site of the Bank of Lucas, Turner & Co.
(Sherman's Bank)

William Tecumseh Sherman established the branch bank of Lucas, Turner & Co. in San Francisco in 1853. He settled the firm in their own building on the northeast corner of Jackson and Montgomery streets in the spring of 1854. Sherman successfully carried the bank through the financial crisis of 1855 and remained until they discontinued business in 1857.

Placed by California Centennial Commission in cooperation with the Society of California Pioneers, 1950.

SAN FRANCISCO (San Francisco Co.)
Dolores St., between 16th and 17th sts.

Mision San Francisco de Asis
(Mission Dolores)

This edifice, the construction of which was started in 1788, was dedicated Aug. 2, 1791. An adobe structure in use since that time, it is the oldest building in San Francisco. Original adobe brick walls and roof tiles are still in place.

Placed by California State Society of Daughters of the American Revolution, 1975.

SAN FRANCISCO (San Francisco Co.)
In lobby, 600 Montgomery St.

The Montgomery Block

This, San Francisco's first fireproof building, erected in 1853 by Henry Wager Halleck, was the headquarters for many outstanding lawyers, financiers, writers, actors, and artists. James King of William, editor of the *Bulletin,* died here after being shot by James Casey, May 14, 1856. Escaping destruction in the fire of 1906, the building is preserved in memory of those who lived and worked in it.

Placed by California State Park Commission in cooperation with Society of California Pioneers.

SAN FRANCISCO (San Francisco Co.)
In lobby, Old Mint, 88 5th st.

Old United States Mint

The old mint (1869), San Francisco's second, is California's only such Federal Greek Revival structure. Due to unsurpassed productivity, it became a sub-treasury in 1874. Intact after the 1906 disaster, it served as clearinghouse bank, thus aiding in the city's reconstruction. Closed in 1937; restored 1972–76 by mint director Mary Brooks.

Placed in cooperation with San Francisco Landmarks Preservation Advisory Board, 1977.

SAN FRANCISCO (San Francisco Co.)
1538 Valencia St.

Original Site of Bancroft Library

Here, from 1881–1906, stood the library of Hubert Howe Bancroft who in 1860 began to collect the wealth of material which was to subsequently result in the writing of his monumental history of western North America. In 1905 the library was purchased by the University of California and removed the following year to its Berkeley campus.

Placed by California State Park Commission in cooperation with Friends of the Bancroft Library, California Historical Society, and St. Luke's Hospital, 1964.

SAN FRANCISCO (San Francisco Co.)
Intersection Mission and College sts.

St. Mary's College

In August 1863, Archbishop Joseph Sadoc Alemany, OP, opened St. Mary's College at this location with a faculty of two diocesan priests, four laymen, and two student teachers. In August 1868, at the invitation of the archbishop, Brother Justin McMahon and seven Christian brothers took charge of St. Mary's. The Christian brothers have manifested the principle characterized by the best education institutions: Excellence.

Placed by California State Park Commission in cooperation with St. Mary's College, its alumni, and California Historical Society, 1962.

SAN FRANCISCO (San Francisco Co.) — *Portsmouth Square Park, Kearny St. between Clay and Washington*

Portsmouth Plaza

On this spot the American flag was first raised in San Francisco by Commander John B. Montgomery of U.S.S. *Portsmouth,* July 9, 1846.

Placed by San Francisco Chapter of Daughters of the American Revolution, 1924.

SAN FRANCISCO (San Francisco Co.) — *SW corner Funston Ave. and Lincoln Blvd.*

Presidio of San Francisco

Formally established on Sept. 17, 1776, the San Francisco Presidio has been administered successively as a military headquarters by Spain, Mexico, and the United States. A major command post during the Mexican War, Civil War, Spanish-American War, World Wars I and II, and the Korean War. It remains a symbol of United States authority in the Pacific.

Placed by California State Park Commission in cooperation with California History Commission and United States Army, 1965.

SAN FRANCISCO (San Francisco Co.) — *NE corner Rincon and Bryant sts.*

Rincon Hill

A fashionable neighborhood in the 1860s, Rincon Hill was the home of William Tecumseh Sherman, William C. Ralston, William Gwin, H. H. Bancroft, and others. By the 1880s the hill, already partially leveled, became a working class district. Today it is nearly invisible beneath the Bay Bridge. This plaque is mounted on the retaining wall of St. Mary's Hospital, built 1861 but destroyed in the fire of 1906.

Placed in cooperation with Yerba Buena Chapter of E Clampus Vitus, and Charles Albert Shumate, 1981.

SAN FRANCISCO (San Francisco Co.) — *First Unitarian Church, Franklin, between Starr King and Geary*

Sarcophagus of Thomas Starr King

Apostle of liberty, humanitarian, Unitarian minister, who in the Civil War bound California to the Union and led her to excel all other states in support of the United States Sanitary Commission, predecessor to the American Red Cross. His statue, together with that of Father Junipero Serra, represents California in the national capitol. His name is borne by a Yosemite Peak—"A man to match our mountains."

Placed by California State Park Commission in cooperation with California Historical Society and First Unitarian Church of San Francisco, 1960.

SAN FRANCISCO (San Francisco Co.)　　　*In sidewalk, NE corner*
Bush and Market sts.

Shoreline Markers

This tablet marks the shoreline of San Francisco Bay at the time of the discovery of gold in California, Jan. 24, 1848. Map reproduced above delineates old shoreline.
Placed by Historic Landmarks Committee of Native Sons of the Golden West, 1921.

SAN FRANCISCO (San Francisco Co.)　　　*555 Montgomery St.*

Society of California Pioneers Organized on This Spot

In a building which stood on this site, known as the Mellus and Howard Warehouse, erected in 1848, the Society of California Pioneers was organized Aug. 31, 1850, its object to collect and preserve the history of California. W.D.M. Howard was its first president. Oldest historical society in State.
Placed by California Centennial Commission with the cooperation of Society of California Pioneers, 1950.

SAN FRANCISCO (San Francisco Co.)　　　*269 Bush St.*

Site of First California State Fair

California's first state fair was held on this site on Oct. 4, 1854. Sponsored by the California State Agricultural Society, the exhibition of "horses, cattle, mules and other stock, and agricultural, mechanical, and domestic manufacture and productions" promoted the new state's growing agricultural industry. A different city held the fair each year, until Sacramento became the permanent location in 1861.
Placed in cooperation with Grand Parlor of Native Sons of the Golden West, 1973.

SAN FRANCISCO (San Francisco Co.)　　　*735 Montgomery St.*

First Jewish Religious Services

In a second-floor room in a store which stood on this location, 40 pioneers of Jewish faith gathered on Yom Kippur (5610) Sept. 26, 1849, and participated in the first Jewish religious services in San Francisco.
Placed by California Centennial Commission in cooperation with Society of California Pioneers, 1950.

SAN FRANCISCO (San Francisco Co.)　　　*728 Montgomery St.*

This Site Marks the Birthplace
of Freemasonry in California

At this location on Oct. 17, 1849, the first meeting of Free and Accepted Masons in the Golden State was held by California Lodge No. 1, F.&A.M.
Placed by California Lodge No. 1 of Free and Accepted Masons, 1948.

SAN FRANCISCO (San Francisco Co.)　　　*608–610 Commercial St.*

Site of First U.S. Branch Mint

The first United States branch mint in San Francisco was authorized by Congress July 3, 1852, and opened for operation Apr. 3, 1854. Dr. L. A. Birdsall was the first superintendent; J. Huston, first minter; and A. Haraszthy, first assayer.
Placed by California Centennial Commission with the cooperation of Society of California Pioneers, 1949.

SAN FRANCISCO (San Francisco Co.) *NW corner Bush and Market sts.*

Liberty Bell Slot Machine

Charles August Fey began inventing and manufacturing slot machines in 1894. Fey pioneered many innovations of coin-operated gaming devices in his San Francisco workshop at 406 Market Street, including the original three-reel bell slot machine in 1898. The international popularity of the bell slot machines attests to Fey's ingenuity as an enterprising inventor whose basic design of the three-reel slot machine continues to be used in mechanical gaming devices today.

Placed in cooperation with E Clampus Vitus, 1984.

SAN FRANCISCO (San Francisco Co.) *Traffic island, N side of Market St., between Bush and Battery sts.*

Site of Invention of the Three-Reel Bell Slot Machine

The first slot machines were manufactured by the inventor Charles Fey just west of this site at 406 Market, from 1896 until the factory was destroyed in the 1906 earthquake and fire. Fey, a Bavarian immigrant, dubbed his invention the "Liberty Bell" in honor of the famous symbol of freedom. Ultimately, the slot machine became the most famous gambling device of all time.

Placed by E Clampus Vitus, 1980.

SAN FRANCISCO (San Francisco Co.) *3333 California St., SE corner California and Walnut sts.*

Former Site of Laurel Hill Cemetery
1854–1946

The builders of the West, civic and military leaders, jurists, inventors, artists, and eleven United States senators are buried here—the most revered of San Francisco's hills.

Placed by California State Park Commission in cooperation with California Historical Society and Fireman's Fund Insurance Co., 1961.

SAN FRANCISCO (San Francisco Co.) *SE corner Mason and California sts.*

Site of the Mark Hopkins Institute of Art

In February 1893, Mr. Edward F. Searles donated the Hopkins mansion to the University of California in trust for the San Francisco Art Institute for "instruction in and illustration of the fine arts, music, and literature," and as San Francisco's first cultural center.

Placed by California State Park Commission in cooperation with San Francisco Art Institute, The Mark Hopkins Hotel, and California Historical Society, 1961.

SAN FRANCISCO (San Francisco Co.) *NE corner Grant Ave. and California St.*

Site of Old St. Mary's Cornerstone 1853—Dedicated 1854
(Plaque at Grant Ave. entrance)

The first building erected as a cathedral in California, Old St. Mary's served the Archdiocese of San Francisco in that capacity from 1854 to 1891. Once the city's most prominent building, much of its stonework was quarried and cut in China and its brick brought "around the Horn" in sailing ships.

Placed by California State Park Commission in cooperation with Paulist Fathers and Grand Parlor of Native Sons of the Golden West, 1966.

SAN FRANCISCO (San Francisco Co.)

SW corner Sacramento and Leidesdorff

Site of What Cheer House

This is the site of the famous What Cheer House, a unique hotel opened in 1852 by R. B. Woodward and destroyed by the fire of 1906. The What Cheer House catered to men only, permitted no liquor on the premises, and housed San Francisco's first free library and first museum.

Placed by California State Park Commission in cooperation with California Historical Society and American Trust Company, 1959.

SAN FRANCISCO (San Francisco Co.)

Coit Tower lobby, Telegraph Hill

Telegraph Hill

On the top of this hill stood the inner signal station, 1849, and the first western telegraph station, 1853.

Placed by Sequoia Chapter of Daughters of the American Revolution, 1929.

SAN FRANCISCO (San Francisco Co.)   *Naval Station, Treasure Island*

Treasure Island

This artificial island was constructed of bay sand in 1936–37. It was the site of the Golden Gate International Exposition, Feb. 18, 1939–Sept. 29, 1940. Tall towers, gigantic goddesses and dazzling lighting effects turned the island into a "magic city." The Exposition celebrated the ascendancy of California and San Francisco as economic, political, and cultural forces in the increasingly important pacific region. From 1939 to 1944 the island was the landing site for flights of the China Clipper. Treasure Island has been a U.S. Naval Station since 1941.

Placed in cooperation with U.S. Navy, Treasure Island Museum, GGIE Research Associates, and Art Deco Society of California, 1990.

SAN FRANCISCO (San Francisco Co.)

NW corner Geary and Powell sts.

Union Square

This was the center of San Francisco in pioneer days, deeded for public use Jan. 3, 1850, during the administration of John White Geary, first mayor and postmaster and later governor of Kansas and Pennsylvania. The name originated in 1860 when public meetings were held here in support of the Union.

Placed by California State Park Commission in cooperation with City of San Francisco and Francisco Landmarks Council, 1958.

SAN FRANCISCO (San Francisco Co.)　　　　601 Montgomery St.
Western Headquarters
of Russell, Majors, and Waddell

This was the site of the western business headquarters of Russell, Majors, and Waddell—founders, owners, and operators of the Pony Express, 1860–61. The firm's main office was in Leavenworth, Kansas. W. W. Finney was the western representative in San Francisco.

Placed by California State Park Commission in cooperation with Society of California Pioneers, 1960.

SAN FRANCISCO (San Francisco Co.)　　　　SW corner Mission
and Duboce sts.

Site of Woodward's Gardens

Woodward's Gardens occupied the block bounded by Mission, Duboce, Valencia, and 14th streets, with the main entrance on Mission Street. R. B. Woodward opened his gardens to the public in 1866 as an amusement park catering to all tastes. It was San Francisco's most popular resort until it closed in 1892.

Placed by California Centennial Commission with the cooperation of Society of California Pioneers, 1949.

SAN GABRIEL (Los Angeles Co.)　　　　537 W. Mission Dr.
Mission San Gabriel Arcangel

Founded Sept. 8, 1771, marked June 5, 1938, California Parlor No. 247 Native Daughters of the Golden West.

Private plaque.

SAN GABRIEL (Los Angeles Co.)　　　　616 S. Ramona St.
Ortega-Vigare Adobe

Erected during mission days 1792–1805. Second oldest adobe in this region. Originally "L" shaped, it is now only half original size. In 1859 became property of Don Jean Vigera. In early 1860s became San Gabriel's first bakery and was separated from mission's lime orchard by high cactus wall.

Placed by California Centennial Commission in cooperation with San Gabriel Valley Parlors No. 291 of Native Sons of the Golden West and No. 281 of Native Daughters of the Golden West, 1950.

SAN JACINTO (Riverside Co.)　　　　3 mi. W, near Cottonwood
and Sanderson sts. intersection

Soviet Transpolar Landing Site

Three miles west of this site on July 14, 1937, three Soviet aviators completed a transpolar flight from Moscow in 62 hours, 17 minutes, establishing a new world's nonstop distance record of 6,305 miles. The huge single-engine aircraft, an ANT-25 military reconnaissance monoplane, was shipped back to the Soviet Union and placed in a museum. Aircraft commander Mikhail Gromov, co-pilot Andrei Yumashev, and navigator Sergei Danilin became generals in World War II.

Placed in cooperation with San Jacinto Valley Transpolar Flight Committee, City of San Jacinto, Riverside County Historical Commission, Billy Holcomb Chapter of E Clampus Vitus, and Museum Associations of San Jacinto and Hemet, 1991.

SAN JOSE (Santa Clara Co.)   *1530 Blossom Hill Rd.*
Almaden Vineyards
On this site, in 1852, Charles LeFranc made the first commercial planting of fine European wine grapes in Santa Clara and founded Almaden Vineyards. LeFranc imported cuttings from vines in the celebrated wine districts of his native France, shipping them around the Horn under sail.
Placed by California State Park Commission.

SAN JOSE (Santa Clara Co.)   *432 S. 8th St.*
Site of Edwin Markham Home
Where the poet lived 1869–89. It now stands at the rear, preserved by Poet Laureate Bland, Markham Landmark Association, and Associated Students of San Jose State College.
Placed by the Edwin Markham Poetry Society, 1937.

SAN JOSE (Santa Clara Co.)   *San Jose State University,*
on Tower Hall in Washington Square,
NE corner San Carlos and 4th sts.
First Normal School
Founded as "Minns' Evening Normal School" in 1857, the school became the state normal school by act of the State Legislature on May 2, 1862. In 1870 the State Legislature chose Washington Square as a permanent location. Destroyed by fire on Feb. 11, 1880, and heavily damaged by the Apr. 18, 1906, earthquake, the school was rebuilt after each disaster to remain California's first public institution of higher learning.
Placed in cooperation with Sourisseau Academy, San Jose University Alumni, and Mountain Charlie Chapter No. 1850 of E Clampus Vitus, 1982.

SAN JOSE (Santa Clara Co.)   *Front parking lot planter,*
City Hall, 151 W. Mission St.
First Site of El Pueblo
de San Jose de Guadalupe
Within a year after the opening of the first overland route from Mexico to Alta California, Governor Felipe de Neve authorized establishment of California's first civil settlement in the state on lands including and surrounding the present civic center. Lieutenant Jose Joaquin Moraga, with 14 settlers and their families, arrived in the Santa Clara Valley to found el Pueblo de San Jose de Guadalupe on Nov. 29, 1777.
Placed in cooperation with San Jose Historic Landmarks Commission, 1977.

SAN JOSE (Santa Clara Co.)   *Main entrance, San Jose Intl. Airport,*
1661 Airport Blvd.
First Honeybees in California
Here, on the 1,939-acre Rancho Portrero de Santa Clara, Christopher A. Shelton in early March 1853 introduced the honeybee to California. In Aspinwall, Panama, Shelton purchased 12 beehives from a New Yorker and transported them by rail, "bongo," pack mule, and steamship to San Francisco. Only enough bees survived to fill one hive, but these quickly propagated, laying the foundation for California's modern beekeeping industry.

Placed in cooperation with Mountain Charlie Chapter No. 1850 of E Clampus Vitus, 1982.

SAN JOSE (Santa Clara Co.) 160 N. 3rd St.
First Unitarian Church
This building, designed by George W. Page in 1891, became the permanent home of a congregation that first met in City Hall in 1866. A version of Richardsonian Romanesque style, the innovative structure withstood the earthquake of 1906 and became a shelter for the injured. In 1906 the church women organized San Jose's first day nursery.

Placed in cooperation with members of the congregation, 1979.

SAN JOSE (Santa Clara Co.) 1481 Saratoga Ave.
Gubserville
Named after Frank Gubser, a German immigrant and barber, Gubserville was an important stage, mail, and teamster stop on the road between San Jose and Saratoga. Gubser served as the village's first and only postmaster, beginning July 5, 1882. Gubserville ceased to exist officially when the post office was discontinued on Apr. 15, 1897.

Placed in cooperation with Alan R. and David R. Pinn and Mountain Charlie Chapter No. 1850 of E Clampus Vitus, 1986.

SAN JOSE (Santa Clara Co.) 200 Edenvale Ave.
Hayes Mansion
Jay Orley and Everis A. Hayes built this Mission Revival style mansion, designed by George W. Page in 1904. The Hayes brothers were early *San Jose Mercury* publishers and prominent Valley politicians, and were actively involved in establishing the Santa Clara Valley fruit industry. The mansion consists of 62 rooms and 11 fireplaces, and was paneled in over a dozen different woods.

Placed in cooperation with Stella B. Gross Charitable Trust and Mountain Charlie Chapter No. 1850 of E Clampus Vitus, 1986.

SAN JOSE (Santa Clara Co.) 184 W. St. John St. and 50 N. Almaden
Luis Maria Peralta Adobe
The last vestige of El Pueblo de San Jose de Guadalupe. The simple adobe, rehabilitated in the mid-19th century, is believed built before 1800 by Manuel Gonzalez, an Apache, who was one of the pobladores (founders). Later owned and occupied by Sgt. Peralta, pueblo comisionado from 1807 to 1822. Both men came to California with the Anza expedition in 1775–76.

Placed in cooperation with Peralta Adobe Restoration Committee and San Jose Historic Landmarks Commission, 1976.

SAN JOSE (Santa Clara Co.) Evergreen College entrance, .5 mi. E of San Felipe and Yerba Buena rds. intersection
Montgomery Hill
Three-quarters of a mile northeast is Montgomery Hill, site of the 55 successful flights of the "aeroplane" of John Joseph Montgomery which demonstrated aero-

dynamic developments still indispensable to modern aircraft. Here the basic principles of aerodynamics discovered by Montgomery were combined by his engineering skill and technology to produce a heavier-than-air flying machine which had complete control: the cambered wing, rear stabilizer, flexible wingtips, and wing-warping aileron.

Placed in cooperation with County of Santa Clara and University of Santa Clara, 1967.

SAN JOSE (Santa Clara Co.)   *110 S. Market St.*
United States Post Office

Constructed in 1892, this was the first federal building in San Jose. It served as U.S. post office from 1892 to 1933. Designed by Willoughby Edbrooke and constructed of locally quarried sandstone, this Romanesque-style structure, built by the U.S. government, is the last of its kind on the West Coast.

Placed in cooperation with Fine Arts Gallery Association, San Jose Historic Landmarks Commission, and San Jose Historical Museum, 1972.

SAN JOSE (Santa Clara Co.)   *770 Lincoln Ave.*
Roberto-Sunol Adobe

This historic adobe was built in 1836 by a native Californian, Roberto Balermino, on Rancho de los Coches. The property was officially granted to him by Governor Micheltorena in 1844. A larger one-story dwelling was built in 1847 by the new owner, Antonio Sunol. The second-story frame structure and balcony were added in 1853 by Capt. Stefano Splivalo.

Placed in cooperation with Santa Clara County Historical Heritage Commission, 1977.

SAN JOSE (Santa Clara Co.)   *4335 Payne Ave.*
Moreland School

Oldest known rural school district in California. Established 1851 as subscription school, meeting in private homes. First teacher, Charles Lafollette, 1851, term three months. Through efforts of Samuel Curtis Rodgers, third teacher, 1852–54, first public school building, formerly home of Zechariah Moreland, obtained 1852. In 1853 Rodgers secured organization of school as Santa Clara Township School District No. 2. Renamed in Moreland's honor, 1862.

Placed by California State Park Commission in cooperation with Moreland School District, 1953.

SAN JOSE (Santa Clara Co.)   *On N. Monterey Rd. (old Hwy. 101),*
.5 mi. S of Ford Rd.
12 Miles
New Almaden Quicksilver Mine

From this cinnabar hill the Indians used pigment for paint; mercury mined, 1845. Gold discovery made mercury indispensable and mine became world famous, most productive in America. Sold for $1,700,700 in 1864.

Placed by Public Division of Works, Division of Highways.

SAN JOSE (Santa Clara Co.) 90 S. Market St.
St. Joseph's Roman Catholic Church
Established in 1803, St. Joseph's was the first non-mission church in a Spanish civil settlement in California. The present edifice, designed in Italian Baroque style by noted architect Bryan J. Clinch, is the fourth to be built on the original site. The cornerstone was laid Mar. 19, 1876, and the building dedicated Apr. 22, 1877.

Placed in cooperation with San Jose Historic Landmarks Commission and St. Joseph's Church Centennial Committee, 1977.

SAN JOSE (Santa Clara Co.) City Park Plaza, 100 block S. Market St.
Site of California's First State Capitol
Directly opposite this tablet was located the first state capitol building in which California's first legislature assembled in December 1849. San Jose was the seat of government from 1849 to 1851.

Placed by Historic Landmarks Committee of Native Sons of the Golden West, 1923.

SAN JOSE (Santa Clara Co.) 100 block W. St. James St.
Site of "City Gardens"—Nursery of Louis Pellier
Pellier, native of France and founder of California's prune industry, came to California in 1849. In October 1850 he established a nursery called "City Gardens" on this site. Here, aided by his brothers Pierre and Jean, he introduced the French prune "La Petite D'Agen" during the winter of 1856–57.

Placed in cooperation with San Jose Historic Landmarks Commission, 1977.

SAN JOSE (Santa Clara Co.) SW corner First and San Fernando sts.
Site of World's First Broadcasting Station
On this corner stood the Garden City Bank Building, where Charles D. Herrold established Station FN, the first radio broadcasting station in the world. As a pioneer in wireless telephony (radio), Herrold established the first station in 1909 to transmit radio programs of music and news to a listening audience on a regular basis.

Placed in cooperation with California Pioneers of Santa Clara County and Mountain Charlie Chapter No. 1850 of E Clampus Vitus, 1984.

SAN JOSE (Santa Clara Co.) 525 S. Winchester Blvd.
Winchester Mystery House
Built by Sarah Winchester, widow of rifle manufacturer William Winchester, this unique structure includes many outstanding elements of Victorian architecture and fine craftsmanship. Construction began in 1884 and continued without interruption until Mrs. Winchester's death in 1922. The continual building and remodeling created a 160-room house that sprawls over an area of six acres.

Placed in cooperation with Winchester Mystery House, Inc., 1974.

SAN JUAN BAUTISTA (San Benito Co.) San Juan Bautista State Historic Park, 2nd and Washington sts.
Castro House
This adobe bulding erected about 1838 on a grant of 1500 Spanish varas from the Mexican government to Don Jose Maria Castro, interim governor of Alta California

1835–36. Deeded by him Feb. 7, 1849, to Patrick Breen, Sr., pioneer and member of the Donner party of 1846. Has since remained in the possession of his family.

Placed by Historic Names and Sites Committee of California Historical Society, 1932.

SAN JUAN BAUTISTA (San Benito Co.)   *Fremont Peak State Park, 11 mi. S of SH 156*

Fremont Peak

(Plaque in Abbey Park,
SE corner Fourth and Muckelemi sts.)

In March 1846, Jose Castro, Mexican military commander, ordered John C. Fremont from the county and with Kit Carson and 60 men he moved to top of peak, built entrenchments, raised flag, and waited attack. Bear Flag incident and Mexican War followed. State Historical Monument.

Placed by Department of Public Works, Division of Highways.

SAN JUAN BAUTISTA (San Benito Co.)   *Mariposa and 2nd sts.*

Mission San Juan Bautista

Founded June 24, 1790
by
Fr. Fermin Francisco de Lasuen

Placed by California State Society of Daughters of the American Revolution, 1969.

SAN JUAN CAPISTRANO (Orange Co.)   *NW corner Ortega Hwy. and Camino Capistrano*

San Juan Capistrano Mission

Founded in 1776 by Padre Junipero Serra. The seventh in the chain of 21 missions established in Alta California to Christianize and civilize the Indians. Stone church was destroyed in 1812 earthquake. Expropriated during Mexican rule. Returned to the Catholic church in 1865 by proclamation of President Abraham Lincoln.

Placed by California State Park Commission.

SAN LEANDRO (Alameda Co.)   *550 W. Estudillo Ave.*

Estudillo Home

Site of the last home of Jose Joaquin Estudillo, grantee of Rancho San Leandro, and his wife, Juana Martinez de Estudillo. It was built about 1850. The family founded San Leandro, built a hotel, and donated several lots, including the original site of St. Leander's Church.

Placed by California State Park Commission in cooperation with St. Leander's Parish Centennial, 1964.

SAN LEANDRO (Alameda Co.)   *561 Lafayette at Leo Ave.*

Peralta House

The first brick house built in Alameda County. Constructed 1860 by W. P. Toler for Ignacio Peralta, early San Leandro Spanish settler whose father, Don Luis Maria Peralta, received land grant from Spanish Governor Don Pablo Vicente de Sola, Oct. 20, 1820.

Placed by California Centennial Commission, 1949.

SAN LEANDRO (Alameda Co.)

In City Park, NW corner
E. 14th and Hays sts.

Rancho San Antonio

Governor Pablo de Sola, last Spanish governor of California, awarded the San Antonio grant to Don Luis Maria Peralta on Aug. 3, 1820, in recognition of forty years of service. From this point northward, the grant embraced over 43,000 acres, now occupied by the cities of San Leandro, Oakland, Alameda, Emeryville, Piedmont, Berkeley, and Albany.

Placed in cooperation with City of San Leandro, Club Iberico Espanol, Sociedad de Agustina de Aragon, and Supreme Council U.P.E.C., 1970.

SAN LEANDRO (Alameda Co.)

San Leandro Marina,
S end of N. Dike Rd.

San Leandro Oyster Beds

Oysters were the mainstay of the California fishing industry at the turn of the century. Along this site (the original Mulford Canal), the San Leandro oyster beds flourished. In 1892 William Roberts filed title to the beds south along San Lorenzo Canal, and in 1895 Thomas Mulford filed title here at Mulford Canal. The beds were often plagued by "oyster pirates" such as Jack London.

Placed in cooperation with local civic and historical organizations, 1971.

SAN LUIS OBISPO (San Luis Obispo Co.)

800 Palm St.

Site of Ah Louis Store

Here in 1874 was established Ah Louis' Store. The first Chinese store in the county, it sold general merchandise and herbs and served as a bank, counting house, and post office for the numerous Chinese coolies who dug the eight tunnels through the mountains of Cuesta for the Southern Pacific Railroad, 1884–94.

Placed in cooperation with San Luis Obispo County Historical Society and Sons and Daughters of Ah Louis, 1965.

SAN LUIS OBISPO (San Luis Obispo Co.)

1309 Toro

Dallidet Adobe

This was the home of Pierre Hyppolite Dallidet, native of France, who settled in San Luis Obispo in 1853 and became a vineyardist. It was given by Paul Dallidet, his son, to the San Luis Obispo County Historical Society in 1953, in memory of the Dallidet family who had occupied it for a century.

Placed by California State Park Commission in cooperation with San Luis Obispo County Historical Society and San Luisita Parlor No. 108 and San Miguel Parlor No. 94 of Native Daughters of the Golden West, 1960.

SAN LUIS OBISPO (San Luis Obispo Co.)

On Monterey St., between
Chorro and Broad sts.

Mission San Luis Obispo de Tolosa
1772

A Spanish mission founded by Fray Junipero Serra, OFM, first president of the California missions, this was the fifth in a chain of 21 missions stretching from San Diego to Sonoma. Built by the Chumash Indians living in the area, its combination of belfry and vestibule is unique among California missions. In 1846 John C. Fremont and his California battalion quartered here while engaged in the war with Mexico.

Placed in cooperation with California Historical Landmark Advisory Committee, San Luis Obispo County Historical Society, and Parlors No. 290 and 108 of Native Sons and Daughters of the Golden West, 1966.

SAN MARINO (Los Angeles Co.)   *1912 Montrobles Pl.*
"Los Robles" (The Oaks)

This was the site of "Los Robles," the 400-acre estate of Gov. George Stoneman. Here in 1880 President Rutherford B. Hayes was entertained. The first schoolhouse in the San Gabriel Valley, California's first tennis club, and the first municipal Christmas tree of San Marino were located here.

Placed by California State Park Commission in cooperation with Region 14, Conference of California Historical Societies, 1959.

SAN MATEO (San Mateo Co.)   *El Camino Real (SH 82) to W. 3rd Ave.,*
½ block N on Arroyo Ct.,
turn left to plaque 300 ft. W
Historic Camp Site

Here on the banks of San Mateo Creek, Capt. J. B. de Anza camped Mar. 29, 1776, after exploring the peninsula and selecting the sites for the Mission and Presidio of San Francisco. Here also the party of families, soldiers, and priests, on the way to found San Francisco, camped for three days, June 24–27, 1776.

Placed by California Centennial Commission, City of San Mateo and San Mateo County Historical Association, 1949.

SAN MATEO (San Mateo Co.)   *SW corner El Camino Real*
and Baywood
"The Hospice"

Here stood the Mission Hospice built around 1800 by the Spanish padres on El Camino Real to break the journey from Santa Clara and to serve the Indians of Mission Dolores, California, 1800.

Placed by Anson Burlingame Chapter of Daughters of the American Revolution.

SAN MIGUEL (San Luis Obispo Co.)   *SW corner Mission St.*
and San Luis Obispo Rd.
Mission San Miguel Arcangel

Selecting this site because of the great number of Salinan Indians living hereabouts, Fray Fermin Francisco de Lasuen, OFM, second president of the California missions, founded San Miguel Arcangel on July 25, 1797. The sixteenth in a chain of 21 Franciscan missions, its influence has played not only upon the native population but upon the history of California as a whole.

Placed by California State Park Commission in cooperation with San Luis Obispo County Historical Society and Parlors No. 150 and 94 of Native Sons and Daughters of the Golden West, 1966.

SAN MIGUEL (San Luis Obispo Co.)

*700 Mission St.,
US 101 to Mission St. off ramp*

Rios-Caledonia Adobe

This imposing building is an excellent example of California's Mexican era architecture. Using Indian labor, Petronilo Rios built the two-story adobe about 1846 as his residence and headquarters for sheep and cattle operations. Named "Caledonia" in the 1860s, it served as a hotel and stagestop between Los Angeles and San Francisco until 1886. Restoration was begun in 1968 by the Friends of the Adobes.

Placed in cooperation with Friends of the Adobes, 1981.

SAN PABLO (Contra Costa Co.)

*Civic Center, NW corner San Pablo
Blvd. and Church Ln.*

Alvarado Adobe

Site of adobe house, grape arbor, and gardens built in 1842 by Jesus Maria Castro for his mother, Doña Gabriela Berryessa de Castro, widow of Francisco Maria Castro, grantee, 1823, of Rancho (Cuchiyunes) San Pablo. Doña Gabriela died in 1851, deeding the adobe to her daughter, Martina Castro de Alvarado whose husband, Juan Bautista Alvarado, was governor from 1836 to 1842.

Placed by California State Park Commission in cooperation with Exchange Club of San Pablo, 1961.

SAN PEDRO (Los Angeles Co.)

*Middle Reservation, Fort MacArthur,
2400 block Pacific Ave., 300 ft. S of
Meyler and Quartermaster rds. intersection*

Casa de San Pedro
Hide House Site

The first known commercial structure on the shore of San Pedro Bay was built here in 1823 by the trading firm of McCulloch and Hartnell to store cattle hides from the San Gabriel and San Fernando missions. Richard Henry Dana described this adobe hide house in *Two Years Before the Mast*. Thus began the development of the Port of Los Angeles.

Placed in cooperation with San Pedro Bay Historical Society, 1979.

SAN PEDRO (Los Angeles Co.)

*Fisherman's Dock,
off Sampson Way*

Timms' Point and Landing

In 1852 German immigrant Augustus W. Timms obtained Sepulveda's landing on the mudflats near here. He built a wharf, added a warehouse, corral, and other facilities to service shipping and the running of stages to Los Angeles. Timms was a pioneer in the development of the harbor and for over fifty years this area was known as Timms Point.

Placed in cooperation with San Pedro Bay Historical Society and Port of Los Angeles, 1993.

SAN RAFAEL (Marin Co.) *Marin County Civic Center*
Marin County Civic Center
The Civic Center complex was designed by Frank Lloyd Wright (1869–1959) near the end of his long career. The Administration Building was completed in 1962 and the Hall of Justice in 1970. They are the only government buildings designed by the distinguished architect that were ever actually constructed. The project fully embodied Wright's ideal of organic architecture—a synthesis of buildings and landscape. In Wright's words, the structures were planned to "melt into the sunburnt hills."

Placed in cooperation with Citizens of Marin County, 1992.

SAN RAFAEL (Marin Co.) *Corner 5th Ave. and A St.*
San Rafael Arcangel Mission
(Plaque located at NE corner
of Merrydale and S bound US 101 San Pedro Rd. off ramp)
One and a half miles southwest was the San Rafael Arcangel Mission, established in 1817 by the Franciscans. This was the twentieth in the chain of 21 California missions. After the "decree of secularization" in 1834, the buildings gradually fell into ruin. Reconstruction of the mission on the original site took place in 1949.

Placed by California Centennial Commission in cooperation with Marin County Historical Society, 1950.

SAN RAFAEL (Marin Co.) *4 mi. N, .7 mi. E of US 101, on St. Vincent Dr.*
St. Vincent's School for Boys
In 1853, Timothy Murphy, Irish-born pioneer of Marin County, gave 317 acres of land to Archbishop Alemany for educational purposes. Here the Sisters of Charity in 1855 founded a school. Now called St. Vincent's School for Boys, it has been maintained and enlarged by successive archbishops of San Francisco.

Placed by California State Park Commission in cooperation with Marin Committee on History and Landmarks of the Native Sons and Native Daughters of the Golden West, 1958.

SAN SIMEON (San Luis Obispo Co.) *On SH 1*
Hearst San Simeon State Historical Monument
(Plaque at entrance to rest area)
Here on the historic Piedra Blanca rancho, William Randolph Hearst created La Cuesta Encantada (The Enchanted Hill), including La Casa Grande and adjacent buildings, with their rare art treasures and beautiful gardens, 1919–47. Presented to the State of California in 1958 by the Hearst Corporation as a memorial to William Randolph Hearst, and donated in the name of his mother, Phoebe Apperson Hearst.

Placed by California State Park Commission in cooperation with Citizens of San Luis Obispo and Monterey counties, 1958.

SAN SIMEON (San Luis Obispo Co.) *On San Simeon Rd.*
Sebastian Store
This is the oldest store building along the north coast of San Luis Obispo County. Built in 1852 at Whaling Point, one-half mile westward, it was moved in 1878 to

its present location. Operated by the Sebastian family for half a century, it is now owned and operated by J.C. and Louise Sebastian.

Placed by California State Park Commission in cooperation with San Luis Obispo County Historical Society and El Pinal Parlor No. 163 of Native Daughters of the Golden West, 1960.

SANTA ANA (Orange Co.) 211 W. Santa Ana Blvd.
Orange County Courthouse
Built in 1900 of Arizona red sandstone, this is the oldest existing county courthouse in Southern California. Significant and far-reaching court decisions were handed down here, including the "Whipstock" case dealing with slant oil drilling, interpretation of farm labor law, and the overall trial resulting in law regulating explosives.

Placed in cooperation with Orange County Board of Supervisors and Let's Improve Santa Ana, 1970.

SANTA ANA (Orange Co.) Red Hill Elementary School, 11911 Red Hill Rd.
Red Hill
A promontory which served as a landmark for early travelers. It was called "Katuktu" by the Indians.

Placed by Katuktu Chapter of Daughters of the American Revolution, 1969.

SANTA BARBARA (Santa Barbara Co.) 129 W. Mason St.
Burton Mound
Thought to have once been Indian village of Syujtun, this site has yielded some of the most important archeological evidence found in California. In 1542 the village was recorded by Cabrillo while on his voyage of discovery, and again in 1769 by Father Crespi and the redoubtable Portola. Don Luis Burton, after whom the mound was named, acquired the property in 1860.

Placed in cooperation with California Historical Landmarks Advisory Committee, Grand Parlor of Native Sons and Daughters of the Golden West, and the City of Santa Barbara, 1966.

SANTA BARBARA (Santa Barbara Co.) 11 E. Carrillo St.
Hill-Carrillo Adobe
Built in 1826 by Daniel Hill of Massachusetts for his bride, Rafaela Luisa Ortega y Olivera, granddaughter of Jose Francisco Ortega, founder and first comandante of the Royal Presidio of Santa Barbara. Later occupied by the family of Guillermo Carrillo. Here in 1850 the first city council met. Preserved and presented to Santa Barbara Foundation by Major and Mrs. Max C. Fleischmann.

Placed by California State Park Commission in cooperation with Santa Barbara Foundation, 1960.

SANTA BARBARA (Santa Barbara Co.)

El Paseo Plaza, SE corner
De La Guerra St. and
De La Guerra Plaza

De La Guerra Plaza
1850–1950

Near this site, Aug. 26, 1850, two weeks before California statehood, duly elected common council, City of Santa Barbara, held first official meeting. Here in 1875, first city hall erected and area still center of city's governmental activities. Plaza scene early Santa Barbara fiestas, and De La Guerra house set standards for Santa Barbara hospitality.

Placed by California Centennial Commission in cooperation with Old Spanish Days of Santa Barbara, and Santa Barbara Historical Society, 1950.

SANTA BARBARA (Santa Barbara Co.)

715 N. Santa Barbara St.

Casa Covarrubias

Built by Indian labor in 1817 for Don Domingo Carrillo whose daughter married Don Jose Maria Covarrubias in 1838. Descendants of these families, many of them leaders in public affairs, occupied this house for over a century. Don Jose Maria was the first federal elector from California in 1852. John R. Southworth moved and rebuilt the "historic adobe" here in 1924 as part of a civic program of historic preservation. Los Adobes de Los Rancheros acquired the property in 1938 as headquarters for Los Rancheros Visitadores and for the use and enjoyment of the people.

Placed by California State Park Commission in cooperation with Los Adobes de Los Rancheros, 1959.

SANTA BARBARA (Santa Barbara Co.)

412 W. Montecito St.

Trussell-Winchester Adobe

Built in 1854 by Capt. Horatio Gates Trussell of Orland, Maine. Partly constructed of material from wreck of the S.S. *Windfield Scott* on Anacapa Island. Acquired by the Winchesters in 1882. Bequeathed in 1955 to the Santa Barbara Historical Society by Katherine Bagg Hastings, niece of Miss Sarah Winchester.

Placed by California State Park Commission in cooperation with Santa Barbara Historical Society, 1957.

SANTA BARBARA (Santa Barbara Co.)

2201 Laguna St.

The City of Santa Barbara
Mission Historical Park

(Plaque at Mission Historical Park, 1,000 ft. W
at old reservoir)

Santa Barbara Mission was founded Dec. 4, 1786. Portions of five units of its extensive waterworks, built by Indian labor, are preserved in this park—a filter house, Spanish grist mill, sections of aqueducts, and two reservoirs. The larger reservoir, built in 1806, is used today as part of the city water system. Ruins of the pottery kiln and tanning vats are here also. The fountain and lavadero are nearby in front of the old mission. A dam, built in 1807, is located in the Santa Barbara Botanic Garden, one and one-half miles up Mission Canyon.

Placed by California State Park Commission, 1957.

SANTA BARBARA (Santa Barbara Co.)   33 E. Canon Perdido St.
Old Lobero Theatre
1873

Jose Lobero opened the region's first legitimate theatre on this site on Feb. 22, 1873. For many years the old theatre was the center of social life in Santa Barbara. A new Lobero Theatre, opened in 1924 on the same site, continues to serve the cultural interests of the area.

Placed in cooperation with County of Santa Barbara, Lobero Theatre Foundation, and Tierra de Oro Parlor No. 304 of Native Daughters of the Golden West, 1974.

SANTA BARBARA (Santa Barbara Co.)   NW corner Canon Perdido and Santa Barbara sts.
Site of Royal Spanish Presidio of Santa Barbara

This presidio was established under orders of King Carlos III, Apr. 19–21, 1782, by Gov. Felipe de Neve, Padre Junipero Serra, and Lt. Jose Francisco Ortega, to provide the benefits of government for the inhabitants of the Santa Barbara Channel region of California.

Placed by California State Park Commission in cooperation with City of Santa Barbara, Grand Parlors of the Native Daughters and Native Sons of the Golden West, Santa Barbara Historical Society, and Boy Scouts of America, 1958.

SANTA CLARA (Santa Clara Co.)   981 Fremont St.
Charles Copeland Morse Residence

"The house that seeds built" was constructed in 1892 by Charles Copeland Morse, co-founder of one of the largest vegetable and flower seed companies in the world, the Ferry-Morse Seed Company. This outstanding Queen Anne residence is the most elaborate remaining Victorian structure in the City of Santa Clara.

Placed in cooperation with City of Santa Clara Historical Landmarks Commission and Chamber of Commerce, 1977.

SANTA CLARA (Santa Clara Co.)   In front of church, University of Santa Clara, The Alameda and Lexington St.
Mission Santa Clara

Santa Clara, the first California mission to honor a woman, Clare of Assisi, as its patron saint, was founded nearby on the Guadalupe River on Jan. 12, 1777. It once had the largest Indian population of any California mission. Floods and earthquake led to successive relocations. Its fifth church was dedicated on this site in 1825. In 1851 Santa Clara College was established in the old mission buildings.

Placed in cooperation with William L. Gates, Class of '64, and Mountain Charlie Chapter No. 1850 of E Clampus Vitus, 1980.

SANTA CLARA (Santa Clara Co.)   3260 The Alameda
Santa Clara Women's Club Adobe

This adobe, among the oldest in Santa Clara Valley, was one of several continuous rows of homes built in 1792–1800 as dwellings for the Indian families of Mission Santa Clara. It links the Franciscan padres' labors with California today.

Placed by California State Park Commission in cooperation with Santa Clara Women's Club, 1961.

SANTA CLARA (Santa Clara Co.)   *SE corner Central Expressway and De la Cruz Blvd.*
Mission Santa Clara de Thamien
The first mission in this valley, Mission Santa Clara de Thamien, was established at this site by Franciscan padres Tomas de la Pena and Joseph Antonio Marguia, Jan. 17, 1777. Here, at the Indian village of So-co-is-u-ka, they erected a cross and shelter of worship and brought Christianity to the Costanoan Indians.

Placed by California State Park Commission in cooperation with City of Santa Clara Historical and Landmarks Commission, 1962.

SANTA CLARA (Santa Clara Co.)   *Civic Center Park, NE corner El Camino Real and Lincoln St.*
Santa Clara Campaign Treaty Site
After an armed confrontation nearby on Jan. 2, 1847, and a truce meeting the following day, Marine Capt. Ward Marston, Commander of the U.S. Expeditionary Force, and Francisco Sanchez, leader of Mexican-Californian ranchers, agreed to a treaty here on Jan. 7, 1847. United States forces were to recognize rights of Californians and to end seizures of their personal properties.

Placed in cooperation with City of Santa Clara and Descendants of California Participants, 1980.

SANTA CLARA (Santa Clara Co.)   *SE corner Lawrence Expressway and El Camino Real*
Amistrice Oak Tree Site
Here on Jan. 8, 1847, Francisco Sanchez, leader of a California band, surrendered himself and some American prisoners and arms to Lt. Grayson, thus ending the Battle of Santa Clara or "The Battle of the Mustard Stalks," of Jan. 2, 1847. This armistice ended the last uprising against the tide of American conquest in the Santa Clara Valley.

Placed by California State Park Commission in cooperation with City of Santa Clara Historical and Landmarks Commission, 1962.

SANTA CRUZ (Santa Cruz Co.)   *400 Beach St.*
Santa Cruz Beach Boardwalk
A local landmark since 1907, this boardwalk was one of the first amusement parks in California. It is now the only oceanside amusement park operating on the West Coast. The boardwalk is the site of two rare attractions: the 1911 carousel and the 1924 giant dipper roller coaster. Both were manufactured by members of the Looff family, some of the nation's earliest and most prominent makers of amusement rides.

Placed in cooperation with Santa Cruz Seaside Company, 1990.

SANTA CRUZ (Santa Cruz Co.)

SW corner Water St. and Branciforte Ave.

Branciforte

These school grounds were center of Villa de Branciforte, founded in 1797 by Gov. Diego de Borica of California on orders from Spain through Viceroy Branciforte in Mexico. Settlement existed as political entity until American occupancy of California. Remained as township until 1905 when annexed to City of Santa Cruz.

Placed by California Centennial Commission in cooperation with Santa Cruz County Historical Society, 1950.

SANTA CRUZ (Santa Cruz Co.)

Plaza Park, NE corner Mission and Emmet sts.

Site of Santa Cruz Mission

Mision la Exaltacion de la Santa Cruz, the 12th Franciscan mission, was consecrated by Father Fermin Lasuen in August 1791. In 1793 the adobe church was built where the Holy Cross Catholic Church is now located. The mission was damaged by several earthquakes and finally collapsed in 1857. Plaza Park is located at the center of the mission complex which contained 32 buildings at the time of its secularization in 1834; the last building remains on School Street.

Placed in cooperation with Monterey Viejo Chapter 1846 of E Clampus Vitus and Santa Cruz Historical Society, 1982.

SANTA MARIA (Santa Barbara Co.)

15 mi. SE, SW corner Foxen Cyn. and Tepusquet rds.

Chapel of San Ramon

This redwood frame chapel, erected in 1875 by Frederick and Ramona Foxen Wickenden for area residents, illustrates the transition between the architecture of the old missions and the frame churches of the later American settlers. It is a unique example of the use of wood to create strong, simple forms that had formerly been executed in adobe.

Placed in cooperation with San Ramon Chapel Preservation Committee and Santa Barbara County Historical Landmarks Advisory Committee, 1976.

SANTA PAULA (Ventura Co.)

Santa Paula Boys Club Recreation Center, 1400 block Harvard Blvd.

Portola Expedition Campsite

On Aug. 13, 1769, reaching the junction of the Arroyo Mupu with the river, the place was named The Holy Martyrs, Ipolito and Casiano. Upon founding the Mission of San Buenaventura, the priests established here an asistencia and christened it Santa Paula where they frequently held services for the conversion of the Mupu Indians.

Private plaque.

SANTA PAULA (Ventura Co.)

4 mi. E, SH 126 at Hall Rd.

Sycamore Tree

In 1846 Gen. John C. Fremont passed this site of the sycamore tree on his way to sign a treaty with Gen. Andres Pico to secure California for future annexation to the

United States. It served the padres as a resting place; the community as a polling place and a temporary post office, and as a location for religious services.

Placed in cooperation with Ventura County Historical Society, and El Aliso Parlor No. 314 and Santa Paula and Poinsettia Parlor No. 313 of Native Daughters of the Golden West, 1961.

SANTA ROSA (Sonoma Co.)

8 mi. W, SW corner Mirabel and River rds.

First Power Commercial Sawmill

In 1834 Mariano G. Vallejo's brother-in-law, John B. R. Cooper, constructed California's first known power-operated commercial sawmill. In addition to sawing redwood lumber, the mill and settlement served as a barrier to Russian encroachment from the west. Located one-third mile east on Mark West Creek, the water-powered mill was destroyed by flood in the winter of 1840–41.

Placed in cooperation with California Division of Forestry and Forest Products Industries of California, 1970.

SANTA ROSA (Sonoma Co.)

Hood Mansion, Santa Rosa Jr. College, 7501 Sonoma Hwy.

Hood House

This was the site of Rancho los Guilucos (18,833 acres), granted in 1839 by Gov. Juan Bautista Alvarado to John Wilson and his wife, Ramona Carillo, sister-in-law of Gen. Mariano Guadalupe Vallejo. The house, constructed in 1858 by William Hood for his bride, Elisa Shaw of Sonoma, incorporates the original bricks fired on the property and has been in continuous use. The property was purchased in 1943 by the California Department of Youth Authority for Los Guilucos School for Girls.

Placed by California State Park Commission in cooperation with Los Guilucos Citizens' Advisory Committee and the Sonoma Valley Historical Society, 1960.

SANTA ROSA (Sonoma Co.)

200 block Santa Rosa Ave.

Luther Burbank
March 1849–April 1926
Home and Experimental Gardens

In memory of our citizen of the world, whose love for youth and growing things was expressed in the work done in these gardens. The perpetual ownership of these grounds is now vested, through the generosity of Mrs. Burbank, in the City of Santa Rosa.

Private plaque.

SANTA ROSA (Sonoma Co.)

5000 Medica Rd.

John Medica's Castles and Garden

"Trying to make it look better," John Medica spent 20 years transforming a barren hillside into a magical garden of plants and creative stone works. Castles were his greatest triumph. A native of Yugoslavia, the self-taught Medica created an oasis for people and animals to enjoy. This imaginative assemblage is one of California's remarkable Twentieth Century Folk Art Environments.

Placed in cooperation with Saving and Preserving Arts and Cultural Environments (SPACE), 1987.

SANTA VENETIA (Marin Co.)   *China Camp State Park, N. San Pedro Rd., 5.3 mi. SE of US 101, at entrance to China Camp Village*

Wa Jen Ha Lio

One of the earliest, largest, and most productive Chinese fishing villages in California, China Camp was in operation by 1870. The Chinese immigrants and their descendants introduced the use of commercial netting to catch bay shrimp off Point San Pedro. The shrimp were then dried and exported to Chinese throughout the world. China Camp represents the last surviving Chinese shrimp fishing village in California.
Placed in cooperation with Marin Chinese Cultural Group, 1980.

SANTA YSABEL (San Diego Co.)   *1.4 mi. N, on SH 79*

Site of Chapel of Santa Ysabel

This plaque marking the site of the first chapel of Santa Ysabel Indian Mission, founded on Sept. 20, 1818, by Father Fernando Martin as an asistencia of the Mission San Diego de Alcala, is dedicated to the memory of the faith and courage of the mission fathers and the Indians of this area Jan. 29, 1974, by the members of districts 11, 12, and 14.
Placed by California State Society of Daughters of the American Revolution, 1974.

SANTEE (San Diego Co.)   *10726 Woodside Ave., NE corner Woodside and Magnolia aves.*

5 Miles
Mission Dam and Flume

Earliest irrigation works in California, supplying water to the San Diego mission fields and gardens. Probably begun late in the 18th century, completed early in the 19th century. Designed by Alberto de Cordoba, Spanish engineer here in 1795–97.
Placed by Department of Public Works, Division of Highways.

SARATOGA (Santa Clara Co.)   *Off SH 9, .3 mi. N on Pierce Rd, 1.2 mi. on Paul Masson Mtn. Winery Rd.*

Paul Masson Mountain Winery

From the winery that bears the name of Paul Masson, premium wines and champagne have flowed continuously since 1852, even during prohibition under a special government license. Twice partially destroyed by earthquake and fire, the original sandstone walls still stand. The 12th-century Spanish Romanesque portal came around the Horn.
Placed in cooperation with San Francisco Landmarks Council and Sainte Claire Club, 1960.

SARATOGA (Santa Clara Co.)   *In park, SE corner SH 9 and SH 85 junction*

Saratoga
(Formerly Toll Gate, McCartysville, Bank Mills)

Anza exploring party passed through Mar. 25, 1776. Lumbering in mountains which began 1847 and continued many years brought first settlers 1850. Among other industries established were lime quarry 1850s, grist mill 1854, tannery 1863, paper mill 1868, and pasteboard mill 1870. Pacific Congress Springs, popular resort, 1866–1942. Pioneered in fruit industry. Blossom festivals began in 1900.

Placed by California Centennial Commission, 1950.

SAUGUS (Los Angeles Co.)

9.2 mi. N, San Francisquito Power Plant No. 2, 32300 N. San Francisquito Canyon Rd.

St. Francis Dam Disaster Site

The St. Francis Dam, part of the Los Angeles aqueduct system, stood one and one-half miles north of this site. On Mar. 12, 1928, the 185-foot high concrete dam collapsed just before midnight, sending 12 and one-third billion gallons of water roaring down the Santa Clara River Valley 54 miles to the ocean. This was one of California's greatest disasters; over 450 lives were lost.

Placed in cooperation with Los Angeles Department of Water and Power, U.S. Forest Service, and Santa Clarita Valley Historical Society, 1978.

SEAL BEACH (Orange Co.)

NE corner Seal Beach Blvd. and Electric Ave.

Anaheim Landing

Soon after the founding of the Mother Colony at Anaheim in 1857, Anaheim Landing was established as a port of entry for the Santa Ana Valley by the Anaheim Landing Company. Despite treacherous entrance conditions which caused several disasters, regular coastwise trade was carried on for about 15 years.

Placed by California State Park Commission.

SELMA (Fresno Co.)

S bound Old Hwy. 99, just N of Highland Ave.

18 Miles
Mussell Slough Tragedy

Dispute over land settlement and railroad rights-of-way resulted in bloodshed. Two deputy marshals, five settlers were killed May 11, 1880. Frank Norris' novel *The Octopus* is based on this tragedy.

Placed by Department of Public Works, Division of Highways.

SHAFTER (Kern Co.)

5 mi. E, Lerdo Hwy., entrance to Shafter Airport

Site of Gossamer Condor Flight

This plaque at Shafter Airport commemorates the world's first manpowered flight to complete the Kremer Circuit, Aug. 23, 1977. The circuit, a figure eight around two pylons one-half mile apart, was completed in six minutes, 22 seconds. The plane was designed by Dr. Paul MacCready, Jr. and flown by Bryan Allen. A cash prize of 50,000 pounds was awarded by the Royal Aeronautical Society, London, England.

Placed in cooperation with Kern County Museum, Kern County Department of Airports, and Kern County Historical Society, 1979.

SHASTA (Shasta Co.)   *NW corner Red Bluff Rd. and Crocker Alley*

Father Rinaldi's Foundation of 1856

Registered State Historical Landmark
No. 483
Foundation of Catholic Basilica
Cornerstone laid on May 1857
by
Archbishop Joseph Alemany O.P.
Rev. Raphael Rinaldi, Pastor

Private plaque.

SHASTA (Shasta Co.)   *Shasta State Historic Park, SH 299,*
NW corner Main St. and Trinity Alley

Shasta

Founded 1849 as Reading's Springs. Named Shasta June 8, 1950. Second county seat Shasta County 1851–88. Metropolis Northern California during 1850s. End road and beginning Oregon pack trail until 1861. Present home Western Star Lodge No. 2, F.&A.M., whose charter brought across plains Peter Lassen party 1848. Shurtleff House built 1851. Business section destroyed, fire 1853. *Shasta Courier* founded 1852.

Placed by California Centennial Commission and Shasta County Centennial Committee, 1950.

SHASTA (Shasta Co.)   *.75 mi. W, on SH 299*

Pioneer Baby's Grave

Charles, infant son of George and Helena Cohn Brownstein of Red Bluff, died Dec. 14, 1864. He was buried near land established by the Shasta Hebrew Congregation as a Jewish cemetery in 1857, one of the earliest such cemeteries in the region. Since there was no Jewish burial ground in Red Bluff, Charles' parents made the arduous journey to Shasta to lay their baby to rest. Concern for the fate of the grave led to the rerouting of Highway 299 in 1923.

Placed in cooperation with Shasta Historical Society, Kevin Hollis Moss Historical Fund, and Trinitarianus Chapter 62 of E Clampus Vitus, 1990.

SHINGLE SPRINGS (El Dorado Co.)   *Mother Lode Dr.,*
near post office

Camp Site of Boston-Newton Party

On this site the Boston-Newton Joint Stock Association encamped on Sept. 26, 1849. The company left Boston Apr. 16 and arrived at Sutter's Fort Sept. 27, after a remarkable journey across the continent. A rich store of written records preserved by these pioneers has left for posterity a fascinating picture of the gold rush.

Placed by California Centennial Commission and Descendants of Boston-Newton Party, 1950.

SIGNAL HILL (Los Angeles Co.)   *NE corner Temple Ave. and Hill St.*
Discovery Well
Signal Hill Field
Shell Oil Company-Alamitos No. 1
June 25, 1921

One of the world's most famous wells, Alamitos No. 1, was started on Mar. 23, 1921, and was completed June 25, 1921, at a depth of 3,114 feet, flowing 590 barrels of oil a day.

This discovery well led to the development of one of the most productive oil fields in the world and helped to establish California as a major oil producing state. This monument commemorating Alamitos No. 1 is a tribute to the petroleum pioneers for their success here; a success which has, by aiding in the growth and expansion of the petroleum industry, contributed so much to the welfare of mankind.

Placed by Shell Oil Company and Petroleum Production Pioneers, 1952.

SILVERADO (Orange Co.)   *1.1 mi. W of post office, at entrance of Silverado Community Church, Silverado Canyon Rd.*

Site of Carbondale

In 1881, after the Southern Pacific took over the Santa Clara coal mine northeast of here, a bustling mining camp complete with hotel, saloons, shacks, store, and post office sprang up on these flats. Three years later the mine played out and Carbondale disappeared without a trace.

Placed by Orange County Board of Supervisors and Orange County Historical Commission, 1976.

SILVERADO (Orange Co.)   *3.4 mi. E of post office, next to fire station No. 2, end of Silverado Cyn. Rd.*

Silverado

Located in Cañada de la Madera (Timber Canyon) was a mining boomtown founded in 1878 when silver was discovered nearby. During the colorful life of its boom, 1878–81, miners flocking to the area established a thriving community, served daily by stage from Los Angeles and Santa Ana.

Placed by California State Park Commission.

SIMI VALLEY (Ventura Co.)   *Robert P. Strathearn Historical Park, 137 Strathearn Pl.*

El Rancho Simi (1795)

This is the site of the headquarters of the Spanish Rancho San Jose de Nuestra Señora de Altagracia y Simi. The name derives from "Shimiji," the name of the Chumash village here before the Spanish. At 113,000 acres, Rancho Simi was one of the state's largest land grants. Two prominent Spanish and Mexican family names are connected with the Rancho: Santiago Pico who first received the grant, and Jose de La Guerra who purchased the Rancho in 1842. Two rooms of original adobe remain, part of the Strathearn home built in 1892–93.

Placed in cooperation with Simi Valley Historical Society, 1989.

SIMI VALLEY (Ventura Co.)   *4595 Cochran St.*
Grandma Prisbrey's Bottle Village

This fantastic assemblage is one of California's remarkable twentieth century folk art environments. In 1956 Tressa Prisbrey, then nearly 60 years old, started building a fanciful "village" of shrines, walkways, sculptures, and buildings from recycled items and discards from the local dump. She worked for 25 years creating one structure after another to house her collections. Today, Bottle Village is composed of 13 buildings and 20 sculptures.

Placed in cooperation with Preserve Bottle Village, 1984.

SLOUGHHOUSE (Sacramento Co.)   *On Meiss St.,*
                                                across from post office
Sloughhouse

Sloughhouse, prominent hotel and stage station on the road to the Amador mines, was a favorite stopping place for travelers, notably Leland Stanford. Constructed in 1850 by Jared Dixon Sheldon, it was destroyed by fire in 1890 and rebuilt the same year. Many descendants of pioneers of the community of Sloughhouse, which developed near Sheldon's establishment, still reside in this fertile valley of the Consumnes.

Placed by California State Park Commission in cooperation with Liberty Parlor No. 213 of Native Daughters of the Golden West, 1957.

SMARTVILLE (Yuba Co.)   *1 mi. W, on Timbuctoo Rd.*
5 Miles
Timbuctoo
(Plaque located on SH 20)

1855. Largest town in eastern Yuba County and at height of its prosperity contained a church, theater, stores, hotels, and saloons. Old Wells Fargo office and Stewart Brothers store restored 1928 and dedicated to pioneer men and women of Timbuctoo.

Placed by Department of Public Works, Division of Highways.

SNELLING (Merced Co.)   *Main St., between Second and Third sts.*
First Courthouse in Merced County
Erected 1857

This monument commemorates the 75th anniversary of the organization of Merced County and is dedicated to the memory of our pioneers.

Placed by Yosemite Parlor No. 24 of Native Sons of the Golden West, 1930.

SODA SPRINGS (Placer Co.)   *8 mi. W, Big Bend Ranger Station,*
                                  2008 Hampshire Rocks Rd.
Overland Emigrant Trail

It is estimated more than 30,000 settlers came into California over this trail in the year 1849. Near this site outcroppings of rock still bear the marks of wagon wheels. For those travelers who reached this point, the next ordeal was the torturous descent into Bear Valley.

Placed in cooperation with Placer County Historical Society, 1976.

SOLEDAD (Monterey Co.) *2.5 mi. W, on Fort Romie Rd.*
Mission Nuestra Señora Dolorosisima
de La Soledad

This mission, founded Oct. 9, 1791, by Father Fermin Francisco de Lasuen, ministered to the Indians of the Salinas Valley. Governor Jose Joaquin de Arrillaga died here July 24, 1814, and was buried in the chapel. Prosperous in its early years, Soledad declined after 1825. Father Vicente Francisco Sarria, who stayed on in poverty, faithfully served the Indians until his death in 1835. Secularized in 1835, the mission was regranted to the Bishop of Monterey in 1859. In ruins after 1874, the chapel was reconstructed and dedicated under the auspices of the Native Daughters of the Golden West, Oct. 9, 1955.

Placed in cooperation with Grand Parlors of Native Sons and Native Daughters of the Golden West, 1956.

SOLEDAD (Monterey Co.) *1.5 mi. S, Los Coches Rancho Wayside Campground, NW corner US 101 and Arroyo Seco Rd.*
Los Coches Rancho
(Richardson Adobe)

Los Coches Rancho (8,994.2 acres) was granted to Maria Josefa Soberanes de Richardson by the Mexican government in 1841. Her husband, William Brunner Richardson, a native of Baltimore, Maryland, built the adobe house here in 1843 and planted the nearby locust trees in 1846. This was the site of Capt. John C. Fremont's encampment in 1846 and 1847. The adobe was used later as a stage station and post office. It was donated to the State of California in 1958 by Margaret Jacks.

Placed by California State Park Commission in cooperation with Mrs. Adeline Richardson O'Brien and the Grand Parlor of Native Daughters of the Golden West, 1959.

SONOMA (Sonoma Co.) *Sonoma Plaza, E. Spain and 1st St. E.*
Bear Flag Monument

This monument was erected by Native Sons of the Golden West and the State of California to commemorate the raising of the Bear flag on this spot June 14, 1846, by the Bear Flag Party and their declaration of the freedom of California from Mexican rule. On July 9, 1846, the Bear flag was hauled down and the American flag here raised in its place by Lt. Joseph W. Revere, U.S.A., who was sent to Sonoma from San Francisco by Commander John B. Montgomery of the U.S. Sloop-of-War *Portsmouth,* following the raising of the American flag at Monterey July 7, 1846, by Commodore John Drake Sloat.

Private plaque.

SONOMA (Sonoma Co.) *Sonoma State Historic Park, 133 E. Spain St.*
Blue Wing Inn

Erected by Gen. Mariano G. Vallejo about 1840 for the accommodation of emigrants and other travelers. Purchased in gold rush days by Cooper and Spriggs, two retired seafaring men, and operated as hotel and store. Among first hostelries in Northern California. Notable guests, according to local tradition, included John C. Fremont, U. S. Grant, Gov. Pio Pico, Kit Carson, "Fighting Joe" Hooker, William T.

Sherman, Phil Sheridan, and members of Bear Flag Party. Classed among the notorious visitors were bandit Murietta and "three-fingered" Jack.

Placed by Historic Landmarks Committee of Native Sons of the Golden West, 1941.

SONOMA (Sonoma Co.) 2 mi. E, 18000 Old Winery Rd.
Buena Vista Winery and Vineyards

Birthplace of California wine. Founded in 1857 by Col. Agoston Haraszthy, father of the state's wine industry. Limestone tunnels were dug into the hillside and vineyards were also established. Haraszthy toured Europe in 1861 to gather the cuttings that developed California's wine industry.

Placed in cooperation with Buena Vista Winery and Vineyards, 1980.

SONOMA (Sonoma Co.) Sonoma State Historic Park, Spain St. at 3rd St. W.

Lachryma Montis
Home of General M.G. Vallejo
Erected 1851
Purchased by
State Park Commission
through funds furnished by
The General Vallejo Memorial Association
and the people of the State of California
Donors names within building
Placed by Historic Landmarks Committee of Native Sons of the Golden West, 1933.

SONOMA (Sonoma Co.) Sonoma State Historic Park, NW corner Spain St. and 1st St. E.

Mission San Francisco Solano

On July 4, 1823, Padre Jose Altmira founded this northernmost of California's Franciscan missions, the only one established under independent Mexico. In 1834 secularization orders were carried out by military commandant Mariano G. Vallejo. San Francisco Solano became a parish church serving the pueblo and Sonoma Valley until it was sold in 1881. This plaque replaces one originally dedicated by the Historic Landmarks Committee, Native Sons of the Golden West, 1926.

Placed by California State Park Commission in cooperation with Sonoma Parlor No. 111 of Native Sons of the Golden West, 1963.

SONOMA (Sonoma Co.) 579 1st St. E.
Nash-Patton Adobe

This house was built by H. A. Green in 1847. Here John H. Nash was taken prisoner by Lt. William T. Sherman in July 1847 for refusing to relinquish his post as alcalde to Lilburn W. Boggs. It was restored in 1931 by Zolita Bates, great-granddaughter of Nancy Patton Adler, who lived here after her marriage in 1848 to Lewis Adler, pioneer merchant of San Francisco and Sonoma.

Placed by California State Park Commission in cooperation with Sonoma Valley Historical Society, 1959.

SONOMA (Sonoma Co.)   *Sonoma State Historic Park,*
                              NW corner E. Spain St. and 1st St. E.
Sonoma Barracks
Erected in 1836 by Gen. M. G. Vallejo. Headquarters of Bear Flag Party which on June 14, 1846, proclaimed a "California Republic" and raised the Bear flag on Sonoma's plaza. Twenty-three days later, July 7, 1846, Commodore John Drake Sloat, representing the United States government, took possession of California. In April 1847 Stevenson's regiment, Company "C," U.S.A., occupied the barracks.
Placed by Historic Landmarks Committee of Native Sons of the Golden West, 1937.

SONOMA (Sonoma Co.)   *421 1st St. W.*
Salvador Vallejo Adobe
Home of Capt. Salvador Vallejo. He was the brother of Gen. Mariano G. Vallejo, Sonoma's founder. Built by Indian labor, 1836–46. Occupied by Capt. Vallejo and family until Bear Flag Party seized Sonoma, June 14, 1846.
Cumberland College, Presbyterian coeducational boarding school, located here 1858–64.
Placed by California State Park Commission.

SONOMA (Sonoma Co.)   *394 4th St. E.*
Samuele Sebastiani Vineyard and Winery
Here in 1825 the Franciscan fathers of San Francisco Solano de Sonoma Mission planted the first vineyard in Sonoma Valley. The grapes were used for making sacramental wines. After secularization of the mission in 1835, Gen. Mariano G. Vallejo, comandante of Alta California's northern frontier, produced prize-winning wines from these grapes. Samuele Sebastiani and his wife, Elvira, purchased this property in the early 1900s. A young immigrant from Italy, he had come here to make his fortune. Since that time he and his family have successfuly continued with distinction the traditions handed down to them through the years. Much of the originial mission vineyard is still planted to choice wine grapes.
Placed by California State Park Commission in cooperation with Sonoma Valley Historical Society, 1960.

SONOMA (Sonoma Co.)   *18 W. Spain St.*
Swiss Hotel
Constructed about 1850 by Don Salvador Vallejo, this adobe adjoined his first Sonoma dwelling built in 1836. Occupied by various pioneers, it was the house in 1861 of Dr. Victor J. Faure, vintner of prize-winning wines made from the grapes of the Vallejo family vineyards. Later it became known as the "Swiss Hotel" because of its use for hotel and restaurant purposes.
Placed by California State Park Commission.

SONOMA (Sonoma Co.)   *3 mi. SW, Temelec Adult Community,*
                                          220 Temelec Circle
Temelec Hall
This structure was erected in 1858 by Capt. Granville P. Swift, a member of the Bear Flag Party. The stone in the building was quarried here by native Indian labor.

General Persifor F. Smith, U.S. military commander-in-chief in California, lived in the little house nearby in 1849.
Placed by California State Park Commission.

SONOMA (Sonoma Co.) — 35 Napa St. W.
Site of Union Hotel and Union Hall

On this site between 1849 and 1957 stood the Union Hotel and Hall. Built by three veterans of the Mexican War, the hotel was a one-story adobe and the hall a one-story frame building. These were destroyed by fire in 1866 and replaced by two-story structures of stone and wood. The hotel was a rendezvous for such noted soldiers as William T. Sherman, Joseph Hooker, George Stoneman, and George Derby. The hall was also a focal point for theatrical, social, musical, and political events in Sonoma. The Bank of America built its Sonoma branch on this site in 1957.
Placed in cooperation with Sonoma branch of Bank of America, 1982.

SOULSBYVILLE (Tuolomne Co.) — NW corner Soulsbyville Rd. and Community Dr.
Mark Twain Bret Harte Trail
Soulsbyville

The first community in Tuolumne County to be founded (1855) entirely upon the operation of a lode mine. Site of the famous Soulsby Mine (discovered by Benjamine Soulsby) which produced over $6,500,000 by 1900. The first hardrock miners who worked the mine were from Cornwall, England. First group of 499 arriving in 1858.
Placed by Citizens of Soulsbyville and Tuolumne County Gold Centennial Celebration Committee, 1950.

SPRING VALLEY (San Diego Co.) — NE corner Memory and Bancroft Dr.
Bancroft Ranch House

Adobe built about 1850 by A. S. Ensworth. Home of Capt. Rufus K. Porter and family. Curved timbers brought from the *Clarissa Andrews,* famed coaling hulk formerly of the Pacific Mail Steamship Co. Historian Hubert Howe Bancroft later owned this estate and here wrote a part of his monumental *History of California.*
Placed by San Diego County Board of Supervisors and Historical Markers Committee, 1958.

SQUAW VALLEY (Placer Co.) — Squaw Valley Sports Center, Squaw Valley Rd., NE corner Blyth Olympic Arena Bldg.
Pioneer Ski Area of America

The VIII Olympic Winter Games of 1960 commemorate a century of sport skiing in America. By 1860 the Sierra Nevada, particularly at the California mining towns of Whiskey Diggings, Poker Flat, Port Wine, Onion Valley, La Porte, and Johnsville, some 60 miles north of Squaw Valley, saw the first organized ski clubs and competition in the western hemisphere.

Placed by California State Park Commission in cooperation with California Historical Society and Organizing Committee of VIII Olympic Winter Games, 1960.

STOCKTON (San Joaquin Co.)   *1100 E. Weber St.*

John Brown
(California's Paul Revere)

In 1846, during American conquest of California, John Brown, nicknamed "Juan Flaco," rode from Los Angeles to San Francisco in four days to warn Commodore Stockton of the siege of Los Angeles. As a result troops were sent and the city secured. This "Paul Revere of California" lived in Stockton from 1851–59 and is buried in the former citizen's cemetery near this site.

Placed in cooperation with local civic and historical organizations, 1969.

STOCKTON (San Joaquin Co.)   *Near Memory Chapel, Stockton Rural Cemetery, Cemetery Ln. and E. Pine St.*

The
Soldiers' Friend
Ruel C. Gridley,
Born Jan. 23, 1829
Died Nov. 24, 1870

Erected by Rawlins Post No. 23, Grand Army of the Republic, and the citizens of Stockton, Sept. 19, 1887, in gratitude for services rendered Union soldiers during the Rebellion in collecting $275,000 for the Sanitary Commission by selling and reselling a sack of flour.

Private plaque, placed 1887.

STOCKTON (San Joaquin Co.)   *City Hall, on Civic St. between El Dorado and Miner sts.*

Site of the First Building in Stockton

In August 1844 the first settlers arrived at Rancho del Campo de Los Franceses. One of the company, Thomas Lindsay, built the first dwelling, a tule hut, on this site. He was later murdered by Indians and buried here by travelers. The Point was formed by the junction of McLeod's Lake and Miner's Channel.

Placed in cooperation with local civic and historical organizations, 1969.

STOCKTON (San Joaquin Co.)   *Administration Bldg., County Fairgrounds, Airport Way*

Stockton Assembly Center

Here, within the confines of San Joaquin County Fairgrounds, enclosed by barbed wire and housed in temporary barracks, 4,271 San Joaquin County residents of Japanese ancestry, predominately American citizens, were interned from May 10 to Oct. 17, 1942, under Executive Order 9066. May such usurpation of civil, social, and economic rights, without specific charges or trial, never again occur.

Placed in cooperation with Japanese American community of San Joaquin County, 1984.

STOCKTON (San Joaquin Co.) *On E. Acacia St., between N. Pilgrim and N. Union sts.*

Temple Israel Cemetery

This hallowed ground was donated by Capt. Charles M. Weber in 1851 for use as a cemetery by the Jewish community of Stockton. It is the oldest Jewish cemetery in continuous use in California and west of the Rocky Mountains.

Placed by California State Park Commission in cooperation with Temple Israel and Union of American Hebrew Congregations, 1961.

STOCKTON (San Joaquin Co.) *On Center St., between Miner and Channel sts.*

Weber Point

Site of a two-story adobe and redwood home built by Charles M. Weber, founder and pioneer developers of Stockton. One of the first elaborate residences and landscaped gardens in the San Joaquin Valley. Completed in 1850. It remained Capt. Weber's home until his death in 1881.

Placed in cooperation with Stockton City Council and Cultural Board, 1976.

STONYFORD (Colusa Co.) *18.5 mi. SW, Letts Lake Campground, Fouts Springs Rd.*

Letts Valley

This valley was settled in 1855 by Jack and David Lett. The present lake spillway is the site of a tunnel built by them to facilitate drainage. Both brothers were killed in 1877, at the site of the present campgrounds, in an attempt to prevent squatters from settling on their land.

Placed by California State Park Commission in cooperation with Colusa County Board of Supervisors and Colusa Historical Society, 1960.

SUGARVILLE (Tuolumne Co.) *On SH 108, at Sugar Pine cut off*

Mark Twain Bret Harte Trail
Sonora Pass-Mono Road

Toll gate, fine hotel, and stables near this spot 1850s. Jedediah Smith reputed to have been first white man to cross over or near Sonora Pass, 1827. Portion of road built by Tuolumne County Water Company, 1852. Surveyed to Bridgeport, Mono County, 1860. Completed 1864 when six-horse team took three weeks for round trip, Sonora to Bridgeport.

Placed by California Centennial Commission and Sonora Lions Club, 1949.

SUN VALLEY (Los Angeles Co.) *10340 Keswick Ave.*

Old Trapper's Lodge

Old Trapper's Lodge is one of California's remarkable twentieth century folk art environments. It represents the life work of John Ehn (1897–1981), a self-taught artist who wished to pass on a sense of the Old West, derived from personal experiences, myths, and tall tales. From 1951 to 1981, using his family as models, and incorporating memorabilia, the "Old Trapper" followed his dreams and visions to create the lodge and its "Boot Hill."

Placed in cooperation with Saving and Preservation Arts and Cultural Environments (SPACE), 1985.

SUNNYVALE (Santa Clara Co.)

Corner N. Sunnyvale and California aves.

Home of Martin Murphy, Jr.

Martin Murphy, Jr., arrived in California with his family in 1844 in the first wagon train to cross the Sierra Nevada. The founder of Sunnyvale, he constructed here his house of prefabricated lumber, brought around the Horn in 1849. Members of the Murphy family lived here continuously until 1953 when the property was acquired by the City of Sunnyvale.

Placed by California State Park Commission in cooperation with City of Sunnyvale and Sunnyvale Historical Society, 1960.

SUSANVILLE (Lassen Co.)

Lassen Memorial Park, S side Adaline and North sts.

Noble Emigrant Trail

This meadow, now a city park, was a welcome stopping place on the Noble Emigrant Trail, pioneered by William H. Noble in 1851 and first used in 1852. Here emigrants en route to the Northern California mines were able to rest, recruit their stock, and obtain needed provisions at Isaac Roop's establishment, from which grew the city of Susanville.

Placed by California State Park Commission in cooperation with Lassen County Historical Society and Citizens of Susanville, 1960.

SUSANVILLE (Lassen Co.)

5 mi. SE, 2550 Wingfield Rd., via Richmond Rd.

Peter Lassen Grave

In memory of Peter Lassen, the pioneer who was killed by Indians Apr. 26, 1859. Aged 66 years.

Private plaque.

SUSANVILLE (Lassen Co.)

Memorial Park, N. Weatherlow at Nevada St.

Roop's Fort

Built in 1854 by Isaac N. Roop. First called Roop House, and used as stopping place by emigrant trains. It was the locale of the Sagebrush War, fought in 1863, between Plumas County and Lassen County citizens.

Placed by Susanville Parlors No. 2 and 3 of Native Daughters of the Golden West.

SUTTER CREEK (Amador Co.)

81 Eureka St.

Knight Foundry

Knight Foundry was established in 1873 to supply heavy equipment and repair facilities first to the gold mines and later the timber industry of the Mother Lode. Samuel N. Knight developed a high speed, cast iron water wheel which was a forerunner of the Pelton wheel design. Knight water wheels were used in some of the first hydroelectric plants in California, Oregon, and Utah. This plant is the last operating water-powered foundry and machine shop in California. The main line shaft is driven by a 42-inch Knight wheel with other machines being powered by smaller water motors.

Placed in cooperation with Carl W. Borgh family and Historic Knight & Company, Ltd., 1992.

SUTTER CREEK (Amador Co.)
Veteran's Memorial Hall, Main and Badger sts.

Sutter Creek

In memory of Gen. John A. Sutter, benefactor of the great State of California, who mined here and gave Sutter Creek its name and under whose regime gold was discovered. Also to those pioneer mothers, fathers, and miners of the Mother Lode which has produced millions in gold.

This rock used in Mother Lode champion hand drilling contests.

Placed by Sutter Creek Chapter of Native Sons and Native Daughters of the Golden West, 1942.

SYLMAR (Los Angeles Co.)
SW corner Foothill Blvd. and Bledsoe St.

The San Fernando
Pioneer Memorial Cemetery

This cemetery, earlier known as Morningside Cemetery, is the oldest nonsectarian cemetery in San Fernando Valley. It was established in the early 1800s and burials continued until 1939. The cemetery was legally abandoned in 1959. In this same year Mrs. Nellie S. Noble donated this site in memory of the pioneers of San Fernando as a pioneer memorial park.

Placed by California State Park Commission in cooperation with San Fernando Mission Parlor No. 280 of Native Daughters of the Golden West and History and Landmarks Association of San Fernando and Antelope Valley Parlors of Native Sons and Native Daughters of the Golden West, 1961.

TAFT (Kern Co.)
8 mi. E, 1.1 mi. N of Buena Vista pumping station, 300 ft. SE of Block House No. BV4

Old Yokuts

Village of Tulamniu named Buena Vista by Spanish Commander Fages, 1772. (One of first place names in South San Joaquin Valley.) Father Zalvidea again recorded site 1806. This village was occupied for several centuries. 1933–34 site excavated by Smithsonian Institution.

Placed by Kern County Historical Society, Micocene Parlor No. 228 of Native Daughters of the Golden West, Kern County Chamber of Commerce, and Kern County Museum, 1950.

TAHOE CITY (Placer Co.)
73 N. Lake Blvd. (SH 89), at SW corner Truckee River Bridge

Lake Tahoe Outlet Gates

Conflicting control of these gates, first built in 1870, resulted in the "Tahoe Water War" between lakeshore owners and downstream Truckee River water users which lasted two decades. The dispute was settled in 1910–11 when techniques for determining water content in snow were developed by Dr. James E. Church, Jr., and made possible accurate prediction and control of the seasonal rise in lake and river levels.

Placed by California State Park Commission in cooperation with Western Snow Conference and Sierra Pacific Power Company, 1965.

TEHACHAPI (Kern Co.)

7.4 mi. SE, 4.6 mi. S of Tehachapi Blvd.,
on Willow Pass Rd.

Oak Creek Pass

Father Francisco Garces used the Oak Creek Pass in 1776 to return to the Mojave after exploring the San Joaquin Valley, as did Fremont in 1844–45. Until the Tehachapi Pass in 1876, Oak Creek Pass was the only route used through the Tehachapi Mountains.

Placed by Bakersfield Parlor No. 42 of Native Sons of the Golden West, Bakersfield Parlor No. 239 of Native Daughters of the Golden West, Kern County Historical Society, and Kern County Chamber of Commerce, 1937.

TEHACHAPI (Kern Co.)

2.5 mi. W, 1.3 mi. N of SH 202,
NE corner Old Town and
Woodford-Tehachapi rds.

Old Town

The oldest settlement in Tehachapi Valley, known as "Old Town," was established here during the 1860s. It was long an important station on the road between Southern California and the San Joaquin Valley. The community began to decline when residents gradually moved to nearby Greenwich, later renamed Tehachapi, after completion of the Southern Pacific Railroad in 1876.

Placed by California State Park Commission in cooperation with Kern County Historical Society, El Tejon Parlor No. 239 of Native Daughters of the Golden West, and Kern County Museum, 1958.

TEHACHAPI (Kern Co.)

6.5 mi. W, 3.2 mi. E of Keene exit,
on old SH 50

Tehachapi Loop

From this spot may be seen a portion of the world-renowned "Loop." It was completed in 1876 under the direction of William Hood, Southern Pacific railroad engineer. In gaining elevation around central hill of Loop, a 4,000-foot train will cross 77 feet above its rear cars in tunnel below.

Placed by Kern County Historical Society, Bakersfield Parlor No. 42 of Native Sons of the Golden West, El Tejon Parlor No. 239 of Native Daughters of the Golden West, Kern County Museum, and Southern Pacific Railroad, 1953.

TEHAMA (Tehama Co.)

75 ft. E of 2nd and D sts. intersection

First Seat of Tehama County Government

Tehama County's Board of Supervisors and other county officials first met in rented rooms in the Union Hotel, later called Heider House. The county seat remained here from May 1856 to March 1857, when it was moved to Red Bluff. The Heider House was destroyed by fire in 1908. This property is part of original land grant to Robert Hasty Thomes, 1844.

Placed in cooperation with Pair-o-Dice Chapter No. 7-11 and Trinitarianus Chapter No. 62 of E Clampus Vitus, 1981.

177

THORNTON (San Joaquin Co.) *3 mi. N, 200 ft. N of Cameron and Thornton rds. intersection*

Benson's Ferry and Mokelumne City
Pop. Feb. 1862—0

E. Stokes and A. M. Woods operated a ferry here in 1849. Sold to John Benson in 1850; he operated it until he was murdered in February 1859. Nearby Mokelumne City, founded in 1850, was the second largest city in the county until washed away in the great flood of January 1862.

Placed by Tuleburgh Chapter 69 of E Clampus Vitus, 1979.

TIBURON (Marin Co.) *Angel Island State Park, Hospital Cove*
Angel Island

In 1775 the packet *San Carlos,* first known Spanish ship to enter San Francisco Bay, anchored in this cove while her commander, Lt. Juan Manuel de Ayala, directed the first survey of the bay. Ayala named this island Isla de Los Angeles. The island has been a Mexican rancho, U.S. military post, bay defense site, and both a quarantine and immigration station.

Placed in cooperation with City of Tiburon, 1970.

TRACY (San Joaquin Co.) *9 mi. SW, Carnegie State Vehicular Recreation Area, 5.9 mi. W of I-580, on Corral Hollow Rd.*
Carnegie

A city of 3,500 population from 1895–1912 and the site of the Carnegie Brick and Pottery Company, served by the Alameda and San Joaquin Railroad. The plant had 45 kilns and 13 tall smokestacks and the town had a post office, company store, hotels, saloons, bandstand, and hundreds of homes. Clay was used from the famous Tesla Coal Mine, four miles to the west.

Placed by California State Park Commission in cooperation with Tracy District Chamber of Commerce, 1961.

TRACY (San Joaquin Co.) *6.5 mi. SW, 1.5 mi. W of I-580, on Corral Hollow Rd.*
Corral Hollow

The Edward B. Carrell home was built here at the site of an Indian village on El Camino Viejo, an old Spanish trail. Through here passed the '49ers and the first mail to the Tuolumne mines. Men and animals received food and drink at Wright's Zink House five hundred yards north of here.

Placed by California State Park Commission in cooperation with Tracy District Chamber of Commerce, 1961.

TRACY (San Joaquin Co.) *Manthey Rd. interchange from I-5, W side frontage rd. N 1 mi. to N bank of San Joaquin River*
The Comet—1846—First Sail Launch

(Plaque at entrance to Mossdale Crossing Park and Ramp, 2 mi. N of I-5 and I-205 intersection)

First known sail launch to ascend San Joaquin River from San Francisco landed here autumn, 1846. Carried 20 Mormon pioneers who founded New Hope Agricultural Project on Stanislaus. A yoke of oxen and span of mules were driven from Marsh's Landing (Antioch) by two men who followed a crude map drawn by Merritt the Trapper. Two years later Doak and Bansell operated here the first ferry on San Joaquin River.

Placed by California Centennial Commission and Alameda County Camps of Daughters of Utah Pioneers, 1949.

TRACY (San Joaquin Co.)
Manthey Rd. interchange from I-5, 1 mi. N to N bank of San Joaquin River

Site of Completion of First Transcontinental Railroad

(Plaque at entrance to Mossdale Crossing Park and Ramp, 2 mi. N of I-5 and I-205 intersection)

The construction of the San Joaquin River bridge completed the last link of the transcontinental railroad. Building had simultaneously proceeded from the Bay Area and Sacramento and met at the San Joaquin River. The first train crossed the bridge on Sept. 8, 1869.

Placed in cooperation with local civic and historical organizations, 1969.

TRACY (San Joaquin Co.)
SE of Tracy, 1.4 mi. N of county line on CH J3

Site of San Joaquin City

This river town was established in 1849. Pioneers and freight wagons crossed the river at nearby Durham's Ferry, following post roads to the southern mines. As terminal for riverboats, it played an important part in development of the westside grain farming and cattle raising.

Placed by California State Park Commission in cooperation with San Joaquin County Historical Society, 1962.

TRINIDAD (Humboldt Co.)
NW corner Edwards and Hector sts.

Town of Trinidad

Founded Apr. 8, 1850, Trinidad is the oldest town on the Northern California coast. During the 1850s, it served as a vital supply link between ships anchored at Trinidad Bay and miners in the Klamath, Trinity, Salmon River, and Gold Bluff mines. It was the county seat of Klamath County (now disbanded) from 1851 to 1854, but its population declined as Eureka and other area port cities developed.

Placed in cooperation with Eureka Chapter No. 101 of E Clampus Vitus, 1981.

TRINIDAD (Humboldt Co.)
1.5 W of US 101, U.S. Coast Guard Station

"Carolus III, Dei G. HYSPANIARUM REX"

June 9, 1775
Replaced by Club women of
Humboldt Co.
Sept. 9, 1913

TRINIDAD (Humboldt Co.) *SW corner Ocean and Edwards sts.*
Tsurai
Directly below was located the ancient Yurok village of Tsurai. A prehistoric, permanent Indian community, it was first located and described by captains Bodega and Heceta June 9–19, 1775. The houses were of hand-split redwood planks designed for defense and protection. The village was occupied until 1916.
Placed in cooperation with Heritage Trinidad and Humboldt County Historical Society, 1970.

TRONA (Inyo Co.) *5.5 mi. NE, Trona Wilderness at Valley Wells rds.*
Valley Wells
In this area, several groups of midwestern emigrants who had escaped from hazards and privations in Death Valley in 1849 sought to secure water from Searles Lake. When they discovered its salty nature, they turned northward and westward in despair, and with travail crossed Argus and other mountains to reach settlements of Central and Southern California.
Placed by California Centennial Commission and Death Valley '49ers, 1949.

TRONA (San Bernardino Co.) *Roadside rest area,*
Trona Rd. at Center St.
Searles Lake Borax Discovery
Borax was discovered on the nearby surface of Searles Lake by John Searles in 1862. With his brother Dennis, he formed the San Bernardino Borax Mining Company in 1873 and operated it until 1897. The chemicals in Searles Lake, which included borax, potash, soda ash, salt cake, and lithium, were deposited here by the runoff waters from melting Ice Age glaciers. John Searles' discovery has proved to be the world's richest chemical storehouse, containing half the natural elements known to man.
Placed by California State Park Commission in cooperation with Death Valley '49ers, Inc., American Potash and Chemical Corporation, and West End Chemical Division of Stauffer Chemical Corporation, 1962.

TRUCKEE (Nevada Co.) *Donner Memorial State Park,*
old Hwy. 40 at I-80 and Truckee exit
Donner Party
Near this spot stood the Breen cabin of the party of emigrants who started for California from Springfield, Illinois, in Apr. 1846, under the leadership of Capt. George Donner. Delays occurred, and when the party reached this locality on Oct. 29, the Truckee Pass emigrant road was concealed by snow. The height of the shaft of the monument indicates the depth of the snow which was 22 California-bound emigrants, who wintered here in 1846–47; many died of exposure and starvation.
Placed by Native Sons and Native Daughters of the Golden West, 1918.

TRUCKEE (Nevada Co.) *Southern Pacific Depot, 70 Donner Pass Rd.*
First Transcontinental Railroad—Truckee
While construction on Sierra tunnels delayed Central Pacific, advance forces at Truckee began building 40 miles of track east and west of Truckee, moving supplies

by wagon and sled. Summit Tunnel was opened in December 1867. The line reached Truckee Apr. 3, 1868, and the Sierra was conquered. Rails reached Reno June 19, and construction advanced eastward one mile daily toward the meeting with Union Pacific at promontory May 10, 1869, to complete the first transcontinental railroad.

Placed in cooperation with Conference of California Historical Societies and Nevada County and Truckee-Donner Historical Societies, 1969.

TULE LAKE (Modoc Co.)   *7.5 mi. S, NE corner SH 139 and CR 176*
May 1942—Tule Lake—March 1946

Tule Lake was one of ten American concentration camps established during World War II to incarcerate 110,000 persons of Japanese ancestry, of whom the majority were American citizens, behind barbed wire and guard towers without charge, trial, or establishment of guilt. These camps are reminders of how racism, economic and political exploitation, and expediency can undermine the constitutional guarantees of United States citizens and aliens alike. May the injustices and humiliation suffered here never recur.

Placed in cooperation with Northern California-Western Nevada District Council, Japanese American Citizens League, 1979.

TULE LAKE (Siskiyou Co.)   *8.3 mi. S, Lava Beds National Monument, 6.6 mi. W of NE entrance*
Canby's Cross
14 Miles

General E. R. S. Canby was murdered here in April 1873 while holding a peace parley under flag of truce with Capt. Jack and Indian chiefs. Reverend Eleazer Thomas, peace commissioner, was likewise treacherously slain.

Placed by Department of Public Works, Division of Highways.

TULE LAKE (Siskiyou Co.)   *8.3 mi. S, Lava Beds National Monument, 3.8 mi. W of NE entrance*
Captain Jack's Stronghold
11 Miles

From this fortress Capt. Jack and his Indian forces successfully resisted capture by U.S. Army troops from Dec. 1, 1872, to Apr. 18, 1873. Other nearby landmarks of the Modoc Indian War are Canby's Cross and Guillem's Graveyard.

Placed by Department of Public Works, Division of Highways.

TULE LAKE (Siskiyou Co.)   *4 mi. S, Lava Beds National Monument, 7.5 mi. W of NE entrance*
Guillem's Camp Cemetery

The bodies of 36 enlisted men were buried here in April 1873 following the disastrous ambush of the Thomas-Wright patrol at Hardin Butte. In 1888 the bodies were removed to the Presidio near San Francisco where they remain, remembered only as "the unknown dead of the Modoc War."

Private plaque.

TUOLUMNE (Tuolumne Co.) *2 mi. N, on*
Confidence-Tuolumne City Rd.

Cherokee

First placer camp in East Belt section of Mother Lode. Gold discovered here in 1853 by Scott brothers, descendants of Cherokee Indians. Scars of placer "diggins" in every little arroyo in Cherokee Valley healed over by Mother Nature, later replaced by quartz mines. Present day productive farms in this area were once rich placer grounds.

Placed by California Centennial Commission and Tuolumne County Progressive Association, 1949.

TUOLUMNE (Tuolumne Co.) *Carter St. and Tuolumne Rd.*
intersection, in center island

Tuolumne
(formerly called Summerville)

Geographical center of East Belt Placer Gold Rush, 1856–57. First white settlers, the Ranklin Summers family, arrived in 1854 and built log cabin half mile west. James Blakely, in 1858, discovered first quartz lode, half mile east, naming it "Eureka," which mine became nucleus of town of "Summersville," later called "Carters" and, finally, "Tuolumne." Other mining towns lively in gold rush days were Long Gulch, two miles south, and Cherokee, two miles north.

Placed by California Centennial Commission and Tuolumne City Progressive Association, 1948.

TUTTLETOWN (Tuolumne Co.) *2 mi. NW, at end of*
Jackass Hill Rd., .7 mi. N of SH 49

Mark Twain Bret Harte Trail
Mark Twain Cabin

Stopping place of packers carrying supplies to miners. Often 200 jackasses on hill overnight furnishing concept suggesting name "Jackass Hill." Very coarse gold found here. $10,000 taken from 100 square feet of ground. Quartz found containing three-quarters of total weight in gold. Mark Twain, Steve, Jim and Bill Gillis, and Dick Stoker, the "Dick Baker" in *Roughing It*, were cronies. Mark wrote here *Jumping Frog of Calaveras* from notes made at Angels Camp Tavern.

Placed by Tuolumne County Chamber of Commerce, 1929.

TUTTLETOWN (Tuolumne Co.) *1 mi. NW, on SH 49,*
N and S of exit to cabin

Mark Twain Cabin
1 Mile

Replica, with original chimney and fireplace. Here on Jackass Hill, young Mark Twain, while guest of Gillis brothers, 1864–65, gathered material for *Jumping Frog of Calaveras*, which first brought him fame, and for *Roughing It*.

Placed by Department of Public Works, Division of Highways.

TUTTLETOWN (Tuolumne Co.)   *On SH 49, at Wilcox Ranch Rd.*
Mark Twain Bret Harte Trail
Tuttletown

Early day stopping place for men and mounts. Named for Judge Anson A. H. Tuttle, who built first log cabin here in 1848. Stones used in this base from old Swerer store, built in 1854, remains of which still exist, 1949. Mark Twain traded here. Tuttletown Hotel, built in 1852 and still standing in 1949, was last operated by John Edwards.

Placed by California Centennial Commission and Sonora Lodge No. 1587 of Elks, 1949.

UKIAH (Mendocino Co.)   *431 S. Main St.*
Sun House

This house, constructed in 1911–12, is a unique Craftsman-style redwood building which incorporates northwestern designs into its architecture. The Sun House was designed by George Wilcox and John W. and Grace Carpenter Hudson. Dr. Hudson was a recognized authority on American Indians, and especially California Pomo Indians. Mrs. Hudson, an outstanding artist, became widely known for her paintings of Pomo life.

Placed in cooperation with Cultural Arts Commission of City of Ukiah, 1979.

UKIAH (Mendocino Co.)   *2701 Vichy Springs Rd.*
Ukiah Vichy Springs Resort

Native Americans used these springs for thousands of years before Frank Marble "discovered" them in 1848. William Day established the resort here in 1854. Ukiah Vichy represents one of the oldest continuously operating mineral springs resorts in California. Its waters remain among the most important of the thermal, alkaline-carbonated waters so highly valued by both European and American believers in hydrotherapy. It is the only mineral spring in California that resembles the famed Grand Grille Springs of Vichy, France.

Placed in cooperation with Vichy Springs Resort, 1991.

UNION CITY (Alameda Co.)   *30977 Union City Blvd.*
First County Courthouse

Site of first courthouse where Alameda County government began, June 6, 1853. Officials met in two-story wooden building erected by Henry C. Smith and A. M. Church as merchandise store. Seat of government moved to San Leandro in 1856, following vote of people of County in December 1854.

Placed by California State Park Commission in cooperation with Alameda County Parlors of Native Sons and Daughters of the Golden West, 1953.

UNION CITY (Alameda Co.)   *30849 Dyer St.*
Site of Nation's First Successful Beet Sugar Factory

The factory was built in 1870 by E. H. Dyer, "father of the American beet sugar industry." Located on a corner of Dyer's farm, the small factory began processing sugarbeets on Nov. 15, 1870, and produced 293 tons of sugar during its first operating season. The plant has since been completely rebuilt on the original site.

Placed by California State Park Commission in cooperation with Holly Sugar Corporation, 1962.

UPPER LAKE (Lake Co.)
1.7 mi. SE, SH 10 and Reclamation Rd. intersection

Battle of Bloody Island

One-fourth mile west was Bloody Island, now a hill surrounded by reclaimed land. On the island, in 1850, U.S. soldiers nearly annihilated all its inhabitants for the murder of two white men. Doubt exists of these Indians' guilt. In 1851 a treaty between whites and Indians entered into.

Placed by California Centennial Commission and County of Lake, 1950.

VACAVILLE (Solano Co.)
Pena Adobe Park, off I-80, .5 mi. NE on Pena Adobe Rd.

Rancho Los Putos

This is the site of Rancho Los Putos, of 10-square leagues, granted in 1845 by Gov. Pio Pico to Juan Felipe Peña and Manuel Cabeza Vaca. The Peña adobe erected here in 1842 is still owned by descendants of the Peña-Vaca families. The town of Vacaville, nearby, was established in 1851 on land sold by Vaca to William McDaniel.

Placed by California State Park Commission in cooperation with Vacaville Parlor No. 293 of Native Daughters of the Golden West, 1955.

VALENCIA (Los Angeles Co.)
SW corner "The Old Road" and Henry Mayo Dr., .2 mi. S of I-5 and SH 126 interchange

Rancho San Francisco

Approximately one-half mile south of this point was the adobe headquarters of Rancho San Francisco, originally built about 1804 as a granary of Mission San Fernando. The rancho was granted to Antonio del Valle in 1839. Here William Lewis Manly and John Rodgers, in January 1850, obtained supplies and animals with which they rescued their comrades of a California-bound, gold-seeking emigrant party, then stranded and starving in Death Valley some 250 miles northeast.

Placed by California State Park Commission in cooperation with Los Angeles County Board of Supervisors and Death Valley '49ers, 1958.

VALLECITO (Calaveras Co.)
Church St. and Cemetery Ln. intersection

Vallecito Bell Monument

One of California's important early-day mining towns named by Mexicans, meaning "little valley." Gold was discovered here by the Murphy brothers in 1849. It was originally called "Murphys' Old Diggings." This bell was cast at Troy, New York, in 1853. After being brought around the Horn, it was purchased from the ship with funds contributed by early-day residents, then brought to Vallecito and erected in a large oak tree in 1854. It was used to call the people together for all purposes until Feb. 16, 1939, when a severe wind blew the old tree down.

Placed by Grand Parlor of the Native Sons of the Golden West, 1939.

VALLEJO (Solano Co.)

Mare Island Naval Shipyard,
main gate entrance, SW corner
Tennessee St. and Mare Island Way

First U.S. Naval Station in the Pacific

Mare Island Navy yard was established Sept. 16, 1854, by then Commander David G. Farragut, USN. Site selected in 1852 by a commission headed by Commodore John D. Sloat, USN. Mare Island had the Navy's first shipyard, ammunition depot, hospital, marine barracks, cemetery, chapel, and radio station in the Pacific.

Placed by California State Park Commission in cooperation with Solano County Historical Society, 1960.

VALLEJO (Solano Co.)

NW corner of city parking lot,
200 block of York St., between
Sacramento and Santa Clara sts.

Site of State Capitol at Vallejo

Vallejo was the official seat of state government from Feb. 4, 1851, to Feb. 4, 1853. The capitol, shown above, within which the legislature convened in 1852 and 1853, stood near this spot.

Placed by Historic Landmarks Committee of Native Sons of the Golden West, 1938.

VALLEY SPRINGS (Calaveras Co.)

3.7 mi. E, on SH 12

Double Springs
2 Miles

(Additional plaque one mi. from site)

Founded Feb. 18, 1850. Became county seat of Calaveras County. Old courthouse said to be constructed of lumber brought from China. Still standing but not on the original site.

Placed by Department of Public Works, Division of Highways.

VALLEY SPRINGS (Calaveras Co.) *3.6 mi. E, on Double Springs Rd.*

Double Springs
First County Seat of Calaveras County
Feb. 18, 1850

Land located in 1847 by Charles L. Peck. Claimed under preemption notice to the alcalde of San Francisco, recorded Sept. 19, 1850, at Page 69, in Record B, Third Archives of San Francisco.

Surveyed and platted as Double Springs townsite in 1850. First county courthouse of imported Chinese panels, erected 100 feet southwest of this monument. Honorable W. Fowle Smith, first county judge, and L.A. Collier, first county clerk.

Placed by Calaveras County Chamber of Commerce, 1930.

VENTURA (Ventura Co.)

4200 Olivas Park Dr.

Olivas Adobe

This adobe is the only early two-story adobe in the Santa Clara River Valley. A small one-story adobe, built in 1837, was enlarged in 1849 by Don Raimundo Olivas, a prosperous cattle rancher. Continuous use has preserved the adobe for public viewing.

Placed in cooperation with City of San Buenaventura, 1976.

VENTURA (Ventura Co.)   *Grant Park, at end of Ferro Dr.*

San Buenaventura Mission Cross
Restored September 9, 1912,
by
the Alice M. Bartlett Club
of San Buenaventura, California,
to take the place of the mission cross erected
on this spot by the Franciscan missionary
Padre Junipero Serra, 1782

Private plaque.

VENTURA (Ventura Co.)   *501 Poli St.*

Old County Courthouse
This imposing building was designed by Albert C. Martin and built in 1912 as the Ventura County Courthouse. It is an outstanding example of neoclassic architecture, considered the proper style for public buildings of the early 20th century. The courthouse was purchased by the City of San Buenaventura in 1971 for use as the city hall.
Placed in cooperation with City of San Buenaventura, 1973.

VERNON (Los Angeles Co.)   *4490 Exchange Ave.*

La Mesa Battlefield
On this spot was fought La Batalla de La Mesa—Battle of La Mesa—Jan. 9th, 1847. Commodore Robert Field Stockton, USN, in command of American forces, and Gen. Jose Maria Flores, commanding the Californians.
Private plaque.

VISALIA (Tulare Co.)   *7 mi. E, .3 mi. W of SH 180,*
on Charter Oak Dr.

Tulare County Election Tree
Under this tree a party commanded by Maj. James D. Savage, on July 10, 1852, conducted an election by which Tulare County was organized. Woodsville, site of Wood's cabin, the first small town settled by white men in Tulare County, and first county seat, was located about one-half mile south of this marker. This general area, the delta of Kaweah River, was also known as the "Four Creeks Country."
Placed by California Centennial Commission and Tulare County Historical Society, 1949.

VISTA (San Diego Co.)   *3.3 mi. N, Rancho Guajome*
Regional Park, 2210 N. Santa Fe Ave.

Rancho Guajome
Formerly attached to Mission San Luis Rey, this 2,219-acre ranch passed through brief ownership by two mission Indians, then Don Abel Stearns, and into possession of Ysidora Bandini upon marriage to Col. Cave Johnson Couts. The adobe ranch house, built in 1852–53, is one of the finest extant examples of the traditional Spanish-Mexican one-story hacienda with an inner-outer courtyard plan. It was acquired by San Diego County in 1973 for the Guajome Regional Park.
Placed in cooperation with Squibob Chapter of E Clampus Vitus, 1981.

186

VOLCANO (Amador Co.)
4 mi. N, on Shake Ridge rd., .9 mi. W of Volcano-Daffodil Hill Rd. intersection

Astronomical Observatory

On the knoll behind this marker George Madeira built the first amateur astronomical observatory of record in California and there discovered the great comet of 1861 with a three-inch refractor telescope.

Placed in cooperation with Stockton and Sacramento Astronomical Societies, 1968.

VOLCANO (Amador Co.)
Main and Consolation sts. intersection

Volcano
4 Miles

Started 1848 by soldiers of Col. Stevenson's regiment. Named by miners because of apparent volcanic appearance. Here the first California rental library, 1850, was established and one of the first "little theaters" founded by the "Volcano Thespian Society," 1854. Interesting Civil War history.

Placed by Department of Public Works, Division of Highways.

WALKER'S PASS (Kern Co.)
At summit on SH 178, 8.4 mi. NW of SH 14

Walker's Pass

Discovered by Joseph R. Walker, American trailblazer, who left the San Joaquin Valley through this pass in 1834. This area was traversed by topographer Edward M. Kern, after whom the Kern River was named, while accompanying the Fremont Expedition of 1845. After 1860 it became a mining freight route to Owens Valley.

Placed by Bakersfield Parlor No. 42 of Native Sons of the Golden West, El Tejon Parlor No. 239 of Native Daughters of the Golden West, and Kern County Chamber of Commerce, 1937.

WARNER SPRINGS (San Diego Co.)
4 mi. SE, on CH S2, 7 mi. E SH 79 junction

Warner Ranch House

In 1844 Gov. Manuel Micheltorena granted 44,322 acres to Juan Jose Warner, who built this house. General Kearny passed here in 1846; Mormon Battalion in 1847. First Butterfield Stage stopped at this ranch on Oct. 6, 1858, en route from Tipton, Missouri, to San Francisco; 2,600 miles, time 24 days. This was the southern overland route into California.

Placed by San Diego County Board of Supervisors and Historical Markers Committee, 1964.

WASHINGTON (Nevada Co.)
Omega Rest Area, SH 20, 6 mi. E of Washington Rd.

Alpha and Omega

One mile north of here were the towns of Alpha and Omega, named by gold miners in the early 1850s. The tremendous hydraulic diggings, visible from near this point, engulfed most of the original townsites. Alpha was the birthplace of famed opera singer Emma Nevada. Mining at Omega continued until 1949, and lumbering operations are carried on there today.

WEAVERVILLE (Trinity Co.)   4 mi. W, on SH 299
The La Grange Mine

This mine, originally known as the Oregon Mountain Group of Claims, first operated about 1862. In 1892 the mine was purchased by the La Grange Hydraulic Gold Mining Company, which brought water from Stuart's Fork through 29 miles of ditch, tunnels, and flume, and delivered it to the mine pit under a 650-foot head. Over 100,000,000 yards of gravel were moved and $3,500,000 in gold produced. Large scale operations ceased in 1918.

Placed by California State Park Commission in cooperation with Mt. Bally Parlor No. 87 of Native Sons of the Golden West, Trinity County Historical Society, and Trinitarianus Chapter of E Clampus Vitus, 1963.

WEAVERVILLE (Trinity Co.)   .2 mi. E, on SH 3
Tong War

In the year of 1854 on this site, two belligerent Chinese Tongs fought a pitched battle; 2,000 participated, 26 lost their lives, and many were wounded.

Placed by Mount Balley Parlor No. 87 of Native Sons of the Golden West and Eltapone Parlor No. 55 of Native Daughters of the Golden West. (Unofficial marker)

WEAVERVILLE (Trinity Co.)   SW corner SH 299 and Oregon St.
Won Lim Miao

Hundreds of Chinese miners came to the Weaverville area in the 1850s and prospered despite hardships, discrimination, and tax on foreign miners. The first house of worship burned in 1873; the Chinese continued their religious traditions in the present temple, dedicated Apr. 18, 1874. Moon Lim Lee, trustee and grandson of one of its contributors, gift-deeded the "Temple Amongst the Forest Beneath the Clouds" to the State.

Placed in cooperation with Trinitarianus Chapter No. 62 of E Clampus Vitus, 1980.

WEED (Siskiyou Co.)   14.5 mi. NE, SH 97 at Military Pass Rd.
Emigrant Trail

As early as 1852 wagon trains of overland emigrants crossed six hundred feet to the north into Shasta Valley and Yreka; and at this point the 1857 military pass from Fort Crook emerged to join the westward emigrant road.

Placed by California State Park Commission in cooperation with Siskiyou County Historical Society and County of Sikiyou.

WEST POINT (Calaveras Co.)   2.1 mi. W, on SH 26
Sandy Gulch

Sandy Gulch, 1849 trading center for pioneer miners of northeastern Calaveras County, was named after the gulch where William and Dan Carsner found large nuggets embedded in the coarse sands. Water for mining was brought from Middle Fork of Mokelumne River through Sandy Gulch and Kadish ditches. Quartz mining began in early fifties and first custom stamp mill in the district was at head of Sandy

Gulch. School and election precincts were established early. Hangman's Tree stood near the center of town. Numerous Indians of Me-Wok tribe originally lived here. Many pioneers are buried in the cemetery.
Private plaque, placed 1941.

WEST POINT (Calaveras Co.)
SH 26 and Main St. intersection
West Point

Named by famous scout Kit Carson while searching for pass over Sierras. One emigrant road forked at Big Meadows and north branch came directly to West Point, a thriving trading post prior to gold discovery. Bret Harte, famous author, lived here for a period.
Placed by California Centennial Commission and Mokelumne Lions Club, 1949.

WESTWOOD (Lassen Co.)
2.5 mi. W, on SH 36
Lassen Emigrant Trail

Through this draw passed many covered wagons and gold seekers en route to California over the Lassen Trail during 1848–51. Approaching this location from the north, the trail passed what is now Bogard Ranger Station. Proceeding southward to Big Springs and Big Meadows (now Lake Almanor), it then turned westward to Deer Creek, which it followed generally to Vina in the Sacramento Valley.
Placed by California State Park Commission in cooperation with Lassen County Historical Society, 1959.

WHEATLAND (Yuba Co.)
Tomita Park, Front St.,
between Main and Fourth sts.
Johnson's Ranch

The first settlement reached in California by emigrant trains using the Emigrant ("Donner") Trail, it was an original part of the 1844 Don Pablo Gutierrez land grant. It was sold at auction to William Johnson in 1845. In 1849 part of the ranch was set aside as a government reserve—Camp Far West. In 1866, the town of Wheatland was laid out on a portion of the grant.
Placed in cooperation with Wheatland Lions Club, 1971.

WHEATLAND (Yuba Co.)
3.9 mi. E of SH 65, on Spenceville Rd.
Overland Emigrant Trail

Approximately 1-1/4 miles east of this site is the historic Johnson's Crossing. This was the first settlement reached west of the Sierra and the last stop on the overland emigrant trail. Used as a camping spot for the pioneers, departure spot for the miners and a sojourning place for trappers, herdsmen, and adventurers. The rescue party for the Donner party was organized and departed from this crossing Feb. 5, 1847.
Placed in cooperation with Yuba County Historical Society, 1976.

WHITTIER (Los Angeles Co.)
Pio Pico State Historic Park,
6003 Pioneer Blvd.
Casa de Governor Pio Pico

Following the Mexican War, Pio Pico, last Mexican governor, acquired 9,000-acre Rancho Paso de Tartolo and built here an adobe home that was destroyed by the floods of 1883–84. His second adobe casa, now known as The Mansion, represents a compromise between Mexican and American culture. While living here the ex-governor was active in the development of American California.

Placed in cooperation with California Historical Landmarks Advisory Committee, Governor Pico Mansion Society, Poppy Trail Parlor No. 266, and Whittier Parlor No. 298 of Native Daughters of the Golden West, 1966.

WHITTIER (Los Angeles Co.)   *12300 Whittier Blvd.*
Paradox Hybrid Walnut Tree
Planted in 1907 as an experiment for the University of California.

Placed by Whittier Area Community Beautiful, Grand Parlor of Native Daughters of the Golden West, and Whittier Chapter of Daughters of the American Revolution, 1963.

WHITTIER (Los Angeles Co.)   *At entrance, Dept. of the Youth Authority, 11850 E. Whittier Blvd.*
Reform School for Juvenile Offenders
The Mar. 11, 1889, Act of the California Legislature authorized the establishment of a school for juvenile offenders. Dedication and laying of cornerstone was done by Governor R.W. Waterman on Feb. 12, 1890. Officially opened as "Whittier State School" for boys and girls on July 1, 1891. Girls were transferred in 1916 and only boys have been in residence since that time. Renamed "Fred C. Nelles School for Boys" in 1941 ("for Boys" was dropped around 1970). This school has been in continuous operation serving the needs of juvenile offenders since 1891.

Placed in cooperation with Department of the Youth Authority, 1984.

WILMINGTON (Los Angeles Co.)   *Banning Park, 401 E. M St., at Banning Pl.*
In memory of General Phineas Banning
August 19, 1830
March 8, 1885
Placed by Long Beach Parlor No. 154 of Native Daughters of the Golden West, 1937.

WILMINGTON (Los Angeles Co.)   *1053 Cary St.*
Drum Barracks
Established at Wilmington in 1862, Drum Barracks became the United States military headquarters for Southern California, Arizona, and New Mexico. A garrison and base for supplies, it was a terminus for camel pack trains operated by the Army until 1863. Abandoned in 1866, its site remains a landmark of the Civil War in California.

Placed by California State Park Commission in cooperation with California History Commission, 1965.

WINTERHAVEN (Imperial Co.)   *Next to St. Thomas Indian School and Church, N of Yuma, on CA side of Colorado River*
Fort Yuma
Originally called Camp Calhoun, the site was first used as a U.S. military post in 1849. A fire destroyed the original buildings. By 1855 the barracks had been rebuilt.

Called Camp Yuma in 1852, it became Fort Yuma after reconstruction. Transferred to the Department of the Interior and the Quechan Indian Tribe in 1884, it became a boarding school operated by the Catholic Church until 1900.

Placed in cooperation with Quechan Tribe and Squibob Chapter of E Clampus Vitus, 1989.

WINTERHAVEN (Imperial Co.)
1 mi. S, St. Thomas Indian Mission, Indian Hill on Picacho Rd., Fort Yuma

Site of Mission Purisima Concepcion, 1780–81

In October 1780, Father Francisco Garces and companions began Mission La Purisima Concepcion. The mission/pueblo site was inadequately supported. Colonists ignored Indian rights, usurped the best lands, and destroyed Indian crops. Completely frustrated and disappointed, the Quechans (Yumas) and their allies destroyed Concepcion on July 17–19, 1781.

Placed in cooperation with Quechan Tribal Council, Catholic Diocese of San Diego, Imperial Valley Pioneers, and Squibob Chapter of E Clampus Vitus, 1982.

WINTERHAVEN (Imperial Co.)
18.2 mi. N, on Picacho Rd.

Picacho Mines

Opened by placer miners after 1852, the gold mines expanded into hard rock quarrying by 1872. Picacho employed 700 miners at its peak from 1895 to 1900. Mill accidents, low ore quality, and the loss of cheap river transport with the building of Laguna Dam led to numerous periods of inactivity. With ores far from worked out, the Picacho Mines, using modern techniques, again resumed operations in 1984.

Placed in cooperation with Squibob Chapter of E Clampus Vitus, and Imperial Valley Pioneers Historical Society, 1985.

WINTERHAVEN (Imperial Co.)
18 mi. W, Algodones San Dunes County Rest Area, south side of I-8

Plank Road
1914 to 1927

This unique plank road, seven miles long, was the only means early motorists had of crossing the treacherous Imperial sand dunes. The eight-by-twelve-foot sections were moved with a team of horses whenever the shifting sands covered portions of the road. Double sections were placed at intervals to permit vehicles to pass.

Placed in cooperation with Imperial Valley Pioneers Association, 1971.

WINTERS (Solano Co.)
1.5 mi. SW, University of California Experimental Farm, Putah Creek Rd.

University of California Experimental Farm,
Wolfskill Grant

In 1842 John R. Wolfskill arrived here laden with fruit seeds and cuttings. He was a true horticulturist and became the father of the fruit industry in this region. In 1937 Mrs. Frances Wolfskill Taylor Wilson, his daughter, bequeathed 107.28 acres to the University of California for an experimental farm. From this portion of

Rancho Rio de Los Putos, the University's research has since enriched the state's horticultural industry.

Placed by California State Park Commission in cooperation with Solano County Historical Society, 1966.

WOODBRIDGE (San Joaquin Co.)   *18500 N. Lilac St.*
San Joaquin Valley College

Built through subscription by the residents of Woodbridge and dedicated as Woodbridge Seminary in 1879 by the United Brethren Church, this was the site of San Joaquin Valley College 1882–97. It was then used as Woods Grammar School until 1922, when the building was dismantled.

Placed by California State Park Commission in cooperation with Northern San Joaquin County Historical Society, 1956.

WOODFORDS (Alpine Co.)   *14.5 mi. W, on SH 88*
Kit Carson Marker

On this spot, which marks the summit of the Kit Carson Pass, stood what was known as the Kit Carson Tree on which the famous scout Kit Carson inscribed his name in 1844 when he guided the then Capt. John C. Fremont, head of government exploring expedition, over the Sierra Nevada Mountains. Above is a replica of the original inscription cut from the tree in 1888 and now in Sutter's Fort, Sacramento.

Placed by Historic Landmarks Committee of Native Sons of the Golden West, 1921.

WOODFORDS (Alpine Co.)   *14.4 mi. W, on SH 88*
The Unknown Pioneer
1849
Here rests one whose name is known only
to our creator. He was one of a valiant
cavalcade who brought honor and stability
to the character of California. They had
faith in God,
faith in themselves,
faith in their fellowmen.
Placed by Odd Fellows of California and Nevada, 1950.

WOODFORDS (Alpine Co.)   *17.3 mi. W, Lake Caples, on SH 88*
Old Emigrant Road

Here the Old Emigrant Road of 1848 swung down across the meadow now covered by Caples Lake (Twin Lakes) and climbed along the ridge at the right to the gap at the head of the valley. From this summit (9,460 feet) it descended to Placerville. This rough and circuitous section became obsolete in 1863 when a better route was blasted out of the face of the cliff at Carson Spur.

Placed by California State Park Commission in cooperation with Silver Lake Camper's Association, 1959.

WOODFORDS (Alpine Co.)

*On SH 89, .1 mi. N of SH 4
and Old Pony Express Rd.*

The Pony Express
Woodfords

During initial five weeks of its operation in 1860, an important remount station of the famous pony express was located a few feet from here at Cary's Barn.

Placed by Historical Society of Alpine County and National Pony Express Centennial Association.

WOODLAND (Yolo Co.)

659 1st St.

Gable Mansion

The Gable Mansion is an outstanding example of 19th-century Victorian Italianate architecture, one of the last of its style, size, and proportion in California. This structure was built in 1885 for Amos and Harvey Gable, pioneer Yolo County ranchers.

Placed in cooperation with Gable family and Robert L. McWhirk, 1974.

WOODLAND (Yolo Co.)

*W side of 2nd St., between Main St.
and Dead Cat Alley*

The Woodland Opera House

The first opera house to serve the Sacramento Valley was built on this site in 1885. The present structure, built in 1895–96, continues to represent an important center for theatrical arts of that period. Erected by David N. Hershey and incorporating the classic American playhouse interior, it served vast agricultural regions of the Sacramento Valley. Motion picture competition hastened its closing in 1913.

Placed in cooperation with Yolo County Historical Society, 1973.

WOODLAND HILLS (Los Angeles Co.)

*Los Angeles Pierce College,
Cleveland Park, 6201 Winnelka Ave.*

Old Trapper's Lodge

(Original location: 10340 Keswick Ave., Sun Valley)

Old Trapper's Lodge is one of California's remarkable twentieth century folk art environments. It represents the life work of John Ehn (1897–1981), a self-taught artist who wished to pass on a sense of the Old West, derived from personal experiences, myths, and tall tales. From 1951 to 1981, using his family as models, and incorporating memorabilia, the "Old Trapper" followed his dreams and visions to create the Lodge and its "Boot Hill."

Placed in cooperation with Saving and Preservation Arts and Cultural Environments (SPACE), 1985.

WOODSIDE (San Mateo Co.)

5 mi. N, Filoli Center, Canada Rd.

Filoli
Fight—Love—Live

This country estate was begun in 1915 for Mr. and Mrs. William B. Bourn, II. Architect Willis J. Polk designed a modified Georgian style country house. Subsequently, the carriage house and garden pavilion were executed by Arthur Brown. The formal gardens were created by Bruce Porter. In 1937 the estate was acquired by Mr. and Mrs. William P. Roth.

Placed in cooperation with National Trust of Historic Preservation, and Filoli Center, 1980.

WOODSIDE (San Mateo Co.)   NW corner Sandhill and Portola rds.
Town of Searsville
Here stood the lumberman's village of Searsville whose first settler, John Sears, arrived in 1854. Across the road, westerly of this monument, stood a hotel. The school, store, blacksmith shop, and dwellings were to the southeast, some on the site of the present lake and others overlooking it. Buildings were removed in 1891, as water rose behind the new dam.

Placed by Board of Supervisors of San Mateo County and San Mateo County Historical Association, 1952.

WOODSIDE (San Mateo Co.)   On Portola Rd., .2 mi. S of Woodside and Portola rds. intersection
First Sawmill
About 300 feet south of this monument, on the banks of the Alambique Creek, stood San Mateo County's first sawmill, built by Charles Brown in 1847. About the same time, Dennis Martin was building a second mill on San Francisquito Creek. Both were run by water power and were similar in structure to the famous Sutter's Mill at Coloma.

Placed by Board of Supervisors of San Mateo County and San Mateo County Historical Association, 1952.

WOODSIDE (San Mateo Co.)   SW corner Tripp and Kings Mint rds.
Woodside Store
Built in 1854 among sawmills and redwood groves by Dr. R. O. Tripp and M. A. Parkhurst; operated by Dr. Tripp in person (who also served as dentist, librarian, postmaster, and community leader) until his death in 1909. Purchased by the County of San Mateo 1940, opened as a public museum Sept. 7, 1947.

Placed by California Centennial Commission, San Mateo County Board of Supervisors, and San Mateo County Historical Association, 1949.

WOODY (Kern Co.)   7.7 mi. W, on SH 155
Garces Baptismal Site
Three miles north of this point was the site of the first recorded Christian baptism in the San Joaquin Valley. On May 3, 1776, Padre Francisco Garces, earliest white man in this area, baptized an Indian boy whom he called "Muchachito" at a Yokuts rancheria in Grizzly Gulch.

Placed by Kern County Historical Society, Alila Parlor No. 321 of Native Daughters of the Golden West, and Kern County Museum, 1958.

WOODY (Kern Co.)   6.3 mi. SW, Dry Creek, on Bakersfield-Glennville rds.
Mountain House
One and one-half miles north of this point stood the site of the Butterfield Stage station known as Mountain House. Operating through present Kern County during

1858–61, this famous line ran from St. Louis, Missouri, to San Francisco until the outbreak of the Civil War.

Placed by California State Park Commission in cooperation with Kern County Historical Society, El Tejon Parlor No. 239 of Native Daughters of the Golden West, and Kern County Museum, 1957.

YERMO (San Bernardino Co.)   *4 mi. NW of I-15, on Ghost Town Rd.*
Town of Calico

Centered about the "Town of Calico," the Calico Mining District, with a peak population of 3,000, produced $13–$20 million in silver and $9 million in borate minerals between 1881–1907. On Apr. 6, 1881, several claims were located which formed the largest mine in the district, the Silver King. Profitable mining of silver ceased in 1896.

Placed in cooperation with San Bernardino County Regional Parks Department, 1973.

YORBA LINDA (Orange Co.)   *NE corner Esperanza Rd. and Echo Hill Ln.*
Don Bernardo Yorba Ranchhouse Site

Site of Don Bernardo Yorba hacienda on this land, portion Santa Ana Grant, awarded by King of Spain 1810 to Jose Antonio Yorba, and additional grants to his son by Gov. Jose Figueroa 1834, was created hacienda of Don Bernardo Yorba. Greatest ranchero of Golden Age, Bernardo Yorba was third son of Jose Yorba, who came to California with Don Gaspar de Portola 1769, and established California's first family.

Placed by California Centennial Commission and Placentia Round Table Club, 1950.

YOSEMITE NATIONAL PARK (Mariposa Co.)   *Visitor Center, on entrance wall of auditorium bldg.*
1864—Yosemite Valley—1964

On June 30, 1864, the United States guaranteed the Yosemite Valley and the Mariposa Big Tree Grove to the State of California to "be held for public use, resort, and recreation . . . inalienable for all time." This Act, signed by President Abraham Lincoln, was the first federal authorization to preserve scenic and scientific values for public benefit. It was the basis for the later concept of state and national parks systems. In 1906 the State of California returned the land, considered the first state park in the country, so that it could become part of Yosemite National Park.

Placed by California State Park Commission in cooperation with California History Commission, and National Park Service, 1964.

YOUNTVILLE (Napa Co.)   *1 mi. N, NE corner Cook and Yount Mill rds.*
Site of George Yount's Blockhouse

In this vicinity stood the log blockhouse constructed in 1836 by George Calvert Yount, pioneer settler in Napa County. Nearby was his adobe house, built in 1837, and across the bridge his grist and saw mills, erected before 1845. Born in North

Carolina in 1794, Yount was a trapper, rancher, and miller, and grantee of the Ranchos Caymus and La Jota. He died at Yountville in 1865.

Placed by California State Park Commission in cooperation with Napa County Historical Society, 1958.

YOUNTVILLE (Napa Co.)   George C. Yount Pioneer Cemetery, Lincoln and Jackson sts.

Grave of George C. Yount

George Calvert Yount (1794–1885) was the first United States citizen to be ceded a Spanish land grant in Napa Valley (1836). Skilled hunter, frontiersman, craftsman, and farmer, he was the true embodiment of all the finest qualities of an advancing civilization blending with the existing primitive culture. Friend to all, this kindly host of Caymus Rancho encouraged sturdy American pioneers to establish ranches in this area which was well populated before the gold rush.

Placed by California State Park Commission in cooperation with George C. Yount Parlor No. 322 of Native Daughters of the Golden West, Colonel Nelson Holderman Parlor No. 316 of Native Sons of the Golden West, and Yountville Cemetery Association, 1959.

YOUNTVILLE (Napa Valley)   SW corner SH 29 and California Dr.

Veterans Home of California

Established in 1884 by Mexican War veterans and members of the Grand Army of the Republic who recognized the need for a home for California's aged and disabled veterans. In January 1897 the Veterans Home Association deeded the home and its 910 acres of land to the State of California which has maintained it since that date.

Placed in cooperation with State Department of Veterans Affairs, 1969.

YREKA (Siskiyou Co.)   SW corner Miner St. and Broadway

Yreka

Founded in March 1851 with the discovery of gold in the nearby "flats," Yreka quickly became the commercial and transportation hub for the surrounding communities and mining camps. Yreka's tents and shanties gave way to substantial commercial and residential buildings seen on West Miner and Third Streets, which remain as tangible evidence of the town's 19th-century regional prominence.

Placed in cooperation with City of Yreka, 1977.

YUBA CITY (Yuba Co.)   6.7 mi. S, 5320 Garden Hwy.

Sutter's Hock Farm
1 Mile

(Plaque on SH 99 at Messick Rd.)

First white settlement in Sutter County, on banks of the Feather River, established 1844. General John A. Sutter retired to this farm in 1850. Partially destroyed by debris from mines in flood.

Placed by Department of Transportation, Division of Highways.

YUBA CITY (Yuba Co.) — *7.7 mi. W, 9001 Colusa Hwy. (SH 20)*
Site of Propagation
of the Thompson Seedless Grape

William Thompson, an Englishman, and his family settled here in 1863. In 1872 he sent to New York for three cuttings called Lady de Coverly of which only one survived. The grape, first publicly displayed in Marysville in 1875, became known as Thompson's seedless grape. Today thousands of acres have been planted in California for the production of raisins, bulk wine, and table grapes.

Placed in cooperation with family of William Thompson, and Wm. Bull Meek-Wm. Stewart Chapter No. 10 of E Clampus Vitus, 1980.

YUCAIPA (San Bernardino Co.) — *32183 Kentucky St.*
Yucaipa Adobe

Constructed in 1842 by Diego Sepulveda, nephew of Antonio Maria Lugo, this is believed to be the oldest house in San Bernardino County. The land, formerly controlled by San Gabriel Mission, was part of the Rancho San Bernardino granted to the Lugos in 1842. Later owners included John Brown, Sr., James W. Waters, and the Dunlap family, before acquisition by San Bernardino County in 1955.

Placed by California State Park Commission in cooperation with San Bernardino County Museum Association, 1958.

YUCAIPA (San Bernardino Co.) — *20-acre site, E side Ave.*
E and 10th sts.
Yucaipa Rancheria

Yucaipa Valley supported a large population of Serrano Indians. The fertile valley was watered by springs and creeks. The Indians called this area "Yucaipat" which meant "wet lands." These Native Americans lived at this village site most of the year, with occasional excursions to the mountains to gather acorns and other food items during the harvesting season.

Placed in cooperation with San Bernardino County Museum, Yucaipa Lions Club, Yucaipa Valley Historical Society, and Billy Holcomb Chapter of E Clampus Vitus, 1987.

Index

Sutter, John A., 34, 71, 126, 128, 129, 176, 196
Sutter, John A., Jr., 128
Sutter Creek, 175
Sutter's Fort, 126, 128, 129
Sutter's Hock Farm, 196
Sutter's Landing, 129
Sutter's Mill, 34, 118, 126
Swift Adobe, 107
Swift's Stone Corral, 36
Swiss Hotel, 171
Sycamore Grove campsite, 46
Sycamore Tree of Santa Paula, 162
Sylmar, 175

Taft, 176
Tahoe City, 176
Tailholt, 57
Tapia Adobe site, 42
Tehachapi, 177
Tehachapi Loop, 177
Tehama, 177
Tehama County, 53, 119, 177
Tejon Indian Reservation, 90
Telegraph Hill, 147
Temelec Hall, 171
Temple Israel Cemetery, 174
Thompson seedless grapes, propagation site of, 197
Thornton, 178
Tiburon, 178
Timbuctoo, 168
Timms' Point and Landing, 156
Tolowa Indian Settlements, 42
Tracy, 178–179
  last link of transcontinental railroad, 179
  Mormon pioneers at, 178
  site of San Joaquin City, 179
Traver Building, 98
Treasure Island, 147
Treaty of Caheunga, 103
Trinidad, 179–180
Trinity County, 10, 188
Trona, 180
Truckee, 180–181
  transcontinental railroad at, 180
Trussell-Winchester Adobe, 159
Tsurai, prehistoric Indian community, 180
Tulare County, 56–57, 71, 78, 115–116, 186
Tule Lake, 181
Tule River Indian Reservation, 115
Tule River State Station, 116
Tumco, ghost town of, 106
Tuna Club of Avalon, 10
Tuolomne, 182

Tuolumne County, 19, 30–31, 35–36, 64–65, 70, 172, 174, 182–183
Turner/Robertson Shipyard, 16
Tuttletown, 182–183
Twain, Mark, 4, 97, 99, 182–183
Twain Cabin, 182
Two Years Before the Mast, 75

Ukiah, 183
Ukiah Vichy Springs Resort, 183
Union City, 183–184
  first county courthouse, 183
  site of beet sugar factory, 183
Union Hotel and Union Hall, site of, 172
Union Pacific Railroad, 181
Union Square, 147
United States Dragoons, 13, 50, 56
United States Mint, 143
University of California Berkeley campus, 17
University of California Experimental Farm, 191
University of Southern California, 84
Unknown Pioneer, 192
Upper Lake, 184
Upson, Warren (*see* Pony Express)

Vacaville, 184
Valencia, 184
Vallecito, 184
Vallecito Bell Monument, 184
Vallejo, 185
  site of state capitol, 185
Vallejo, Salvador, adobe of, 171
Vallejo Flour Mill, 58
Vallejo Mill Historical Park, 58
Vallejo's Petaluma Adobe, 112
Valley Springs, 185
Valley Wells, 180
Vasquez, Tiburcio, 57, 77
Ventura, 185–186
Ventura County, 100, 113, 162–163, 167–168, 185–186
Vernon, 186
Veterans Home of California, 196
Virginiatown, 101
Visalia, 186
  county election tree, 186
Vista, 186
Volcano, 187
  site of comet discovery, 187
Von Schmidt State Boundary Monument, 99

Wa Jen Ha Lio, early Chinese fishing village, 164

More Traveling Companions
from Gulf Publishing Company

Backroads of Southern California
Bob Howells
18 tours visit coast, mountains, and desert via the region's rustic backroads and secluded byways. Each tour includes a site map, directions, and photos.
April 1995. 256 pages, maps, photos, index, 5 1/2" x 8 1/2" paperback.
ISBN 0-88415-146-8   #5146   **$16.95**

Beachcomber's Guide to California Marine Life
Thomas M. Niesen
This handy, easy-to-read guide identifies the marvelous marine creatures and plants along California's magnificent coast. It's packed with color and black and white photos, beautiful, detailed illustrations, and fascinating facts sure to enlighten and entertain.
1994. 192 pages, color and black-and-white photos, drawings, bibliography, index, 8" x 11" paperback.
ISBN 0-88415-075-5   #5075   **$16.95**

Camper's Guide to California
Mickey Little
This two-volume set provides maps and information on hundreds of federal and state parks; hiking, canoeing, biking, and horse trails; lakes; forest; and recreation areas.

Volume 1: Northern California
176 pages, color photos, maps, checklists, index, large-format paperback.
ISBN 0-87201-152-6   #1152   **$12.95**

Volume 2: Southern California
176 pages, color photos, maps, checklists, index, large-format paperback.
ISBN 0-87201-153-4   #1153   **$12.95**

Birder's Guide to Northern California
Lolo and Jim Westrich
Maps and detailed directions point the way to hundreds of exceptional locations for premier birding adventures.
322 pages, illustrations, maps, appendix, index, California species checklist, 6" x 9" paperback.
ISBN 0-87201-063-5   #1063   **$16.95**

Diving and Snorkeling Guide to Northern California
Steve Rosenberg
1992. 96 pages, full-color throughout, maps, index, 6 x 9" paperback.
ISBN 1-55992-052-1   #2052   **$11.95**

Diving and Snorkeling Guide to Southern California
Darren Douglass
1994. 112 pages, full-color throughout, maps, index, 6" x 9" paperback.
ISBN 1-55992-057-2   #2057   **$11.95**

Visit Your Favorite Bookstore!

Or order directly from:
Gulf Publishing Company

P.O. Box 2608 • Dept. FO
Houston, Texas 77252-2608
713-520-4444 • FAX: 713-525-4647

Send payment or credit card information plus shipping and handling (see chart). CA, IL, NJ, PA, and TX residents must add sales tax on books and shipping total.

SHIPPING/HANDLING	
U.S., Canada, and Outside U.S. Surface add:	
$ 4.95	$10.00-$20
$ 6.15	$20.01-$30
$ 7.75	$30.01-$45
$ 8.65	$45.01-$60
$ 9.95	$60.01-$75

Shipments to Alaska, Hawaii, and Puerto Rico require that an additional $6.50 be added to our normal packing and shipping charges due to the much higher costs of UPS delivery to these locations. (Second day air required.)